THE

SUNSHINE

CHRONICLES

THE SUNSHINE CHRONICLES

JAN BECKER

Jitney Books

#MADEINDADE

#MIAMIFULLTIME

For all my teachers, especially Michael E. Davis, who believed for me when I was faithless & for Sexy Joe Biden who makes me swoon.

THE
SUNSHINE
CHRONICLES

Foreword:

Thursday, August 23, 2016 at 11:40 pm
Conversation with The Editor:

> J.J. Colagrande: Jan Becker— do you have any manuscripts (fiction, nonfiction or short stories) that you feel are collecting digital dust?? And if yes, are they about South Florida in any way?

Friday, August 24, 2016 at 6:53am

> Me: Sorry, J. J., I don't.

Friday, August 24, 2016 at 10:22 am

> J. J. Colagrande: Just wanted to work with you is all. See ya around.

Saturday, August 26, 2016 at 4:37pm

> Me: I did think of something, but I'm nowhere near ready to touch it, and it's an odd project. Lynne Barrett, and Lissette Mendez, and a few other people have been telling me for close to three years that I need to edit my Facebook posts into a book. But like I said, I'm not sure how interesting it would be. And I'm so slow, J. J., It would probably take me another year to get to that.

Saturday, August 26, 2016 at 5:09 pm

> J. J. Colagrande: If Lissette and Lynne say it's a good idea, then it's a good idea. I learned that without question.

> J. J. Colagrande: I was just reading some of your posts. I like this as an idea. A light bulb is lit. A machine is illuminated. A switch is turned on. Churning slowly begins.

Saturday, August 26, 2016 at 9:54pm
Me: (sends Timeline file) Here you go, J. J.

Saturday, August 26, 2016 at 10:07pm

> J. J. Colagrande: I'm gonna make a little book baby with and for you....and it's gonna be dope and a fun ride :)

> Me: Let's hope there's enough there

Sunday, August 27, 2016 at 8:24pm

> J. J. Colagrande: Holy fuck nuggets. This document when double spaced is 2,445 pages and 552,688 words. This is the biggest thing I've ever jumped into editing. Good. I'm happy.
> I'm gonna get it down to 100 pages :)

Sunday, August 27, 2016 at 10:58 pm

> J. J. Colagrande: Maybe 300 pages. This is good stuff, Becker. I'm in it.

Monday, August 28, 2016 at 1:25am

> J. J. Colagrande: Maybe 900 pages. This is going to have to be published in Volumes

> Me: Wow, that's a lot of words.

> J. J. Colagrande: Currently down to 527,719..

Monday, August 28, 2016 at 2:09am

> J. J. Colagrande: I need to double check this with you. Can I make a Jitney book out of this??

> Me: What's a Jitney Book?

> J.J.: Jitney Books, it's a small press I'm starting...

> Me: Yes. Proceed. If you think it would be good for the press, then go forward.

It's not often that an emerging writer receives a call of faith from someone like J.J. Colagrande: Part Neal Cassady at the helm of a Magic City Jitney instead of Furthur. Imagine a sign above him that reads, "J.J. gets things done," as Cassady once had hanging above his driver's seat; part Tom Robbins, a solid wordwright blessed with a vivid imagination; part Voltaire, a philosopher primed for a revolution of thought—there's also a bit bad boy Kerouac/Gonzo hybrid, and perhaps a little Romantic poet, but one like Whitman, out of era, absent the cronyism, tossing off the convention of structured rhyme, sounding his barbaric yawp over the rooftops of Miami—if there was a recipe for J.J., it might look something like that. What would be missing from that curry pot is his yeoman work ethic, endearing charm, unbounded energy, and dedication to promoting the work of South Florida writers and artists.

Through alchemy, and hard work J.J. Colagrande took 552,688 words and shaped them into a 349-page rough draft that landed in my Facebook message box with a solid thud: Boom! Here's your book, ma'am.

I came into this project with no expectation that the book you're holding would capture my affection, or that I'd develop maternal feelings towards it. I was struggling to finish my MFA thesis in memoir at Florida International University. My mantra for over a year had been, "Write the fucking book already." My faith was already weak. But, the process of bringing this baby into the world renewed it, and rather than steal energy from my focus on thesis, this book gave me the resolve I needed to finish it, and begin to put a painful past behind me.

With that loud Boom! J.J. showed me I already had written the book, and when he wrapped her in swaddling designed by Marlene Lopez, featuring Miami artist Luis Berros' lovely "Coppertone Girl." I could not help but love her and insist on further shaping her.

What you're holding in your hands are selected, but largely unedited posts I've made over the past few years on Facebook. The only edits made to the actual text of the posts were for spelling, grammar, or in a few instances to add minor context and clarity. As you'll read, I also changed names to protect privacy, or to better convey character of very real people who inhabit my whacky world.

THE
SUNSHINE
CHRONICLES

Welcome Home.

Friday, October 7, 2016 at 12:56am
#13. The square root of a hurricane is a cycle. Already, the next stage of this one is beginning. In Haiti, Jamaica and the Bahamas they are clearing roads, putting back on the rooftops, and counting too many dead. It's so quiet in my building right now, I want to tiptoe and do everything by candlelight. This kind of quiet can only exist against the bluster of a tempestuous night. Clouds will block the azure for a few more days, but on Sunday, there will be sunshine in Florida, and the birds will fall against the lake as they grab at fish with their talons. An iguana will glow greener on the lawn as he warms himself. One of the hardest lessons I've had to learn is that what I miss most right now has not necessarily vanished forever. I can be certain of little in life, aside from impending sunshine.

Thursday, October 6, 2016 at 11:07pm
#12. Before the storm came, I was bitten by a spider while moving balcony furniture indoors. The storm is growing louder now, sometimes it sounds the way an angry mob turns into an unintelligible roar. The wound from the spider has grown into a furious lump on my shoulder, with a perfect purple circle surrounding the edges. And at the center, there's a blister--or is it an eye?

Thursday, October 6, 2016 at 8:39pm
#11. Don't tell my mother this, but I like to shower outside in big storms.

Thursday, October 6, 2016 at 7:57pm
#10. A hurricane is a kind of tropical cyclone. "Cyclone," from the Greek for "coiled snake." In Zimbabwe, there is an invasive plant called cyclone weed that is choking the fruit trees. It may have blown over from Mozambique during a cyclone. It had been brought from Brazil to lure honeybees. I haven't seen a honeybee in a very long time.

Thursday, October 6, 2016 at 7:43pm
#9. A storm in the dark is more menacing than in the day. It is all sound, growing fury. Right now, it is the rustle of palm fronds, and tapping of raindrops at windows, a stranger becoming bolder at the threshold.

Thursday, October 6, 2016 at 3:50pm
#8. When I search with my zipcode to check the current weather, Haifa, Israel pops up. Pompano Beach is a long way from Israel, where it is a moonlit 73° F right now. When they wake up in Haifa tomorrow, it will be sunny. Here, the storm will have landed, and the sky will be dark, turgid and agitated.

Thursday, October 6, 2016 at 2:32pm
#7. The word "hurricane" comes from the Spanish word huracán, which comes from the name of the Taino storm god, Juracán. The Taínos believed Juracán dwelled on El Yunque mountain and sent strong winds and rain upon them when they pissed him off.

Thursday October 6, 2016 at 12:58pm
#6.: When Hurricane Bob hit Boston, I left my now ex-husband behind in Brighton, for a friend's house in Quincy where there was liquor, marijuana, and a brother with a beautiful smile. Bob was still far away as I inched through traffic in the sublime air of Dorchester. The Scorpions were on the radio when lightning struck my car, a 1984 Plymouth Horizon named Edna, which stalled. Horns began beeping, and a man yelled out, "Hey, you can't pahk the cah now." I was surprised when the engine turned over. My radio was fried, but I've always hated that song anyway.

Thursday, October 6, 2016 at 11:18am
#5. Fact: There has never been a Hurricane Jan. It would be Category 6.

Thursday, October 6, 2016 at 10:16am·
#4. I remember air before landfall as vivid, electric, charged with possibility, and impossibly-colored like the moment the water hits the

absinthe, like the sudden tinge of peridot on a luna moth's wing. Someone should name that color sublime.

Thursday, October 6, 2016 at 9:17am
#3. I have loved men who were like tidal pools, calm and focused, safe places to nurse gashes from being tossed against the rocks. But a man like a hurricane? There is nothing like being swept up in his stormy arms for mutual destruction.

Thursday, October 6, 2016 at 8:40am
#2. In another place, a typhoon and a hurricane might be the same. When we lived in Hawai'i and Dad was off training in Okinawa, a hurricane's cousin hit the island, and our house began to flood. My mother woke me up close to dawn to help her bail. I don't remember before dawn prior to that day. When the sun came up, we took a drive to survey the damage, and it looked like a giant had run over the mountains to play javelin toss with the coconut palms. I still look for the giant in any big storm.

Thursday, October 6, 2016 at 7:50am
13 Ways of Looking at a Hurricane #1. When Gloria hit Massachusetts, the Seabees evacuated the base we lived on, and instead of going to a shelter, we hunkered down in my Dad's office at a recruiting station in Quincy. I looked up at one point, saw a window in the building across the street get sucked out of its pane. It hung there, suspended in the air for a second, and then shattered into tiny bits of glass that peppered the street like snow.

Thursday, October 6, 2016 at 3:59am
I'm up at 4AM, covered in mosquito bites. Ugh. Also, Donald Trump the goose is out on the lake, honking at Matthew to "bring it. You're not so yuge."

Wednesday, October 5, 2016 at 6:07pm
Suddenly, everyone in the building wants clean skivvies. I may be riding out #Matthew commando. #LaundryDay

Wednesday, October 5, 2016 at 3:08pm
I gave 22 students in Miami the offer of an excused absence for storm prep. 16 showed up for class.

Wednesday, October 5, 2016 at 4:27am
Seriously. He knows how to work it. #sexyjoebiden

Wednesday, October 5, 2016 at 2:20am
I just discovered that someone invented a chainsaw on a pole. This may revolutionize my whole life.

Tuesday, October 4, 2016 at 6:55pm
I've been very lucky. In the 7 1/4 years I've lived in South Florida, we've never had a hurricane hit. If the situation at Publix today is any indication of the havoc I can expect should Matthew make landfall here, then it looks like South Florida might turn into some weird (er) post-apocalyptic thunderdome of hell. Also, I forgot to pick up toilet paper, but I'm not going back into that maelstrom of panicked retirees with sharp canes and mobility chairs. God help the person who tries to get between one of them and the last 12 pack of Scott's.

Monday, October 3, 2016 at 12:37am
Weird Miami Greetings I Received this Weekend: Walking to the parking garage downtown, in my combat boots, feeling like a Lucille Clifton poem, "gentlemen" kept yelling out to me, "Hey Girl, you on your way to church?" I pity the men who don't understand I am always in church no matter where I roam.

Sunday, October 2, 2016 at 7:43am
Good morning, Miami. I am 25 floors above your streets, and my nose is telling me--even from this height--cafecito, cortadito, cafe con leche. Dalé.

Saturday, October 1, 2016 at 5:41pm
At Reading Queer Boot Camp
They're massaging writers' cramps. Mission accomplished

Saturday, October 1, 2016 at 12:21pm
The Chef just walked in and saw me strapping myself into my combat boots and started giggling. Then he saw me trying to get my Spanx up and pissed himself. Sigh.

Friday, September 30, 2016 at 8:42am
Random Confession: I may have told myself this while getting dressed to teach this morning: "You go earn those ratemyprofessor chili peppers, JB."

Wednesday September 28, 2016 at 7:49pm
Random Confession: The Chef asked me to run out to Publix to pick up trash bags this evening. But the little girl down the hall, who've I've watched growing since she was born about six years ago is moving out, and while I try to remain detached from my neighbors, I'm afraid if I go out there, I might start crying.

Friday, September 23, 2016 at 4:28pm
My response to the student who shared his religious beliefs with me, and then asked, "What do you believe in?" during my office hours today: Simile and Metaphor

Monday, September 19, 2016 at 8:45am
I spend so much time with The Feline daily, that sometimes I forget how to communicate with people when I'm away from him, and find myself using Feline communication skills with humans. For example, yesterday in Miami, walking down the street, I saw as people approached to walk by me that there was a moment of apprehension, like, is this human going to attack me? And without thinking it through, I did the Feline greeting, that slow blink that means, "I trust you enough to close my eyes

to you." Funny thing though--it seems to work with humans. Each time I did this, I got a smile in response to the slow blink.

Sunday, September 18, 2016 at 9:08am
You might live in South Florida if: At your local grocery store, along with all the other "likely to be shoplifted" products, the Senokot laxative is a behind the counter purchase item. (true story)

Saturday, September 17, 2016 at 11:24pm
I've retired yet another office chair. I've gone through more desk chairs since moving to South Florida in 2009 than the last three popes went through fancy hats. 2. The Chef was supposed to go on vacation this past Thursday, but it was delayed until tomorrow, because someone forgot him. He called me from work around 9:30 to say his car won't shift into gear, and he's waiting to catch a ride home with a dishwasher who lives nearby. Any minute, I'm expecting fresh-sprung Chef to bound through the door untethered from long days under the broiler for a full week of freedom. 3. If I were the party barge captain, I'd be out in this moonlight on the middle of the lake and I'd stay there, until the moon sank below the summit of the landfill near dawn. I'd also have a much better mixtape. I'm sure "Muskrat Love" would be on it somewhere.

Thursday, September 15, 2016 at 6:46pm
Management has posted signs in the elevators asking the residents and visitors to be precautious about flicking cigarette butts in the bushes. I was once precautious, but then I hit puberty.

Friday, September 9, 2016 at 8:58pm
Today's funny puzzler + a true story: While driving north on I-75 earlier, at about 75 mph, with the window half-down, I heard a loud thump and simultaneously, an explosion, and a shower of silver in the passenger compartment of my car, as my driver's side mirror exploded on impact with a duck or other large suicidal waterfowl. There's glass all over the inside of my car. Had I a longer neck, it might've nicked my jugular--but I am fine, and other than the mirror and the poor duck (Could it be

Donald Trump the goose?), there is no real damage. Thankfully, traffic was light, because I lost control of the car for a moment and swerved into the next lane.

Here's what I want to know: Who gets the seven-year debt for breaking the mirror? Does it matter that the duck has sailed off to Byzantium? Damned ducks, man.

Sunday, September 4, 2016 at 3:41pm
Random/maybe Confession: While deciding whether to do a load of laundry, or just buy new underwear instead, I may have discovered a line of panties with secret pockets in them. My first thought may have been: "Pizza pocket?"

Monday, August 29, 2016 at 12:32am
The Chef is not amused that I find it necessary to stand up and shout, "Hey! That's Gordon from Sesame Street!" whenever I see Gordon in a non-Gordon role. (He'll always be Gordon to me).

Friday, August 26, 2016 at 8:41pm
There are new signs in the elevators warning the residents   to stay away from the live animal traps scattered around the perimeter of the building--that the animals will be collected and released in a humane manner over the coming weeks. After a day of being posted, the signs are covered with graffiti from people who reside here, and apparently don't like being told to ignore the cooped-up critters. I'm not sure what they are hoping to trap. We have just about everything living on or in the lake. And I'm happy to report that despite the traps, I had to battle my way past a clutch of juvenile ducklings in the downpour earlier. I hope they catch a maintenance man, and nothing else.

Wednesday, August 24, 2016 at 2:24pm
Conversation in the Elevator with too many Maintenance Men:

(Scene: I enter the elevator. Creepy Maintenance Man #1 is there with another Maintenance Man I've never seen before, who is standing on a step ladder. The door closes. It's hot.)

    Me: Wow, it's awful hot in here.

    CMM#1: Ayuh.

    MM of indeterminate status: Yeah! I like it like this. Hot is good. Yeah, sweat!

    Me: (I look at CMM#1 with a look that says, "is this guy for real?"

    CMM#1: (nods at nothing in particular. Elevator stops on the 2nd floor, unknown MM exits. Doors close)

    Me: New guy?

    CMM#1 No, that's my boss.

Wednesday, August 24, 2016 at 8:08am

I guess insomnia is not a second day of class concern. Woke up this morning, fell back to sleep on the toilet (again). My back does not approve.

Monday, August 22, 2016 at 2:42pm

Along with the inevitable pre-teaching insomnia, I do this thing, where I convince myself I'm not going to get very excited about my students. And then I get there, and there's a student sitting front and center, and she's all tensed up, and when everyone introduces themselves, they are excited and engaged—there's an accountant who left her steady job, because she loves writing so much, and a guy majoring in Sports management, who loves to write poems on the side, and another guy in international relations, who thinks he'll better be able to make peace in the world if he can manipulate the lingo better—and it gets to that one student, and she looks like she'll pop, and she says, "I've been waiting since I was 12 years old to study creative writing." And her cheeks are streaked with a couple happy tears. It's like the time I met Dorothy Allison at the Miami Book Fair (although I am no Dorothy Allison) and I told her how I had been waiting years to meet her, and she took my hands and said, "Oh, honey, I'm so glad you finally made it." I'd have to have a heart made of rusty nails not to get excited—and I don't, so I'm sunk. Completely smitten with my whole class. Dammit.

Monday, August 22, 2016 at 8:58am
I have a rough time getting any sleep the night before I teach a class for the first time. Last night was no exception. I tried. I lay in bed for hours thinking, "what are you forgetting?"(apparently to fall asleep, dumbass). After about two hours of that, I got up and waxed my Birkenstocks, because this is logically the thing to do in the face of insomnia. Anyhow, I tried some miracle eye cream someone gave me that's supposed to remove all my wrinkles and make me look like I've had great plastic surgery. All it did was make the bags under my eyes look greasy. If you're on the south campus of FIU today, keep a look out for me. I'll be the week-long-bender-looking buzzard under the piano in the Graham Center, snoring louder than the undergrad trying to pound out Rachmaninoff. It will be ugly.

Sunday, August 21, 2016 at 9:10pm
I'm eating sriracha and horseradish on everything until further notice. Don't get too close. I'm also breathing fire.

Sunday, August 21, 2016 at 12:37pm
The Feline is insisting that waking up today at all is optional.

Saturday, August 20, 2016 at 1:16pm
The whole world can laugh (The Chef just did), but I'm wearing my "Feel the Bern" t-shirt til the thing falls apart.

Friday, August 19, 2016 at 1:38pm
Fall syllabus done! And as I do anytime I prepare to teach a course, I've looked over their roster photos, and apologized to each student for what I'm about to put them through over the course of the next semester. They all look so innocent and eager to learn. God (Goddess, gods, Universe--whatever higher power applies) help them.

Thursday, August 18, 2016 at 9:47pm
Another quiet evening with the cobbler's glue and the crevice tool.

Thursday, August 18, 2016 at 12:36am
In Syria, they're dropping chlorine gas munitions on hospitals. And little boys.

Wednesday, August 17, 2016 at 10:43pm
The Toddler (who I've been on hiatus from watching) baked me a cake with booze in it. That's love, son. <3 (Thanks, Laura!)

Wednesday, August 17, 2016 at 5:19am
The moon's so pretty right now over the lake. I want to pretend to be an owl, and take my pussycat out in a beautiful pea green boat. We'll sail away for a year and a day, to the land where the Bong-Tree Grows. And we'll eat quince with a runcible spoon. And then dance by the light of the moon, the moon. We'll dance by the light of the moon.

Tuesday, August 16, 2016 at 9:39pm
Today, The Feline faced the consequences of the vandalism he wreaked on my draft yesterday. I vacuumed. Also, he suffered a sponge bath. I should have trimmed his claws first.

Tuesday, August 16, 2016 at 1:02am
I just heard the ominous sound of paper being torn into tiny bits, turned around, and caught The Feline shredding my thesis draft and spitting it all over the floor. Everyone's a critic. #littleshit

Monday, August 15, 2016 at 7:02pm
Janbecker logic: When the only thing accessible on the internet is Facebook, and there is work to be done, the solution is to lie down with The Feline, and dream of #sexyjoebiden in Scranton (Grandma's hometown), at least until the internet starts behaving itself.

Saturday, August 13, 2016 at 2:18pm
Jan Becker feeling crazy.
I'm experiencing that moment when, after 6 hours at the spreadsheet, entering copy, I hit the wrong button and closed out the file without saving, thereby losing all the work I just did.

Saturday, August 13, 2016 at 2:54am
I'd like to swim with a goat.

Thursday, August 11, 2016 at 11:47pm
Jan Becker is drinking a bourbon. Thesis draft #1 (of many, I'm sure) sent.

Thursday, August 11, 2016 at 9:21pm
Jan Becker likes Moonlight.

Wednesday, August 10, 2016 at 9:08pm
They are STILL power-washing the building. And of course, because it is Crystal Lake, things are complicated. One of the exit doors to the apartment was damaged in a tropical storm five years ago, and management hasn't replaced it, despite our pleas. Earlier, I saw Pressure Washer Guy and pointed to the door and asked him to go gently on the door, because it was dry rotted. Apparently, "easy" is a subjective term, because he just power-washed right through the door.

Wednesday, August 10, 2016 at 11:42am
Etsy just sent me an email that says "mermaid crowns" are trending. This is troublesome.

Tuesday, August 9, 2016 at 6:08pm
Creepy Maintenance Man is outside my office door right now at 6:05PM (when many of my neighbors are returning home from work), pressure washing the walkway. Also, this activity is occurring during a violent thunderstorm. Sigh.

Tuesday, August 9, 2016 at 8:22am
File under other unexpected news: Herbert, the Hostile Hermit Hippie
that lives next door smiled at me yesterday. I'm not taking this as a sign
of neighborly affection. I think it was probably more that the "Eff
America" Guy who hates the electric company and the whole effing
building finally moved out. Happy Trails, "Eff America" Guy. I hope you
find the deserted, off-the-grid kingdom of your dreams.

Tuesday, August 9, 2016 at 2:14am
Jan Becker feeling blissful.
Ahhh, that moment when the ingrown toenail that has been an agony for
weeks finally lets go.

Tuesday, August 9, 2016 at 12:26am
Anyone have a "Bud"weiser pun? Big alcohol is working to undermine
marijuana legalization, Wikileaks confirms.

Monday, August 8, 2016 at 10:24am
Jan Becker shared a memory.
Officially, I have been a Florida resident for seven years today (I arrived
after midnight). It was a rough journey. I'm not sure I'm here yet. I still
haven't gotten my coffee down the gullet. The Chef woke me up at 7AM
running the vacuum. Love (for The Chef, for Florida--for most things
that are important and leave an indelible tattoo on one's psyche) is
complicated. Florida living isn't easy--I am covered in fresh mosquito
bites. But the people are top-notch (I always say that in my mind with
clenched teeth and an upper-crust grin), and if my wallet is a little light,
I'm filthy stinking rich with friendship. Thank y'all for putting up with
me these past 7 years.

Sunday, August 7, 2016 at 9:26am
For most of yesterday, I had no phone, no in-house internet and no cable.
I also had a deadline for copywriting work that involves internet
research, so I was using a hotspot. So was everyone else in my building.
After about two hours, trying and failing to upload a file, I gave up, and

did some housework. I could tell the cable had returned when the building started shaking and cheers erupted. It was like the World Cup all over again. And I went to sleep listening to the party barge out on the lake, playing "Rocky Mountain High." Again, I ask, how is this at all appropriate party barge music?

Saturday, August 6, 2016 at 9:55pm
Damn you, Comcast. Damn you.

Saturday, August 6, 2016 at 11:23am
The Feline survived the night. I did too. Here, in South Florida, the local merchants are price-gouging OFF considering the Zika scare, $9.00 for a bottle I normally pay $5.79 for (I'm going with lemon eucalyptus oil instead). Also, seen at the Brazilian market: Banned Kinder Eggs. Of course, I picked one up. I'm a big fan of choking hazards (and all things contraband).

Saturday, August 6, 2016 at 2:17am
Just as the cheering from my neighbors stopped, the party barge blew its foghorn, and has begun its weekly soiree. They're playing Croce, "Time in a Bottle." The Feline just up-chucked a wooden barbecue skewer he chewed up and swallowed. I'll be up all night now wondering about the first thing that I'd like to do, and fretting that the cat might have injured himself with his pica. #nosleep

Saturday, August 6, 2016 at 1:03am
Somehow, I forgot that the Olympics are in Rio, and 90% of my neighbors in the building are Brazilian sports fans. #nosleep

Friday, August 5, 2016 at 9:28pm
Seven years ago today, I left Binghamton for Florida. Tonight, I discovered an infestation of mites in the AC duct that blows right at me when I'm at my desk (EWWW), and my steering wheel melted. Thank you, Florida, for everything. <3

Friday, August 5, 2016 at 12:06pm
There have been some changes here on Crystal Lake with new management: Signs above the mailboxes expressing confidence that the tenants of the building will "govern yourselves in a reasonable manner," signs prohibiting lawn chairs on the lawn, the removal of the docks from the lake shore. But perhaps the most disturbing is that the cleaning woman for the building appears to have been replaced. There is a backstory here. For the past 7 years, our cleaning woman has held a flame for The Chef—and it appeared to me, some jealousy towards me. For example, she would often corner me in the elevator to tell me about her talks with The Chef, about how her first boyfriend made her baked Alaska, and how she was close to getting a second helping of that dessert from my man. Once, she asked me about my job, and when I told her I'm a writer, she looked down her nose at me and told me she could be one too, because once in the 7th grade, she wrote a poem her teacher said was good (and I would lay money on odds it was exceptional). But the big clue to her true feelings was that she always referred to The Chef as "your roommate," no matter how many times I corrected that to "boyfriend" or "partner." I'm sure going to miss her.

Wednesday, August 3, 2016 at 4:12pm
I'm not sure what he's doing, but Creepy Maintenance Man #2 has been banging something with a hammer upstairs for hours now, and it just sounds filthy. #creepy

Tuesday, August 2, 2016 at 2:53pm
My shrink is predicting a Trump presidency. He says it's not that he wants him to win, it's just that he thinks the country has gone mad. I told him a Trump presidency would be the best thing that could happen for him. He asked, "Why would you say something like that?" "You're the shrink," I told him, "job security."

Monday, August 1, 2016 at 9:21pm
Conversation with The Feline: Feline: (In his co-pilot seat next to my desk chair, squints at me and yawns)

Me: Feline, I adore you. You're the best boy ever. I'm promoting you to "Emotional Support Animal."
Feline: (Yawns again and licks his ass. Knocks a pen off my desk. Jumps off his chair, grasps his pilfered pen in his teeth and runs under the bed.)
Me: Sigh.

Monday, August 1, 2016 at 1:27am
#sexyjoebiden

Sunday, July 31, 2016 at 2:50pm
I want to preface what I am about to write with a note saying that this is in no way meant to indict an entire group of people. I have a great deal of empathy for the homeless. I know firsthand exactly how desperate and difficult it can be to not have a home of your own, and normally if I have cash, I have no problem sharing with a panhandler, because I know they aren't walking around with big wads of dough. I also don't subscribe to the notion that if you give a homeless person money, they will spend it on drugs or drink, because for all I know that bump or snort of hooch is the one thing keeping them from dropping dead from withdrawal. However, Florida consistently teaches me that there are exceptions to every rule: I had to make a run to Comcast today to change out some equipment, and as I was walking to the store, a man with a shopping cart approached and asked if I had any change I could spare so he could buy a soda. And I didn't—I'm a writer—I am broke on a regular basis. So, I apologized politely, and tried to continue on my way, and Dude ran up with his shopping cart and started yelling at me, blocking my path, called me an asshole. And I said, Dude, really, I have no money. If I had some I'd give it to you. I tried walking around him, but he kept pushing the cart in my way. So, he's got me cornered against a Cadillac in the parking lot with his shopping cart, and he whips out a roll of bills and starts counting, "Here! Take ten!" And I said, "no I don't want your money, I just want to go exchange my equipment and go home, where I have work waiting for me." And he continues yelling, and blocking and parrying with the shopping cart, raising his bid on how

much money he's willing to give me (he went all the way up $60). All the while, calling me a bitch and an asshole, and a bunch of other things. I said, "Look, you don't know me. You have no clue who I am. Just let me go." And people are just walking by, not paying him any mind... Anyhow. Dude finally dropped his Newports and bent over to pick them up and I made my escape. I should have just taken the $60. Dude has no clue how broke I am. Also, I hate Comcast.

Sunday, July 31, 2016 at 10:27am
The Chef broke the Carafe for the French Press. There is nothing I can add to that.

Saturday, July 30, 2016 at 2:33am
We've reached a new low on Crystal Lake in party barge entertainment music. They are out there right now, playing Gordon Lightfoot. This might work if it were any other song, but no! It is indeed "The Wreck of the Edmund Fitzgerald" keeping me up tonight. How is this at all appropriate?

Friday, July 29, 2016 at 11:24pm
Jan Becker likes Joe Biden.

Thursday, July 28, 2016 at 9:11am
I was about to be wrapped in #sexyjoebiden's arms in my dreams again, when Creepy Maintenance Man #2 interrupted the moment with urgent pounding at the door and a need to inspect my pipes. Sigh. #creepy

Wednesday, July 27, 2016 at 8:47pm
Thank goodness I still have five more months of #sexyjoebiden to look forward to.

Wednesday, July 27, 2016 at 1:39pm
I had a dream last night that I was on the phone with a very dear friend who died about two and a half years ago. It was good to hear his voice

again--and as usual, he gave me the best advice. I just wish I could pick up the phone now that I'm awake and thank him. <3

Tuesday, July 26, 2016 at 11:45pm
I'm a little obsessed with the Saharan dust layer right now (because allergies, wow), but specifically, I'm wondering if there are critters, like dust mites traveling across the Atlantic on the dust clouds--and I'm wondering if they are sentient and freaked out by the journey. Do they miss their dust mite buddies back in the desert? More specifically self-involved, I'm wondering if I have Saharan dust mite poop in my sinuses. Little discomfiting that thought path. <HA CHOO!>

Monday, July 25, 2016 at 9:33pm
I'm thinking of global interconnectedness right now. This might have to do with the Saharan dust that's made its way across the Atlantic and landed in my sinuses, but it also might just be that we need to get our shit together as a planet.

Sunday, July 24, 2016 at 4:22pm
Before I moved into this apartment with The Chef, he had a long history of roommates, most of them of questionable repute (but also, a couple who remain dear friends--and were the best roommates ever). The bathroom sink has never, since I've lived here, drained properly. After 14 hours of plunging and pouring various non-caustic bubbling chemicals (Baking soda and vinegar, OxyClean and boiling water, washing soda and lemon juice) down the drain, I am pleased to announce I have cleared the pipes. More importantly, I have located Jimmy Hoffa's remains.

Sunday, July 24, 2016 at 4:06am
My 4AM attempt at plumbing has thus far been futile, but it's still early (clogged bathroom sink).

Friday, July 22, 2016 at 10:56am
I'm starting to learn Southern code. For example, "Bless your little heart." I'm fairly certain that really means, "Oh, sweetie, you have bricks for brains."

Thursday, July 21, 2016 at 8:49am
And they say writing's an easy gig. Check out the shiner I got working on these revisions.

Thursday, July 21, 2016 at 5:06am
I got a little desperate just now, up all night trying to write, and cut all my hair off again--think Cersei Lannister right before the tomatoes started flying. It's not straight, and I don't care. Aunt Esther (from Lordville) is the wisest woman I've met in a long time, and I'm going with her "no combs" philosophy. This will grow back eventually. For now, my head doesn't feel as heavy.

Wednesday, July 20, 2016 at 6:33pm
Note to Self: There is an increased chance of meeting a man at the Publix named Sam, who does not enjoy green eggs and ham if you are wearing that Dr. Seuss shirt. You will likely engage with him in an on the spot recitation of the book in dialogue at the entrance to the store, after he jumps out at you and shouts, "I am Sam. Sam I am." You won't be the least bit embarrassed.

Wednesday, July 20, 2016 at 3:11am
Jan Becker at Poop Town.
Note to Self: When investigating alternate co-pilot seats for The Feline, so he can sit right next to you while you work, do not type "stool for sale." Instead, try "ottoman." You really want to just type "ottoman." Trust me on this.

Tuesday, July 19, 2016 at 11:49pm
Jan Becker shared Miami Book Fair's event.

Tuesday, July 19, 2016 at 4:21pm
Guy outside on 4th floor is screaming, eff electricity, eff this building, eff this effing country, and all the effing people who live in it. Dude missed his calling. He should be a keynote speaker at a convention in Cleveland.

Tuesday, July 19, 2016 at 1:52am
I just couldn't watch the RNC. I feel like I'm losing brain cells any time I hear anyone connected to that campaign speak. You know the one. The Chef says I should watch, that it's funny. I say yeah. Funny like World War III. I won't watch that either.

Monday, July 18, 2016 at 10:50pm
I'm working through some revisions in my writing, and damn, this is going slow. I'm averaging maybe a page an hour. But it's occurring to me that as I do this, things are starting to make more sense--at least until I open the file again in the morning and read the changes and am puzzled all over again. #amwriting

Monday, July 18, 2016 at 12:12pm
Creepy Maintenance Man #1 and Creepy Maintenance Man #2 are outside my window with chainsaws and sawzalls disassembling the dock on the lake where all my neighbors go to hold hands or fish or smoke pot or have secret conversations. I'm terribly depressed to see the dock go. It was my one steady source of juicy eavesdropping.

Monday, July 18, 2016 at 12:29am
The Feline just noticed that there is a fat juicy gecko in the window between the screen and glass, and has gone into mighty hunter mode. I have a feeling I'm not going to get much sleep tonight. I'm never washing the windows again. NEVER.

Sunday, July 17, 2016 at 11:01pm
With Shamanatrix Missy Galore
Hey, the more you fluff it, the better the vibe. <3

Sunday, July 17, 2016 at 4:17pm
Jan Becker feeling disgusted.
I just got out of the shower, and dried my face, only to realize I'd grabbed The Winemaker's chosen towel from the linen closet. And even though it has been thoroughly washed (several times), it will NEVER lose his odor. #Winemakerchronicles

Saturday, July 16, 2016 at 10:12am
I don't know what a Pokemon is (it's okay, you don't have to fill me in), but apparently, the fad is even spreading into the fiber art/crochet community. Am I going to be devoured by a Pokemon?

Wednesday, July 13, 2016 at 6:27pm
I took a quick nap and had a dream I was laid out flat and Meinhardt Raabe was standing over me singing, "As coroner, I must aver, I thoroughly examined her." And then The Feline poked me in the nose and woke me up.

Tuesday, July 12, 2016 at 2:47pm
Three things: 1. I have FINALLY finished cleaning my windows. 2. I will NEVER wash my windows again. 3. Vertical blinds are evil.

Tuesday, July 12, 2016 at 4:46am
Last year, I was in the stairwell, at around 10 PM, trying to throw some garbage down the trash chute, but it was jammed, so I was struggling, and then startled when I saw someone trying to pass me on the stairs, and I jumped and startled a young Black man. It was the kind of startle that happens when you're not expecting someone behind you in a stairwell--or you don't expect to startle someone wrestling with a bag of trash. Anyhow, we apologized for startling each other, and I said the polite howdoyoudo that I hardly ever get an honest answer to. And my neighbor said, "I'm a Black man living in Broward County, how do you think I'm doing?" I told him that I couldn't presume to know, that I could imagine, but if he wanted to talk about it, the trash chute was jammed anyway, and we were both going to be taking the stairs down together,

he could fill me in. And for about the next 45 minutes, after introducing himself, Michael and I talked about a lot of things, like how he likes to go to the gym at night when he can, but that the Sheriff's Department keeps pulling him over for how darkly his windows are tinted, or because he didn't use a turn signal (nobody in this fucking state uses a turn signal), or whatever reason they can find to mess with him. And I told him that sounded terrifying, and that he shouldn't be subjected to stops on a regular basis, especially by the Broward County Sheriffs, who have plenty more pressing things to occupy themselves with. Michael's a nice kid, about 21-22. He has a good firm handshake. He moved here from Detroit with his family. His bedroom is above my office, and sometimes at night, I hear him running radio controlled somethings or other around the room. He wants to study computer programming, and when I asked him the name of the school he was looking at, he named one of those predatory for-profit colleges that are just looking to steal his money, leave him with a worthless degree that doesn't lead to a job, and a ton of student loan debt, which I explained to him, and suggested an accredited school with a decent program (Broward College). My point with this long story is that in the attached article about Philando Castile, "Fred Friedman, the retired chief public defender for Northeast Minnesota, called it unusual to be stopped so many times with no serious charges. "It's a big deal to get stopped 52 times. You can't find somebody who's been stopped 52 times and doesn't have any felony convictions or drunk driving. That's highly unusual," he said. Bullshit. This is not an anomaly, and it's most certainly not because there is a concern for public safety. Castile's number of pull overs is from a 14 year DMV file. Michael mentioned 4 stops in the space of a month. There's no just cause for that level of harassment and scrutiny, and it pisses me off that my upstairs neighbor is up right now pacing the floor. Not because he is disturbing me, but because he is being terrorized.

Tuesday, July 12, 2016 at 12:28am
The raccoons have apparently been wandering the cow fields, eating the sudden mushrooms, because they are in the trash room three floors below me, giving an impromptu performance of Pagliacci, amplified by

the building's trash chutes. I am still cleaning my windows and thinking of everything. I'm hoping the mockingbirds show up for the second act.

Monday, July 11, 2016 at 6:59pm
When I grow up, I want to be a capybara.

Monday, July 11, 2016 at 6:17pm
I should probably clean my windows more than once every eight years.

Monday, July 11, 2016 at 1:28pm
Few things in life thrill me more than ground-scoring a perfectly ripe mango on a South Florida sidewalk in the sun, and then slicing it and eating it while it's still hot.

Monday, July 11, 2016 at 11:38am
I sometimes have weird dreams in which there's no real action, just an image. For most of my childhood, it was an empty room, all the walls and floors were painted white, and there were no windows at all. In the center of the room, there was a school desk, and for years, no one ever sat at the desk. Last night, I had a different dream, that there was a Kennedy half dollar sitting on the floor and people kept stomping on JFK's face. I don't really have an opinion of JFK that's one way or the other. I'm ambivalent about most things American, and don't understand why this image came up in my dream (except for maybe that lucre is an elusive thing to me). I woke up with this song in my head, and it's not going away.

Sunday, July 10, 2016 at 1:22am
I know that argan oil makes my skin soft, and my hair gleam, but I can't get over knowing it passed through a goat's ass.

Saturday, July 9, 2016 at 10:05pm
Jan Becker shared Game of Thrones Memes's photo.

Saturday, July 9, 2016 at 2:48pm
Another Weird TMI Update: I've mentioned my shrink, and last I posted, he'd managed to skirt the FIU Mafioso in medical services and found hours in another department, AND got me on the schedule. What I didn't mention is that I finally got in to see him this Tuesday, and while I was happy to see him, his crazy stories this week didn't help. (I have severe PTSD, which I refuse to be ashamed of, because I did nothing to bring it on myself.) I mentioned to the good doctor how stressful firecrackers are for me--especially considering the Orlando shootings (this was Tuesday, before I heard about Alton Sterling and Philando Castile). My buddy the shrink then proceeded to give me a step-by-step explanation of how an AR-14 works. Sigh. Anyhow, for self-care, I stopped at Grandma's favorite thrift store and chatted with her spirit. I think she led me to a little naked potted man, because I thought I heard her giggle when I picked him up. I'm planning to hang him next to Naked Allen Ginsberg above the bed to remind me of how silly Grandma was. If she was alive, I'd teach her to say, "pinga." It would be her new favorite word.

Saturday, July 9, 2016 at 11:05am
I had been awake for close to 40 hours when I finally crashed last night. (No vivid dreams, Leslie). I'm not sure what, other than my brain not wanting to stop, and allergy eyes kept me up that long. There's no logic after 40 hours of awake, and while the mind trip was fun, it's not something I want to do very often. Anyhow, The Feline puked a hairball on my foot before I got coffee this morning. Poor thing, he's all worked up from the firecrackers on the Fourth of July. It's been 5 days and he still refuses to go out to his catnip/grass garden on the balcony to sun himself. It doesn't help that the heat index is crazy hot, and that five days past the holiday, the kids are still making explosions out back.

Thursday, July 7, 2016 at 12:55pm
Jan Becker shared Black Lives Matter Alliance Broward's event.

Thursday, July 7, 2016 at 10:22am
In the interest of better understanding America's ills, I'm coining a new term for one of our biggest (or over-esteemed) diseases. I'm calling it "coq blanche." (This term is Chef approved).

Wednesday, July 6, 2016 at 7:07pm
Somehow, I think if Jesus (or Mohammed or another Buddha or whoever) shows up, they're going to look around at the mess and say, "You had just one job." #love

Wednesday, July 6, 2016 at 12:55pm
Jan Becker feeling annoyed.
Frustrated by numerous interruptions in my attempt at a morning writing routine, I am resorting to the only thing I can think of to make the day better, that is, I'm whipping out the cobbler glue and vise grips, and since I can't line the whole office with cork, I'm going to be very satisfied lining my desk with it. And if The Chef shreds any more paper, I may line him with cork as well--or at least subject him to the vise grips.

Monday, July 4, 2016 at 8:37pm
Judging by the number of bangs I'm hearing right now, before it has even gone completely dark, The Feline and I are in for a long, loud night. There is, however, hope. I see a line of dark clouds, just across the lake, and they look thick with lightning. I'm pulling for Mother Nature, that she'll show up and school these dilettantes on what real fireworks look like.

Monday, July 4, 2016 at 8:47am
Jan Becker updated her profile picture.
My Spirit Animal. The Lordville Polar Bear. She was rescued from a sex-trafficking ring, found by an adult video store in a g-string and pasties, and now guards the back entrance to the Kilgore Hotel in Lordville.

Monday, July 4, 2016 at 12:29am
The party barge out on the lake is back, and I'm beginning to think they need a new, hipper DJ. So far tonight I've heard "I Will Always Love You," followed by "America the Beautiful," followed by "Yes, Jesus Loves Me." I don't have an issue with Jesus per se (or even America occasionally), but in this case, Sir Mix A Lot might be a more upbeat choice. Also, I hope they aren't dunking people out there in an effort to baptize them. There's been a recent spike in cases of brain eating amoebae (which now that I think of it, might explain the GOP candidate for president).

Sunday, July 3, 2016 at 6:55pm
Not sure what's up with the tummy, but I can't even get coffee down my gullet this weekend. As a result, I am more ugly and gruesome than usual. Don't even try to talk to me.

Saturday, July 2, 2016 at 12:07pm
Some 4th of July weekend ramblings: I'm not sure if it's that every article I opened while I was drinking my coffee this morning was abysmal and cynical about the state of the world, or that people are throwing quarter sticks into the lake out back, scaring the hell out of me and The Feline (firecrackers freak us out), or that it is summer and the air in South Florida is so thick and heavy, it feels like a pot of soup in my lungs, but I'm homesick for last summer, the river, my friend Buck (my other friends there too, but mostly Buck, because he is good and makes the best coffee in the world), and nights spent battling bats. The 4th of July weekend has always been a bummer for me, except for the ones I spent in Lordville. In other news, not even the mafia could completely rid FIU of my shrink (long story, his delusion, not mine), and I've managed to get an appointment to see him next week. This is positive, because his stories about Jesus and Jeb Bush are probably the only things that make me feel sane some days.

Friday, July 1, 2016 at 4:01pm
Random Confession: There's a store in my neighborhood that I'd like to check out, because I'm due for new skivvies, but I'm completely freaked out by its name. "Lingerie Liquidators"—it's just too intimidating for me.

Monday, June 27, 2016 at 8:39pm
While this does not completely unwind my frustration from earlier, The Chef brought me home griot (and PIKLIZ!) from the local Haitian restaurant, so I'm feeling a little kinder tonight.

Monday, June 27, 2016 at 3:36pm
Chef's Day Off & I'm working in the office & if he comes in here one more time to try to talk to me, I will teach The Feline to gnaw off his face. #premenstrualwritingjones

Sunday, June 26, 2016 at 9:22pm
One thing I hate about living in a big apartment building is being put in the position where, like just now, I witness one of my neighbors beating the crap out of their wife/girlfriend/lover/other and am forced to pick up the phone and call 9-1-1. I hate that. But what I'd hate worse is wondering what happens if I don't make that call. (Also, how can ANYONE beat the crap out of anyone during the GOT season finale? Beastly person, that one.)

Saturday, June 25, 2016 at 11:31pm
It took me 46 years, but finally, I have discovered the joy of a dirty martini. <hiccup>

Saturday, June 25, 2016 at 5:10pm
There is nothing so pathetic as the look The Feline gives me when I try to squeeze into my Spanx.

Thursday, June 23, 2016 at 1:55pm
Oh, goodness, Heart, you clichéd muscle. So many ways to pain you, but I suspect you function best when allowed to be repeatedly broken.

Wednesday, June 22, 2016 at 2:35pm
It is probably a good idea to just continue my day, and not reply,
"PLEASE, YES!" to a Freecycle offer for a unicycle (rusty, but works).

Wednesday, June 22, 2016 at 2:24pm
Jan Becker shared John Lewis's post.
John Lewis knows a thing or two about sit-ins.

Wednesday, June 22, 2016 at 12:16am
Driving to an LGBTQA reading in a Miami downpour is as harrowing as
a NY blizzard. But then, rainbows over @BooksandBooks @readingqueer!

Tuesday, June 21, 2016 at 3:23pm
Random Confession: All this CB lingo is coming up, because growing
up, we had a base unit in my home. My CB handle was "Chubby
Cheeks." I have to warn you, if you ever call me that to my face, I may
have to give you a noogie.

Tuesday, June 21, 2016 at 12:11pm
The trouble with being awakened at 3AM by a Broward County Sheriff
helicopter out on the lake, shining its lights in my windows and heavy
police activity all around the apartment building is not so much that I'm
talking to myself in CB lingo. It's more that I can't get enough mud in my
cup, and I'm stuck with this damned song, "Convoy," in my head, where
I suspect it will remain for the next several weeks. I should probably
watch this movie again sometime, because land sake's alive, Kris
Kristofferson.

Tuesday, June 21, 2016 at 4:34am
Disconcerting 3AM Full Moon Solstice Wakeup in a nearly forgotten
lingo: I jumped up to pay the water bill & it's open season out my
bedroom window. There's a flying donut riding heavy on my donkey
and wall to wall bear, rolling discos and meat wagons out on Boulevard
95. I'm checking my eyelids for pinholes, but the Broward County

Mounties and their gumball machines are keeping me out of my nightgown. I need to get horizontal, press my sheets, & cut some Zs, but the Cub Scouts are disrupting my nap trap with their eyeballs. It is going to take many many forty weight 100 mile cups of mud to get me through tomorrow.

Monday, June 20, 2016 at 5:20pm
Some thoughts on elections in general: In both of the major party political campaigns, the front-runners are both so slick with PR posturing, it is hard to get a good look at what is holding up the façade they each present to the public. Who are these people really? Really? What is the thought that wakes them at 3AM? And why the hell would they want to want the awful job they're applying for?

Sunday, June 19, 2016 at 11:51pm
Hodor.

Sunday, June 19, 2016 at 6:52pm
At my neighborhood Publix, there's a customer named Al. That I know his name should be an indication of what a regular fixture he is in the place. He's elderly, and wears black socks with shorts that always drift past his ass, not because he likes loose shorts, but because he has no ass. He has this voice that sounds like a brass instrument, sort of like William Burroughs, but louder and brassier. And he's bossy. I'm guessing that in his retirement, he doesn't have much that keeps him feeling useful, so he spends his afternoons wandering the grocery store, yelling at the stock clerks that they don't know how to place cans on the shelves. He's not mean; he's just very critical, and wants everything in the store to be neat, stocked and in order. But there's something I noticed about his interactions with the people who work there. They love him. They smile at him when he gives them hell, and thank him for pointing out that they forgot to face the iced tea. He even bitched at me once for leaving my cart parked in the middle of the aisle for two seconds so I could retrieve something I'd dropped. I asked my cashier today how it felt to have him come in every day for his inspections (she assured me, he never misses a

day), and she said she wouldn't know how to work in his absence, because he belongs there. I don't generally go to the grocery store to learn how to love people, but I won't discount a lesson so profound and wondrous if I stumble over it in the clearance bin either.

Friday, June 17, 2016 at 7:04pm
Day 5 of the burn from the 5-gallon pot of boiling OxyClean (Do Not EVER Boil OxyClean): Up til now, it really hasn't been too awful, just a couple blisters, some redness and sore. Today, my skin decided to start falling off. And it's raw under there. #housebolton

Thursday, June 16, 2016 at 10:31am
Morning Two with my Creepy Peeper and his mothertrucking bucket truck. Super Creepy. Creepy Super. I just want to drink my coffee in peace.

Thursday, June 16, 2016 at 4:50am
Cookie Monster Searches Deep Within Himself and Asks: Is Me Really Monster?

Wednesday, June 15, 2016 at 11:41am
It's tree trimming time in preparation for hurricane season (albeit late) here on Crystal Lake. This means that there's a Creepy Maintenance Man or two in a bucket truck directly outside my bedroom window, even though there aren't any trees within arms' length. I haven't yet had my coffee, and he's talking to me. Good God, this morning. #Creepy

Wednesday, June 15, 2016 at 3:57am
(Thank you, Stephanie for posting this article). Dear queer friends who are hurting or scared or pissed off or whatever you're feeling (and you may be feeling these things at once). I enjoy the hell out of times with you when you're laughing and covered in glitter, but I'm also going to love you when you're down or bitchy or blue. And if you need someone who doesn't expect you to be strong all the time, you let me know. You're important to me, and I've been so blessed to have loved and been

loved by so many of you. My whole heart would be so much smaller without you. You don't have to be lonely through any of this. <3

Monday, June 13, 2016 at 1:55pm
I just spoke to the new building manager, who was polite, patient and kind on the phone. I have a feeling he won't last very long.

Monday, June 13, 2016 at 11:13am
I am about as sore as one woman can be. Aside from the heartache, I'm literally burnt and blistered, my back feels broken, and I can barely move. I dropped a cast iron skillet on my big toe on top of everything else I did to myself yesterday, and just want to crawl back to bed. But, it's The Chef's day off, and he said, "Curry?" Miracle cure, that turmeric.

Sunday, June 12, 2016 at 8:40pm
The only thing that seeing men kissing in Miami ever compelled me to do is sing praises and write poetry. #beproud #lovewins

Sunday, June 12, 2016 at 1:03pm
Jan's jackass move of the day, or why I am not online: Somehow, I managed to give myself a serious scalding (possibly) chemical burn by dumping a 5-gallon pot of boiling OxyClean on my writing hand. I'm okay--or will be once I stop screaming about this horrible day (and damn, it feels like I woke up screaming) --but do not do this at home. Also, boiling OxyClean does terrible things to nail polish as well as to skin. #effyouDIYwebsites

Sunday, June 12, 2016 at 8:59am
Oh, hell. Orlando.

Saturday, June 11, 2016 at 7:55pm
Four years ago today, The Feline returned from his Chef-imposed exile and moved back in with me (The Chef didn't have cats growing up, and so feared them). In celebration, I gave The Feline a nice hunk of oil packed tuna, brushed his coat and told him how happy I was that he'd

moved back in with me, how I can't imagine spending my days with any cat but him glaring at me from his chair next to me when I write. I told him that when people ask me about him, I say that he is the love of my life, and my very best friend. And the little shit bit me.

Saturday, June 11, 2016 at 5:03pm
Epsom salts, and a tub filled with hot water are my new best friends.

Saturday, June 11, 2016 at 3:20am
I have no memory of a dream attached to this, but I just woke up with a fat lip--and I'm going right back in there for more.

Thursday, June 9, 2016 at 4:58pm
Jan Becker likes Publix.

Thursday, June 9, 2016 at 12:13pm
Jan Becker at Publix at Winston Park Center.
Random confession before I go do something productive: Sometimes I go to the Publix that's not right in my neighborhood. It's not a better Publix. I wind up spending twice as much time there, because the layout is so confusing. And sometimes, getting there can be a hassle because of traffic. However, there's a very sweet cashier there, and if I get in her line, she always tells me how much she loves me, and kisses my hands and gives me blessings (Jesus may be involved, but I'm cool with whoever wants to bless me). And I know sometimes "I love you" doesn't mean what I think it means. Sometimes it means "I need something from you," or "You're looking rough today, maybe saying this will cheer you up." The thing is, I have no doubt that this sweet, odd cashier loves the hell out of me, and if she's compelled to tell me so, I'll drive a couple more miles to pick up the Brussels sprouts.

Thursday, June 9, 2016 at 8:33am
I am convinced that The Chef's super sharp chef knife is one of those weapons possessed by an evil spirit. Last week, I peeled back the tip of my index finger with it. Last night, it jumped off the counter while I was

draining the whey from the curds, and lopped off just the very tip of my big toe. And then, as if that wasn't enough destruction for it to wreak on a Wednesday night, it also sliced into my favorite pair of Birkenstocks. I should just give it up. I have a perfectly respectable santoku of my own, but I prefer the danger.

Wednesday, June 8, 2016 at 9:26pm
I had a terrible daydream of the future: Trump inauguration, a reanimated/resurrected Ezra Pound reads the inaugural poem. #scarypoems

Wednesday, June 8, 2016 at 12:50pm
Today is The Chef's day off. This begs the question: If he's The Chef, why am I the one making homemade cheese (paneer, for saag) today?

Wednesday, June 8, 2016 at 9:39am
The Feline got into his valerian/honeysuckle/catnip stash, and now he's all eyes and nosiness. He's trying to colonize the cabinet in my desk. He's taken all my freshly finished crochet lacework flowers I'd stacked in a basket, and decorated the interior of his new sassy cat cave with them, and stuffed vermin. And if I listen closely (he's closed the door, so I can't spy), I think he's down there, clackety clack, typing out a Pulitzer. #littleshit

Wednesday, June 8, 2016 at 4:12am
It's always satisfying to locate the vise grips at 4AM.

Tuesday, June 7, 2016 at 3:29pm
Confession: John Irving is one of my favorite writers. I love his early-mid-career work so much, I once vowed to give up an ovary for the chance to see him live, and then had to have my left ovary removed just as he was due to visit Binghamton while I was in school there (and I went anyway, because JOHN IRVING, a week after surgery, all hopped up on pain meds--and it was amazing). He's speaking in Coral Gables at the Congregational Church tonight, and I'd planned to be there, but all

day yesterday and today I've been getting these familiar sharp, stabbing pains on my right side (where I still have one ovary left). God help me, John Irving. I'd give you my whole uterus if you'd do a little more with plot in your next books.

Tuesday, June 7, 2016 at 1:45pm
I think it says something about my character that when told by my shrink that he would no longer be able to see me for monthly appointments because Student Health Services at FIU has been infiltrated by the mafia, and because of a budget issue due to misappropriated student health fees, my first thought was not, "Wow, the doctor needs a doctor." My first thought was, "I'm really going to miss this guy and his stories about how Jesus cured his asthma on the radio, and how Jeb Bush was responsible, not only for 9/11, but ebola and genital warts."

Monday, June 6, 2016 at 7:15am
Jan Becker shared I'm not "Spiritual." I just practice being a good person's post.

Sunday, June 5, 2016 at 3:59pm
Conversation with The Chef Prior to Coffee, and the resultant quandary:
> Chef: (kisses me on the cheek) Game tonight.
> Me: Hell yeah. Game of Thrones, Brienne of Tarth, blah,blah, blah.
> Chef: (looks befuddled) NO! NBA finals. Lebron James, blah, blah, blah.
> Me: (kicks Chef out of bed onto floor) No! Game of Thrones. Valar morgulis, buddy.

Here's the quandary. He didn't set the game to tape, and won't be home until about 10:30 tonight. I could just leave it alone, win the whole argument, and watch Game of Thrones on the night it airs, thus missing all the spoilery mcspoiler updates on social media, but then I'd be stuck with a miserable Chef, who admittedly is in an unrequited bromance with Lebron James. I went ahead and set the basketball game to tape for him, because valar dohaeris, but he is in for some grumpy companionship tonight.

Saturday, June 4, 2016 at 3:22pm
This sombrero is surprisingly fetching and practical.

Saturday, June 4, 2016 at 12:53pm
For years now, when I reach that terrible state of mind where I just can't anymore, I watch this video. I even show it to my students when we reach the point just past midterm, when it is apparent they are lacking the mojo needed to get through the semester. No one did vainglory mixed with poetry and social justice like Muhammad Ali. No one was ever so pretty. No one.

Saturday, June 4, 2016 at 1:10am
RIP, Muhammad Ali.

Friday, June 3, 2016 at 9:16pm
Despite my new sombrero, I'm totally behind the fella from Puerto Rico.

Friday, June 3, 2016 at 8:14pm
Eye of the Tiger is no longer appropriate theme music for boxers. It's like dropping a cliché on a cliché at this point.

Friday, June 3, 2016 at 7:57pm
After a lame KO like that, I find myself asking what would Burgess Meredith do?

Friday, June 3, 2016 at 7:50pm
Oye como va. That's the tune. I could strut to that.

Friday, June 3, 2016 at 7:46pm
I still want theme music to play when I enter the room. Thinking Peaches might be worthy.

Friday, June 3, 2016 at 7:33pm
At the fights again. Last time Viking helmet, this time, sombrero.

Friday, June 3, 2016 at 12:04am
Nothing says "Welcome Home" quite like my upstairs neighbor tonight who dumped their bucket of something foul and fluid over the railing just as I was paused on the walkway beneath, fishing my house key out of my pocket. #itsnotrainingmenhere

Wednesday, June 1, 2016 at 4:10pm
Despite the change in building management, most things seem the same here on Crystal Lake. The Creepy Maintenance Men still convene in the parking lot. The Feline is still pissed that I clipped his nails again. The one notable difference is in Herbert, the Hostile Hermit Hippie who Lives Next Door. He's taken to wearing a man bun. We didn't discuss this. We just nodded at each other, and then he glared at me a bit, as if to say, "You wish you had locks long and luxurious enough to twist into an intricate knot on your thick, empty skull."

Wednesday, June 1, 2016 at 1:00am
This may make no sense, but I'm a woman who takes her vegetables very seriously. I once drove a rutabaga to Ohio for a potluck.

Tuesday, May 31, 2016 at 7:04pm
Random Confession & Other News: 1. Il Confessio: I was so excited about the escarole, that I just stared at it all last night and left it to cook today. Then I got so excited preparing it, I peeled off the tip of my index finger with The Chef's super sharp chef knife while mincing garlic. Thankfully, I was mincing, and not slicing. 2. Other News: The building is abuzz with news that our long-time building manager (the one who leaves notes that encourage tenants to disrobe in the laundry room. "Tenants may remove clothing at any time." And told me once that floors are not included in our rent.) has mysteriously left, only to be replaced by a Mercedes-driving person of ambiguous origin and character. Intrigue and escarole. That's what's for dinner.

Monday, May 30, 2016 at 5:37pm
Friends, I am pleased to announce that, finally, I have procured the escarole. I am complete.

Monday, May 30, 2016 at 2:18pm
No, escarole is NOT a euphemism.

Monday, May 30, 2016 at 11:31am
I'm on a quest for escarole.

Sunday, May 29, 2016 at 11:55am
Having The Chef back on the caffeine may not be such a good thing. By the time I woke this morning (okay, closer to noon), he'd already consumed a full pot and was working on making a second. This was good, in that there was coffee waiting, but the downside is he's all chipper, full of energy, and wants to interact with me, and I'm still in the "kill it if it talks to you" phase of my morning.

Saturday, May 28, 2016 at 1:34pm
Of course, it only begins to rain thunderously when I am walking out of the office supply store with a ream or two of printing paper. And of course, I refused to let the cashier bag it, and left my umbrella in the car. AND MOST ESPECIALLY, of course I parked in the farthest corner of the parking lot. Of course, this was the day I wore cork-soled shoes, and of course, a lake formed all around the car in the downpour.

Friday, May 27, 2016 at 3:56pm
That perfume I'm wearing? Bubble juice and baby burps, Bub.

Thursday, May 26, 2016 at 3:25pm
The children are sleeping and some evil toy somewhere in earshot keeps squeaking out, "jitterbug." This would be fine, if only George Michael would show up and put the boom-boom into my heart.

Wednesday, May 25, 2016 at 5:24pm
I have a removable whistle top for my teakettle and use a French press.
So, if I'm working in the back of the apartment and need to boil water for
the French press, I work while I'm waiting for the water, because
otherwise it takes twice as long to boil. The problem is that I'm not
always careful about where I point the spout of the teakettle, and
sometimes, like just now, when I have a pot prepped with Sumatran
beans, just waiting for the water, I hear the whistle, go running for the
kitchen, and get shot when the whistle top blows right off the teapot,
across the kitchen and into me. My cause of death will likely be coffee
casualty.

Wednesday, May 25, 2016 at 8:17am
Jan Becker is interested in First Draft: A Literary Social.

Sunday, May 22, 2016 at 4:57pm
Occasionally, The Feline climbs into my laundry basket, and buries his
little nose in my dirty clothes. I suppose I should be flattered, but I just
find it creepy.

Saturday, May 21, 2016 at 11:09pm
The Chef was just trapped in our building's elevator for 40 minutes. I
was stuck with him once for 15 minutes. It's good they let him out when
they did. He might have chewed off his arm if he'd been stuck there just
a few minutes longer. It wouldn't have gotten him out of the elevator
any faster, but The Chef's mind goes to some very strange places when
he's trapped in a tight space. In other news, he's giving up his futile
attempt to cut caffeine from his diet. I think there was an epiphany in the
elevator involving the brevity of life, and its miserable nature when
absent caffeine.

Friday, May 20, 2016 at 9:54pm
I fell asleep in the middle of assembling a new floor lamp for the living
room and dreamt I was attacked by a clan of grizzly bears. #stiffneck

Wednesday, May 18, 2016 at 1:15pm
Something very large and fragile just broke into a thousand pieces in the living room. I'm bunkered down in my office with enough supplies to last through the nuclear ice age about to commence here.

Wednesday, May 18, 2016 at 10:05am
Of course, today, when it's chock-full of CV updates, telephone conferences, interviews, editing tasks, and assorted alltheotherthings, is the day The Chef selected as Pre-amp Testing Day. #godhelpme

Tuesday, May 17, 2016 at 2:48pm
Oh, thank goodness. It's about to start pouring. RIP, Ridiculous Pollen Count. You're about to suffer a watery, South Florida-style downpour of a death.

Monday, May 16, 2016 at 8:39am
Monday, fasting bloodwork, case for coffee: Ouch. Ugly sun. Head of sand. No sentences, word sense from mouth tongue. Biting people only option. Pray quick needle nurse. Ouch. Coffee cry.

Sunday, May 15, 2016 at 7:41pm
Toddler logic: Given a plate of peanut noodles and a fork, The Toddler uses the fork as intended, and then combs her hair with it. #Peanutbutterhead

Sunday, May 15, 2016 at 10:33am
The Chef is trying to get off caffeine, and is not drinking coffee. I'm walking around flaunting my Colombian like a drunkard at an AA meeting.

Thursday, May 12, 2016 at 9:12am
I'm taking the pollen count personally now.

Wednesday, May 11, 2016 at 5:25pm
I probably have enough fight in me to take on city hall. FIU Parking? I have a feeling that's too big a behemoth even for me.

Tuesday, May 10, 2016 at 9:28am
Conversation with The Chef:

> Me: How are you feeling today, Chef?
> Chef: Much better. How about you?
> Me: I had a Michelle Obama dream last night, and now feel like I can do ANYTHING.
> Chef: Yeah? I had a nice dream last night too.
> Me: Was Michelle Obama in it?
> Chef: No, all my friends went to jail.
> Me: ...

Tuesday, May 10, 2016 at 8:34am
I had a Michelle Obama dream last night, and everything today seems much better.

Sunday, May 8, 2016 at 1:32am
There's a cockroach in my office (I live in South Florida. Don't judge.) who keeps popping out to say hello and then runs away as soon as I reach for a bludgeoning tool. Intellectually, I understand that this roach might have been my mother (Happy Mother's Day, Mom) in a past life, but tonight, there will be no sleep until the little bugga is mash. Ya no puede caminar porque no tiene porque le falta marijuana que fumar.

Saturday, May 7, 2016 at 1:23pm
Margaritas for breakfast.

Saturday, May 7, 2016 at 10:41am
Woke up all teary-eyed and reached for a tissue to wipe my eyes, but forgot I'd bought the Puff's Plus with Vicks. #ouch

Wednesday, May 4, 2016 at 8:35pm
Jan Becker shared a memory.
Here's something I don't talk about much. Five years ago today, my "little procedure" was in reality, a major, life-altering surgery. When I went under general anesthesia, I weighed 369 pounds, my triglycerides were so high, the lab couldn't get a reading, and I was waking up every day very close to dropping dead from a stroke, because my blood pressure and diabetes were so out of control. Within a day of the gastric bypass, my blood sugars had normalized. Within 3 months, my blood pressure, cholesterol, and triglycerides were normal. Within 6 weeks, my pants were falling off when I reached up to write on the whiteboard while teaching (sorry class). Deciding to have the surgery was the best thing I ever did for myself (other than matriculating), not because I look better, but because I feel better—and bonus—after rerouting my intestinal track, alcohol hits me like a bitch slap, so I'm about the cheapest date you'll ever have. I'm still above my goal weight, but I'm close enough to be happy. I've been thinking lately about how difficult it is to be obese in America (let alone South Florida), how every step outside one's home feels like an examination, and each trip through grocery store aisles feels like walking a catwalk naked, except no one seems to appreciate the body on display. Fuck that. We're all so lovely and miraculous--no matter the size--that if we all looked at each other objectively, we'd fall over from the brilliance of it. (Sorry for the rambling post. I am so tired).

Tuesday, May 3, 2016 at 9:21pm
I just gave The Feline a chunk of Valerian root the size of his head, and while my office now smells like sweat socks that have been brewing in a bucket of armpits for a few weeks, I am pleased to announce that he reports he has met God, and she loves us all very much.

Tuesday, May 3, 2016 at 1:34pm
There are just some things that should not be done in the waiting room at the doctor's office. I did all of them today.

Monday, May 2, 2016 at 9:07pm
Craziest election ever. Heidi Cruz: My Husband Is Not the Zodiac Killer

Monday, May 2, 2016 at 6:00pm
Jan Becker likes New York Grilled Cheese Co.

Monday, May 2, 2016 at 11:23am
Poor Kitty: The Feline has scratched a spot on his neck bald--I think it might be a bug bite. I'm seriously considering placing him in a cone of shame until it heals up.

Sunday, May 1, 2016 at 7:20pm
In thanks to the young man at Publix who makes me feel like Mrs. Robinson (and thus blush) whenever he greets me in the dairy aisle with his, "Hello, Beautiful, how are you today?"

Sunday, May 1, 2016 at 2:50pm
Include Adjuncts in Loan Forgiveness Program

Saturday, April 30, 2016 at 2:12pm
In a past life, I worked a job that required me to carry a service baton (billy club). I was trained in how to use it safely to stop an attack with a single whack to the side of the kneecap--which I had to do twice. I'm mentioning it now, because I took a spill last night and crunked up my kneecap and ankle, and I can't help thinking it is somehow karma calling in the debt I owe for the two men I disabled with my service baton many years ago. And OUCH. Evolution (or Creation, if that's your thing) should have done a better job engineering the human knee.

Friday, April 29, 2016 at 6:09pm
I'm still recovering from yesterday, which was filled with a workshop with Reading Queer and Danez Smith, and a conversation with Tim O'Brien (yes, THAT Tim O'Brien) about Vietnam, Agent Orange, and the Marine Corps.

Wednesday, April 27, 2016 at 8:36pm
Possibly the most important conversation I've ever had with The Chef:
Scene: Our living room just after sunset.

> Chef: Who's your favorite Beatle?
> Me: George, of course.
> Chef: (shakes his head) Of course, yeah, you WOULD say George. Why George?
> Me: Because he was the prettiest Beatle. He had the biggest heart of them; he was a humanitarian. And he was the best musician.
> Chef: Really? You think he was the best musician?
> Me: OF COURSE HE WAS. HE WAS EVERYTHING. Why? Who was your favorite Beatle?
> Chef: George, of course.

Monday, April 25, 2016 at 10:06pm
Note to Self: It will not help the situation if you try to explain Marxism and Socialism to a toddler who has suddenly become enamored of the word "MINE."

Monday, April 25, 2016 at 7:34pm
Every time I see Houston Cypress' name in print, my heart starts doing a mambo in my chest.

Monday, April 25, 2016 at 5:43pm
I have great admiration for how The Toddler just dives right in to a plate of curry. It's a double-fisted kind of activity--and somehow that means every inch of her is covered. The child is going to be sporting turmeric stains in odd places for the next several years.

Saturday, April 23, 2016 at 9:28pm
Of course, now that The Toddler is expressing how "scary" she thinks giants are, all the new Sesame Street episodes are filled with giants. Giant robots, giant dinosaurs, and giant mutant Cookie Monsters. Giant pain in the ass, you, new, Sesame Street.

Thursday, April 21, 2016 at 6:16pm
#sexyjoebiden dreams big.

Thursday, April 21, 2016 at 3:35pm
Jan Becker went to John Dufresne Book Launch.

Wednesday, April 20, 2016 at 6:11pm
Overheard at last night's reading: 1. She had a bright future ahead of her
until she walked into Janbecker's intro to creative writing class. 2. No,
don't drink the Miami tap water! It might have nuclear waste in it.

Wednesday, April 20, 2016 at 11:27am
If you celebrate: Happy Holidaze!

Wednesday, April 20, 2016 at 12:58am
Thank you, South Florida. For everything.

Monday, April 18, 2016 at 1:37pm
After painstakingly removing all the wontons from The Toddler's soup,
and hooking her up with a straw to drink the broth, and a spoon for the
dumplings, and some veggie straws because she asked for them,
EVERYTHING wound back up in the broth. Some of this will no doubt
make it into The Toddler eventually. But for right now, I am totally
ignoring my mother's voice in my head saying, "Hey! Stop playing with
your food." #sorrymom

Saturday, April 16, 2016 at 10:30am
The Chef was up at 8AM to celebrate Record Store Day. He reports (with
a giant Star Trek convention kind of smile) that the stores are all packed
with vinyl nerds. In addition to albums from John Coltrane, Notorious
BIG, Daft Punk with Junior Kimbrough, and a 1967 French remix EP of
the 13th Floor Elevators, he finally received this thing in the mail, after a
year of waiting for it to be built. He says it's a "Decware Phono Preamp."
The thing looks like a miniature nuclear reactor. Please let me know if
you notice I'm glowing.

Friday, April 15, 2016 at 4:50pm
One good thing about spending time with The Toddler is that I can be as scatological as I want to be, and she doesn't judge me. Not one bit. #pooptalk #wetalkshit

Wednesday, April 13, 2016 at 1:30pm
This is the kind of day I open my email and am flooded with unsolicited advice from anti-Planned Parenthood groups, pleas for donations to the Republican Party, an offer for a 47% discount on Viagra, and inquiries about my premature memory loss. I'm not so much troubled by how offensive I find these. I just can't handle all the mangled grammar.

Tuesday, April 12, 2016 at 10:43pm
The fate of my entire week is currently hinged on an absence of proper bookmarks and index tabs.

Monday, April 11, 2016 at 8:21pm
An example of why Jan Becker's brain is just gross: Five minutes before I was due to walk out the door, The Chef downloaded a virus (this is relatively immaterial to the nature of my brain, and really, just an excuse to rat out The Chef.). After scolding him soundly, I walked out the front door into the sunshine, and lo, Creepy Maintenance Man #2 was disrobing in the parking lot, all muscled and sweaty in his barechestedness. And before I could stop it, my brain switched on its internal hi-fi and began blasting Joe Cocker's, "You Can Leave Your Hat On." #Creepy

Monday, April 11, 2016 at 2:17am
"Miami" keeps autocorrecting to "miasma." Make of that what you will.

Sunday, April 10, 2016 at 2:33pm
Jan Becker shared a memory.
I DID finally get to hug this tree.

Saturday, April 9, 2016 at 4:57pm
I imagine that seeing The Winemaker off is a bit like giving birth. When imminent, it seems as though it will be a blessing, and each year, once I've grunted my way through the labor, I conveniently forget the excruciating pain and all the nausea of cleaning out the fridge of his leftovers.

Saturday, April 9, 2016 at 10:42am
The Winemaker's final words to me as he walked out the door for the last time this visit: "Becker, don't cry. I'll be back." Is that not enough to make a woman weep?

Thursday, April 7, 2016 at 2:49pm
Conversation with The Winemaker:
(Scene: I'm getting coffee brewed, in a rush to head out the door. The Winemaker is in the livingroom, crunching a bag of Cheese doodles quite loudly)

> WM: I had a terrible time at the beach today.
> Me: I'm sorry to hear that, what happened?
> WM: This rude guy, he sat down right next to me, and started eating crunchy snacks from his own country. He was right in my face, eating crunchy snacks. I had to move on. (pops a Cheese Doodle into his mouth, crunches)
> Me: I completely understand how you could find that offensive.

Thursday, April 7, 2016 at 2:13pm
Calculating travel time to arrive in Downtown Miami at 5:30 PM at various times of the day: 7AM: Leave now 10AM: Leave now. 11AM: Leave Now 12PM: Call and let them know you'll be late. #traffucked

Thursday, April 7, 2016 at 1:19pm
The Chef announced that he thinks The Winemaker may be returning north this Saturday, though he specifically asked I not quote him on this. In my experience a better indicator of departure date is to do an

inventory of the remaining wine bottles of homebrew in my living room. The current tally is 9 1/2 bottles. At an average consumption rate of three bottles per day, it appears The Chef may be correct in his estimate, unless I throw the scheme off and drink a few bottles myself tonight. However, I like my digestive system too much to do that to myself.

Thursday, April 7, 2016 at 11:28am
Jan Becker went to Working Poet Radio Show.

Thursday, April 7, 2016 at 12:53am
Donald Trump the goose is out on the lake right now, at 1 AM, mocking me.

Wednesday, April 6, 2016 at 9:38pm
The Winemaker wants to watch *The People vs. OJ Simpson* with me. I may have to live tweet this mess.

Wednesday, April 6, 2016 at 9:06pm
48 hours and change after returning from Los Angeles--The List: 1. I have heard The Chef say, "He's only here a few more days," 37 times. 2. Have had three Creepy Maintenance Man encounters. 3. Have 26 fresh insect bites where no insect ought to be biting. 4. Have discovered how very much I love my own bed. 5. Have also discovered how very perfect a bedmate Fabienne Sylvia Josaphat-Merritt is (don't tell the cat).

Tuesday, April 5, 2016 at 3:36pm
You know how people say they wake up with a start and feel like they are drowning? I didn't really understand what that meant until just now, when I woke from my nap and heard The Winemaker showering.

Tuesday, April 5, 2016 at 1:42pm
The Feline has finally forgiven me for leaving him. I also, at long last, slept an entire night, and should be well-rested, full of energy and doing all the things I neglected while away—"should" seems to be my primary operative word today. And so, the suitcase remains full of stinky clothes,

and a nap appears to be the most appealing activity to engage myself in for the afternoon. I'm hoping a more lucid brain wakes me up, but I've been hoping that for more than 40 years to no avail.

Monday, April 4, 2016 at 11:35am
The Winemaker is experiencing a dire "crisis." The air conditioner in his car has gone on the fritz. "I can handle this," he's telling The Chef, "it's a very serious issue, but I'm strong enough." He's here one more week, and is beginning to wonder if it will be more than he can bear. Talk to me in August, Winemaker. I spent two years without air conditioning in my car in South Florida, with a commute through the swamp. I'm going to bed—perhaps for the rest of the month.

Monday, April 4, 2016 at 11:03am
The mystery rash is spreading, and I am still awake. I'd tell you how many hours, but I can't do the math with the time zone change.

Monday, April 4, 2016 at 8:11am
I survived the long red-eye and the football team, who fell asleep fairly early, as did the coach--She was a cuddler. I am covered with a mystery rash. I suspect it may be hives from too much alien space invasion and TSA pat-downs. I'm home now and unable to sleep, because The Feline is airing his grievances over my abandonment of him (he has been at it since 7), and Donald Trump the goose is honking out on the lake. The Winemaker is sound asleep in my office. I'll assess those damages later. Thank you friends and LA for a week filled with everything! And, hey, it's good to be back home again.

Monday, April 4, 2016 at 12:37am
It looks like my red-eye is populated mostly by a high school football team with too much energy and a bunch of exhausted writers. This is going to be great.

Monday, April 4, 2016 at 12:23am
I had the pleasure of a long wait in the airport with Fabienne and
Michele whose flight boarded late at the gate next to mine. As soon as
they left, a Great Dane in a service vest took a piss on the rug in the
waiting area. My thoughts exactly, Mr. Great Dane, my thoughts exactly.
#aloneagainnaturally

Sunday, April 3, 2016 at 11:14pm
TSA screening wasn't so bad this time. I managed to only get a pat
down. My poor laptop though. It's in my backpack weeping after
undergoing the latex-gloved secondary screening.

Sunday, April 3, 2016 at 2:05am
Last night of AWP, I find myself licking the honey off my pajamas before
I crawl into bed.

Friday, April 1, 2016 at 8:17am
4AM during AWP: Janbecker finds herself wide awake with feet that
want to wander, and a room full of sleeping writer-roommates. She
wanders to the hotel lobby, and then outside. Spends a half-hour
pondering a dove perched over the entrance, a chihuahua in a sweat suit,
and the bizarre parking habits of Los Angelenos, gets that cry from the
back of throat for hot, fresh coffee, asks the doorman (who does not
judge her for wandering in public in her pajamas) when the first
coffeehouse in the immediate vicinity opens for the day. He smiles,
points to the registration desk, says, "we just brought out the first pot."
And lo, as if an answered prayer, she spies the steaming pot of joe. Long
skeptical of hotel coffee (Janbecker brings her own grounds on overnight
trips), she takes a chance, and good god. It's the BEST cup ever tasted.
Later, this morning jaunt will be painful, but for right now, it's perfect.

Friday, April 1, 2016 at 3:12am
Clock strikes midnight Pacific time. Outside the front entrance to the
Omni Hotel, the doormen are jamming out to "Dancing Queen," and the
writers begin straggling in for the night. And me in my Cookie Monster

PJs and Ma in her cap are ready to settle down for a long April nap, except these writers are all so pretty, I'm going to have to sit here a bit longer and gawk.

Thursday, March 31, 2016 at 9:51pm
Jan Becker at Bouchon Bistro, Beverley Hills, California.
I feel a little more like the hillbilly I am tonight.

Thursday, March 31, 2016 at 8:44pm
Los Angeles is growing on me. Just saw a Viking riding her bicycle down the street.

Wednesday, March 30, 2016 at 12:54pm
If they are going to grope me every time I fly (hello, fingers in my butt), they could at least sweet talk me a little. We've landed. Watch out, Los Angeles!

Wednesday, March 30, 2016 at 12:39am
What my packing list has come down to: 1. Absinthe spoon. 2. Needle nose pliers. 3. Latex gloves. 4. Armed Forces Survival Manual.

Tuesday, March 29, 2016 at 4:08pm
Oh, good Lord (whatever that means to you). I should not travel. I do stupid things like end a phone call with The Winemaker by saying, "Have fun, love you, Winemaker." #stockholmsyndrome #Winemakerchronicles

Tuesday, March 29, 2016 at 12:26pm
All the things still need to be done before I hand my office over to The Winemaker to sleep in (foolish move, Janbecker), and then fly out to Los Angeles. However frantic it may become, I am delighted by The Toddler's latest milestone. She's learned to say, "cheers." Also, there's a bottle of single malt scotch here with my name on it, but for now, despite how fun that might be, I'm sticking to coffee for my toasts.

Monday, March 28, 2016 at 9:52pm
Jan Becker updated her cover photo.
Saw this on Dragnet. The Chef made me watch it. Weird episode, but I
like the idea of living in a Temple of the Expanded mind.

Sunday, March 27, 2016 at 1:36pm
Easter so far: 1. Donald Trump the goose is making more noise than ever
early in the morning. 2. I woke up The Winemaker this morning while
searching for a pair of professional claw trimmers. 3. I discovered on my
birthday that "out of your hair for most of the day" (Winemaker) means
he will watch television in the living room for four hours, and give me a
slice of pizza for a birthday gift. Today I will learn the true meaning
behind, "I'm taking off for my friend Chuck's place for a few days, but
Chuck doesn't have a television, so I need to watch the Syracuse game at
6PM." How long is a Syracuse game? I am guessing 8 hours. 4. I woke
The Chef up this morning letting out The Feline, then again when I
discovered he'd parked in space #69, which belongs to someone else in
the building, who is pissed at us, because we keep parking there instead
of our space #68, but really, their space is more fun. Anyhow, The Chef
wasn't happy, and barked something about being a working man who
needs his rest. 5. After that exchange, I got in the car and drove to the
cats I am minding, and even though little Ollie was kicked out of the
feline hospital for being incorrigible during pedicures, I managed to trim
his front claws and that of brother Smush Face. Neither of them knicked
me with their razor-sharp claws. I am a working Jan. 6. It is quiet here
now, and I'm packing for AWP. Packing list includes: immersion
blender, soldering iron, cobbler glue.

Thursday, March 24, 2016 at 7:29pm
I drove through a tornado warning (and possibly the tornado itself) only
to find I'm trapped here with The Winemaker (and he's cagey tonight).

Wednesday, March 23, 2016 at 8:03pm
Warm welcome home from The Feline. He took one look at me, and
coughed up a hairball on my foot. That's love right there.

Wednesday, March 23, 2016 at 12:02pm
According to The Toddler, breakfast today included an "offal." Sounds a
mite less appetizing than a waffle.

Wednesday, March 23, 2016 at 9:07am
Jan Becker shared Binghamton University's post.
This was my anthropology professor at Binghamton. He offered extra
credit to anyone in the class who could successfully breed with an ape.
That was a fun class.

Monday, March 21, 2016 at 11:36pm
The highlight of my evening was stumbling into The Winemaker's sack
of soiled skivvies. #nightmaremaker #Winemakerchronicles

Monday, March 21, 2016 at 8:29pm
The Feline is not convinced that Swedish fish count as seafood.

Monday, March 21, 2016 at 4:45am
It makes perfect sense that at 4AM on the first day of spring, when there
is little use for such a thing, I finally locate the plug to the electric
blanket. Boo-yah!

Saturday, March 19, 2016 at 10:04am
The Winemaker's annual visit requires not only personal compromise,
but diplomatic negotiation between species. For years now, we have
been requesting cessation of hostilities between The Winemaker and The
Feline. Finally, this year, we are seeing marked improvement. To wit,
yesterday The Winemaker granted The Feline access to his medicinal
greens on the balcony--unprompted. This morning however, The Feline
again yowled in The Winemaker's ear at dawn, waking him from
slumber filled, no doubt, with reprobate imaginings. Furthermore, when
given access to the balcony this morning, The Feline did not graze his
grasses, but instead glared through the window at sleeping Winemaker,
and proudly sang his battle hymns.

Friday, March 18, 2016 at 8:46pm
Today was "ask Tia for an orange/cheese/cheerios/potato sticks and throw them on the floor day" with The Toddler. Tonight is "I've decided to stay here and watch March Madness" with The Winemaker. #icantgetno

Wednesday, March 16, 2016 at 3:10pm
Observation after freeing The Toddler after she locked herself in her sister's room in the 15 seconds I was on the potty, and I briefly considered calling in the fire department and/or removing the door, and/or finding an implement of destruction to bust a Toddler-sized hole through the door, while having a major panic attack imagining she was starving/suffering/creating the biggest mess in the history of messes: 1. Thank goodness for skeleton keys. 2. Thank goodness I don't have any children of my own. 3. Boarding schools for Toddlers--that should probably be a thing. 4. Oh blessed, relatively uncontested naptime, I cherish you most of all.

Tuesday, March 15, 2016 at 10:19pm
Jan Becker feeling overwhelmed.
If I wind up in hell in the afterlife, my eternity will be spent with an overtired Toddler who no longer believes that naps are necessary.

Tuesday, March 15, 2016 at 10:23am
Jan Becker added 2 new photos.
It seems appropriate that Florida's primary is falling on the Ides of March. The Winemaker returns today. Donald Trump the goose appears to have left the area & The Chef woke very bronchial this morning. We're leaving shortly to vote (Feelin' the Bern). In the meantime, while he has been absent from the apartment, I am having a hard time deciphering Winemaker hieroglyphics on the wine boxes he left behind.

Monday, March 14, 2016 at 12:00pm
Happy Pi Day!

Sunday, March 13, 2016 at 10:58am
This morning, Donald Trump the goose started up his squawking again, and the downstairs neighbors decided they'd had enough. Armed with broomsticks, they chased him away. Trouble is, he didn't fly off very far, just across the lake, and he's pissed now, so his honking is louder than usual, and while there's no canyon here, it seems to me he's echoing. I miss that hour of sleep that was stolen from me last night.

Saturday, March 12, 2016 at 4:12pm
Some notes on the goose named Donald Trump: 1. Listening to Donald Trump gave me back spasms. I'm spending the day with a heating pad. 2. The rally was a whole lot of honking with little substance, and when the Muscovy ducks tried to enter the yard, his flock of followers pushed them around and made even more noise until the ducks just jumped in the water and swam off. 3. I won't even mention what they did to the egrets. 4. I offer as evidence of Donald Trump's lack of moral substance and character the observation that even though he has fresh grass and some juicy catnip on the balcony, if Donald Trump is anywhere near the building, The Feline refuses to go out to graze. 5. Donald Trump hates children. When the kids from the building went out to play, Donald Trump and his supporters all flew away. It's too bad the kids have to do anything but play in the backyard. EVER.

Saturday, March 12, 2016 at 7:02am
Donald Trump the goose is holding a rally this morning. The whole lake is flocking with his ilk. Here he is with one of his endorsers. I think it might be Sarah Palin.

Friday, March 11, 2016 at 10:22pm
From this moment forward, the honking goose in the backyard shall be known as Donald Trump. There's a strong resemblance.

Friday, March 11, 2016 at 6:19pm
I've just figured out the goose that drove The Winemaker out is probably
my "Raven." It hardly seems fair. Poe's tormentor was at least poetic with
his, "nevermore." All this goose says ALL DAY LONG is
"HAHAHAHA." This is probably appropriate.

Friday, March 11, 2016 at 10:32am
I'm having second thoughts about the goose whose honking drove The
Winemaker off. The little pisser was out again at 6AM, and called for
two hours straight. It's enough to give a vegan a craving for roasted fowl.

Friday, March 11, 2016 at 12:45am
Because I slept so sinfully late today, and was happy, I offered to allow
The Winemaker to sleep in my office while I'm in Los Angeles (I may
regret this later, but I usually find interesting things under the bed when
he vacates the room). This means I need to organize my office so he has
room for whatever it is Winemakers do in my absence. Since he's not
here tonight, and I'm not tired, I've pulled all my hardcopy rough drafts
together, and have them spread out all over the living room rug. I didn't
realize what I'd been up to with all this writing business until now, but it
appears I may be partially responsible for the deforestation of the planet.

Thursday, March 10, 2016 at 5:08pm
Wow, Universe is being very kind to me this week. The Winemaker
returned, packed his bags and left for alternative lodging. He may be
back, but for now, my great friend, the honking goose has driven him
away. Also, I got me that ticket for an aeroplane. All booked for AWP! A
week ago, this was inconceivable. It still is. I'm gobsmacked with joy.

Thursday, March 10, 2016 at 1:48pm
I would like to thank the universe for finally granting me a good night's
sleep (I haven't had one in two weeks). As a bonus, I slept so late, I didn't
have to tiptoe in the kitchen to make my morning coffee and risk waking
the Winemaker, nor were my eyes assaulted by the sight of him lounging
in his skivvies while he eats his Lucky Charms or Honey Pops cereal. I

slept so late, the honking goose must have grown hoarse, because he's grazing like he's in a Quaker meeting. The Feline is tripping on catnip on the balcony, basking in the breeze and the sun. The apartment is empty, and I am here alone, in the quiet, rested, drinking the best cup of coffee that has ever been brewed. None of this will last, but for right now, the solitude is perfect.

Wednesday, March 9, 2016 at 6:28pm
In other news: While cleaning in preparation for The Winemaker's arrival, I found the draft of a one-act play from 2002 about a persistent house-guest whose hostess resorts to desperate measures to end his stay. This prefigures my move to Florida and the annual migration. Art as prophecy, I suppose. #Winemakerchronicles

Wednesday, March 9, 2016 at 5:59pm
Earlier I was told of The Winemaker, "He is much closer than we thought." Just now I heard, "Uht, he's here." #Winemakerchronicles

Wednesday, March 9, 2016 at 9:42am
This morning thus far: Was harassed by a squawking goose out on the lake while trying to eke out ten more (OH PLEASE JUST TEN MORE) minutes of sleep. Stepped on the cat's tail, and suffered the consequences. Stabbed myself in the eyeball with tweezers. Happy Winemaker Arrival Day!

Tuesday, March 8, 2016 at 11:41pm
Jan Becker shared John Lewis's photo.
I love this man.

Tuesday, March 8, 2016 at 9:27pm
Wow. Today: Was rear-ended by a young man in Miami with no knowledge of pedestrian right-of-way privileges. Watched a poet get her wings. Was blessed by a random act of kindness that will put me on a plane to Los Angeles for AWP (!). Sat out rush hour with some of my favorite people. Came home to another unexpected gift in the mail from

someone I adore and miss like an amputated limb. Was informed The Winemaker is arriving tomorrow. Let's not think about that right now.

Monday, March 7, 2016 at 1:53am
I just randomly discovered that for the past three days, I've been trying to fix heartburn with my allergy med by mistake, which means I was taking three times the daily dose, and my sinuses didn't benefit the least from it. On a separate note, in a former life, I dispensed medications in a group home I managed for mentally ill/developmentally disabled adults. I had that job several years, and never screwed up. I also did personal care work for about 8 years that involved dispensing meds for my disabled friend Michael, and other than forgetting to pack his meds on a return trip from Florida to Binghamton once (and an incident in Panama with Mexican Farmacia Valium, which wasn't my mistake), I never mixed his drugs up. That's about 13 years almost free of med errors. I think I might need a Nurse Ratchett the next time I run a fever. Or, perhaps just more poetry. I shoulda just stuck with the poetry.

Sunday, March 6, 2016 at 7:45pm
Jan Becker feeling blessed.
Funny how one bit of grace in a day can suddenly turn into a whole whirlwind of good things, like having that pesky ear canal clear after two weeks of being clogged, and being able to breathe through the nose again, and feeling reconnected with fabulous writer friends after a long lonesome quarantine.

Sunday, March 6, 2016 at 9:37am
There HAS to be a better name for this. What is Scrotal Tongue?

Sunday, March 6, 2016 at 6:32am
Thought on being awakened by the prison loudspeaker across the lake announcing morning meds are ready: Someday, I'm going to get hold of a megaphone and read to the inmates from a boat in the middle of the night under a full moon. Maybe if they had more poetry they wouldn't

have to get up so early to take meds. Maybe if they had more poetry there'd be no one in the prison at all.

Sunday, March 6, 2016 at 5:59am
Jan Becker shared Structure and Style's post.
I love a powerful pussy poem.

Saturday, March 5, 2016 at 9:28pm
In approximately 35 minutes, The Chef will be home from a long day at work. It will take him approximately 13 minutes and 47 seconds to wash up from work, grab a big glass of water--or maybe a beer, and sit down in the recliner with his feet up. That means in approximately 48 minutes 49 seconds, we will be watching Harold and Maude. Him for the first time, me for the second of 763 times I plan to watch this movie. I have a bottle of bubbles ready.

Saturday, March 5, 2016 at 2:54pm
I'm spending the weekend on a hippie trail, head full of zombie.

Friday, March 4, 2016 at 8:47pm
I'm watching Harold and Maude for the very first time. I have a feeling this is going to change my life.

Thursday, March 3, 2016 at 4:45pm
Squirting a mixture of eucalyptus oil, menthol, and baking soda up my nose was not my wisest move.

Thursday, March 3, 2016 at 1:10pm
Whoa. #sexymittromney (never thought I'd say that)

Wednesday, March 2, 2016 at 1:14am
67° F outside/ 103.6° F inside Janbecker. #yougivemefever

Tuesday, March 1, 2016 at 6:43pm
My quest for some shuteye continues. My current challenge involves The Chef, testing out his new speaker wires with Morrissey's mean and miserable albums. Sigh.

Tuesday, March 1, 2016 at 1:43pm
I'm sick with a head cold trying to sleep because I got no sleep last night. Creepy Maintenance Man #2 is pressure washing the walkway outside my bedroom. He hit the exit door with the pressure washer, which scared the hell out the cat, who clawed my back trying to take cover. Even worse, CMM#2 managed to pressure wash the inside of my bedroom with his hose. This was probably his aim all along. #Creepy

Tuesday, March 1, 2016 at 6:27am
If the hills have eyes and the trees have ears...we're doomed.

Monday, February 29, 2016 at 11:00pm
I am not leaping. No matter if the day calls for it.

Monday, February 29, 2016 at 5:03pm
I have an estimate from The Winemaker on his arrival date: 9-10 days. Nothing is ever exact where he is concerned. I should have stuck with moonshine gargles a bit later into my Monday. #Winemakerchronicles

Monday, February 29, 2016 at 12:21pm
Starting Monday off gargling with moonshine (sore throat) is not the best use of my talents. I probably shouldn't have swallowed. <hiccup>

Monday, February 29, 2016 at 7:15am
Florida shores yellow, brown and black all over

Sunday, February 28, 2016 at 10:20pm
Investigating alternate vacation rentals for The Winemaker I find myself repeating, "Mea Culpa, mea maxima culpa" to his prospective landlords.

Friday, February 26, 2016 at 4:00pm
Two heartwarming incidents I witnessed today: 1. Leenie Moore nailed her defense. 2. There's a boy with autism in my building named Samir, who finds things like heart shaped leaves in our bushes delightful. He giggles and squeals when he finds something small that excites him. He giggles and squeals over large things that delight him as well. Boarding the elevator just now, as Creepy Maintenance Man was disembarking, Samir took extreme delight in CMM's belly, which has grown into a globe as of late. On seeing CMM, Samir rubbed CMM's belly like he was the Buddha, or a pregnant woman--or the world. CMM was not happy, but I nearly pissed myself with bliss. God bless the child who finds delight in all things great and small.

Friday, February 26, 2016 at 9:51am
Breakfast scene in my living room: The Chef is watching a murder scene on television. A blood-covered man snaps a woman's neck. There is a man writhing on the floor in agony. The blood-covered man approaches him.
>Chef: I can't watch this.
>Me: You watched the Republican debate last night.
>Chef: Oh, yeah. You're right. That was much worse.

Thursday, February 25, 2016 at 11:20pm
Amazing "head" line: Awareness of premature ejaculation can't come soon enough

Wednesday, February 24, 2016 at 2:07pm
HBO is totally gentrifying Sesame Street. Lovely skyline view, they stuffed Big Bird into a new nest, took Oscar's can off the street and put him behind a wooden corral with a recycling bin. Sigh.

Wednesday, February 24, 2016 at 9:17am
Wow, Zuckerberg finally came through with more than a like option.

Monday, February 22, 2016 at 8:41pm
Note to Self on shopping for The Chef and The Feline: 1. If The Chef
sends you to Publix for a very specific wine for cooking (Marsala), do not
pick up the "Holland House Cooking Marsala" even if it's the only bottle
of Marsala in the store and you've been searching the shelves frantically
for the real stuff in such a panic that even the Creepy Stock Guy who
flirts with you will run the other way in fear. The Chef will spit the wine
in the sink and say something rude in French (or Italian, you're not sure
which) that sounds like, "genital farts" would sound in another language.
Next time, get thee to a liquor store and buy REAL Marsala--or better yet
a bottle of bourbon, and forget about dinner altogether. 2. Also, The
Feline will not be amused if you come home with a medium-sized dog
harness because you're convinced that at ten years old, he's ready to start
taking leisurely strolls by the lake. He's not ready. He will never be
ready, and he will hiss at you, and claw your legs, and piss on your feet
if you even attempt to put him in any kind of dog harness. Even if it only
cost you $2.10 on clearance.

Friday, February 19, 2016 at 6:03pm
If I have to get a rejection letter, at least it's from Roxanne Gay—and at
least it says nice things.

Friday, February 19, 2016 at 11:30am
Harper Lee too? RIP

Friday, February 19, 2016 at 7:24am
Regarding efforts to wake this morning: Ouch.

Tuesday, February 16, 2016 at 7:22pm
My brain feels like it's the consistency of pudding right now. This may
have something to do with the well-reasoned argument The Toddler
presented earlier supporting her stuffed Elmo's right to share curry at
lunchtime. Kid refuted all my rebuttals. #starveelmostarve

Tuesday, February 16, 2016 at 2:46pm
For some reason, the dog only seems to bark when the children finally
fall to sleep. #Whatsupwiththat

Tuesday, February 16, 2016 at 8:08am
A Plea for Assistance: I have received word that The Winemaker is
planning his annual visit soon, though, as usual, one cannot pin The
Winemaker down to exact dates. If you are unfamiliar, he comes every
year and stays between a month and six weeks. This year, I have word
that he is looking for a sublet on the beach (Pompano/Ft. Lauderdale
area), and will only be staying with us for as long as it takes him to find
said sublet. I'm sure this is all a ploy, and that there will be no subletting
because: A. The Winemaker is tight in the wallet. B. A move to the beach
will disrupt years of faithful seasonal migration patterns. If anyone
knows of an inexpensive seasonal rental or sublet, please let me know.
However, I cannot guarantee the state of the property post-Winemaker
will be acceptable. Last year, there were exploding bottles of red
homebrew and an incident involving Winn-Dixie meat-flavored pasta
sauce. #Winemakerchronicles

Sunday, February 14, 2016 at 12:13pm
"On Friday, when you left me alone all day, while you were presenting a
paper at UM, and attending a book launch with the literati in Coral
Gables, The Chef locked me in the bedroom when he left for work. As
punishment for this, I pooped in the middle of the bed and tore up the
carpet trying to escape. You're not allowed to leave me alone with The
Chef EVER again." #felinechronicles

Sunday, February 14, 2016 at 9:55am
My downstairs neighbors woke me up at about 7AM with a loud
conversation on their balcony, and it is still going strong. The trouble is,
it's just loud enough to wake me up, but not loud enough that I can
eavesdrop. So what I'm hearing is, "Oh, man she's like blahblahblah."
"I'm telling you, last time I saw her I was like, wompwompwha."

"HAHAHA, did you hear about that time that she blahblahblah?" Sigh. Is it too much to ask for elocution???

Saturday, February 13, 2016 at 6:27am
I'm finally home from my long, wonderful scary yesterday. The conference went well. No one was put off by the poop. Michele Jessica Fievre gave a good keynote, and Fabienne Sylvia Josaphat-Merritt SOLD OUT at her book launch. I crashed on a friend's couch for a few hours because I'd gotten so tired I was seeing things (better to crash on the couch instead of I95). Now that I'm home, the prison is making morning announcements on the other side of the lake via loudspeaker (think morning school announcements with mandatory minimums). They are calling the prisoners to the nurses' office for morning medication, and again, I had to double-check to make sure they aren't talking to me.

Friday, February 12, 2016 at 5:58am
I have a long, wonderful, scary day ahead of me. Long, because it started at 4:30 AM. Wonderful, because I'll get to see Michele Jessica Fievre deliver a keynote address at the Recycling Poetics conference at UM, and then later in the evening Fabienne Sylvia Josaphat-Merritt will launch her novel, Dancing in the Baron's Shadow. It will only be scary for about an hour, because I'm presenting a paper at the conference. I'm posting some links below if anyone is interested in watching any of these presentations via livestream. I know there are some Caribbean scholars on my friends list. Faby and Michele are both amazing Haitian-American writers with powerful words, but one needn't be a scholar to appreciate them. And I'll be talking about elephant poop, Everglades, and poetry.

Thursday, February 11, 2016 at 2:53pm
In answer to the Facebook prompt, "What's on your mind?": 1. Panic and social anxiety, so everything. 2. The fact that the average Asian elephant produces 500 pounds of dung per day, that the Republican party symbol is an elephant, and that I like elephants and their poo much more than Republican policies and their poo. 3. See #1 4. My complicated

relationship with Lyndon Baines Johnson (yes, I know he's dead. That's one of the complications). 5. See #1

Thursday, February 11, 2016 at 9:26am
Jan Becker shared Broward County Cultural Division's post.

Wednesday, February 10, 2016 at 10:13pm
This is stuck in my head tonight. Make of that what you wish. "I'm not afraid of a witch. I'm not afraid of anything. Except a lighted match."

Tuesday, February 9, 2016 at 11:23pm
While searching through the cupboards for something else, i stumbled upon the kava kava tea. this status update would have exclamation points all over it, but i'm way too relaxed for that right now.

Monday, February 8, 2016 at 6:24pm
I'm not sure how this happened, but I went to Publix for half & half, and came home with a pot of curry to make.

Monday, February 8, 2016 at 3:31pm
How did I not know about Calming Manatee? This could put my shrink out of a job.

Sunday, February 7, 2016 at 10:22pm
Long before I entered college, I was rebuked by a supervisor on a job who very publicly belittled my use of the word "poo," and insisted that I needed to matriculate as soon as possible to develop a more professional sounding vocabulary. I feel somewhat vindicated that my first paper for an academic conference is now finished and submitted, and includes the words "poo" "farting" and "panty pulping." #justice

Sunday, February 7, 2016 at 3:18pm
It is entirely possible that my greatest achievement for the day will be sleeping in until 2PM. I'm quite proud of this.

Saturday, February 6, 2016 at 10:49pm
While I'm postulating about poo for this paper, here's a random bit of personal trivia you did not need to know: I must hide prunes if I bring them home, because they mysteriously disappear. I once brought home two 18 ounce containers (buy one get one sale) on a Sunday. By Tuesday, they had vanished.

Saturday, February 6, 2016 at 7:17pm
I should send in a final draft of a paper about elephant poop (among other things) by Monday. Understandably, this has my muscles all up in knots, and I've been hitting up the heating pad, along with various other home remedies to try to get rid of the resultant headache. Nothing has worked. Earlier today, I was rushing in the kitchen, trying to get my coffee made and spotted The Feline sitting on the arm of a chair, tossing me this "come hither" look that signals he wants to be brushed, and then flop onto my lap and purr for a good half hour. So I went thither and did my duties. Whatever medicine The Feline possesses, he willingly squandered on my aches and pain, and much of the tension is gone. I should have just listened to the cat three days ago.

Friday, February 5, 2016 at 11:36pm EST
Here is the question (and a follow up) keeping me up tonight: Is it appropriate to wear my combat boots to present at an academic conference? Follow up: How am I going to get through the conference without my combat boots on?

Friday, February 5, 2016 at 2:27pm
While outside with The Toddler's dog, I again spied the neighbor boy who tried to free the dog from his gilded cage. He was in the driveway in his pajamas with a pair of tighty-whities on his head, spinning in circles, doing what I assume is the skivvy slide.

Friday, February 5, 2016 at 1:29am
If you click "Read-on +" After the first story in "When a Gun Gets Between Mom and Dad," that's my story. No byline, but I'm in The

Atlantic. I posted this earlier in the week, but someone suggested I repost, because it went unnoticed the first time. I like that The Atlantic is covering the whole gamut with this issue.

Thursday, February 4, 2016 at 3:25pm
After three rounds of bloodwork, and a scary scare, the doctor says I'm good. After three days of the most intense headache I've ever had, I finally can see straight again. I'm convinced the headache was caused by my shrink who spent my last appointment explaining to me that the mafia is taking over FIU (I swear this isn't a delusion--he really said this). Jeb Bush is involved in this scheme. But then, per my shrink, Jeb Bush is the source of all the evil in the world.

Thursday, February 4, 2016 at 12:31am EST
Jan Becker shared Gulf Stream Magazine's photo.

Wednesday, February 3, 2016 at 8:13pm
I may have caught The Toddler's neighbor's child trying to open the gate to let The Toddler's dog out today. I also may have told the neighbor child that the dog would chew his face off if released. #ainttooproudtolie

Wednesday, February 3, 2016 at 3:17pm
Every time Jan Becker gets an acceptance email from a lit journal, the day suddenly bursts into sunshine. Thank you, Jai-alai Magazine!

Wednesday, February 3, 2016 at 9:38am
Note to Chef: It could be worse. I could be asking you to shave my neck hair.

Tuesday, February 2, 2016 at 9:55pm
Jan Becker shared Michele Jessica Fievre's photo.
I'm excited to present next week at this conference at UM on a project I'm working on involving elephant poo paper, poetry and Everglades conservation, and to hear Michele Jessica Fievre's keynote address.

Tuesday, February 2, 2016 at 6:25pm
I'm face-humping an ice bag.

Tuesday, February 2, 2016 at 4:42pm
Study: Exposure to fracking activity could make your balls bigger and reduce your sperm count via @FusionNews

Tuesday, February 2, 2016 at 4:21pm
Please pardon my language, but FUCK. FUCK. FUCK.

Tuesday, February 2, 2016 at 12:23pm
This is by no means an indictment. I am quite fond of many of these folks, but it strikes me today that undergrads overwhelmingly tend to smell like armpits.

Tuesday, February 2, 2016 at 12:19pm
Jan Becker likes Alice Walker.

Tuesday, February 2, 2016 at 7:49am
Happy Groundhog Day. The Prognosticator of All Prognosticators has prognosticated. I'm not sure why this matters to me in South Florida, but it does...

Saturday, January 30, 2016 at 7:36pm EST
In other news: The Elevator Urinator is back, apparently with a diet heavy in asparagus and other cruciferous vegetables.

Saturday, January 30, 2016 at 5:33pm EST
In some of my happiest early memories, there were trips to the Rhode Island shore with my Grandma Becker for clam digs and hide and go seek games with my exuberant clan of cousins and their parents, my Uncle Bob and Aunt Ruth. I was just talking about Aunt Ruth last night at dinner with friends, and heard today that she's passed. She was a good woman. The world would be such a better place if more people were that filled with that much love and kindness. I'll miss her. <3

Friday, January 29, 2016 at 5:49am EST
Last night, I slept with The Feline's tail waving in my face. In all my dreams, I had a fabulous, magical moustache.

Wednesday, January 27, 2016 at 11:46am EST
Things The Feline does not appreciate AT ALL (Partial list): 1. The Chef's feet. 2. The Humans' habit of lining the trashcans with plastic bags when the can is emptied. 3. The Humans' habit of emptying a trashcan by pulling out the full plastic can liner. 3. Vacuum cleaners. 4. Maintenance Men (of any sort, creepy or not). 5. Package deliveries. 6. The orange tabby who lives on the first floor and exercises his freedom by chasing squirrels up the tree next to our balcony (to quote The Feline, "That privilege flaunting fuck."). 7. The female human's habit of occasionally taking a shower. ("Barbaric") 8. Thunderbolts. 9. Lightning. 10. Tornadoes on the lake at 9:30 in the morning when he's just easing in to a good snuggle with the less-than-freshly-showered female human.

Monday, January 25, 2016 at 8:49am EST
A thought after having a second round of fasting bloodwork in one week: Considering how, in the last 35 years or so, the medical establishment has come to consider blood a potential bio-hazard and toxin, requiring complicated safety protocols, maybe the rest of the world (especially governments) should take heed and think a little harder before spilling as much of it as we have over those same 35 years or so?

Sunday, January 24, 2016 at 12:24pm
This morning the dream I woke from was one in which Nicholas Garnett found the perfect job for me. It turned out a well-off community of seniors needed an enemauensis (I just made up that word, but it means exactly what you think. Also, thanks, Nick!). I got out of bed, went to the bathroom, remembered the toilet is broken, and fell asleep until The Feline came in and urged me to go back to bed. I love my cat.

Saturday, January 23, 2016 at 5:23pm
Today is the eighth anniversary of The Feline's resurrection from the dead. It's a long story, but I'd come to Florida for an eight week visit, and got a call my second week away that he'd passed. I went into a deep mourning. When I returned to Binghamton I was in the kitchen of the house he'd been staying in while I was away, and heard scratching at the basement door. I opened the door and out he fell, still alive, but very much starved and thirsty after six weeks locked in the cellar. He's ten years old now, and up until last week, he never showed an interest in sitting on my lap. The past week, every time I sit down, he's been climbing up for a cuddle. Today, he did that, and when I petted his belly, the little shit bit me hard enough to draw blood. At least he's not still dead. That was miserable.

Saturday, January 23, 2016 at 12:22pm
This is the kind of morning that I wake from a dream where I've lost the tribute speech I'm supposed to give at a star-studded award-ceremony for Roxane Gay, and then stumble into the bathroom, and discover the toilet is broke, wash my hands and squirt hand soap all over my toothbrush head and then discover The Chef has consumed all the morning coffee. Sigh.

Thursday, January 21, 2016 at 8:51am
I looked in the mirror this morning as soon as I woke, realizing my body is trying to grow the eyebrows of Thufir Hawat. I'm going back to bed.

Thursday, January 21, 2016 at 12:00am
I'm wondering about the sewage that flooded Biscayne Bay, and whatever pollutants/chemicals are left on the Superfund site they built the FIU campus on will mix with contamination from the nuclear power plant. Seems like they're turning the bay into a big nasty teapot of poison.

Wednesday, January 20, 2016 at 12:53pm
The Feline is playing a new game on me. He begs to go out on the balcony for wheatgrass (and rye and barley grasses) and catnip. I let him out, walk away grab coffee, and he starts yowling to be let in because it's so cold out (69°). My fear is that the neighbors will hear this and think he's neglected. In truth, I think I own the least neglected cat in the world—a spoiled brat cat is what I've got (in an impeccably brushed fur coat).

Tuesday, January 19, 2016 at 8:53pm
Because it's cold here in Florida (I had to turn the heat on last night. It dropped into the low 50s), I'm making chili. This means I'm handling hot peppers again. I got them all roasted, remembered to wear my rubber gloves, and went hard to work chopping and mincing. When I got to the skinning part, I clogged up the sink, so I had to plunge. The problem is I'm not good with a plunger, so I created this volcano of hot pepper water that erupted all over me. I'm pretty much soaked, head-to-toe in capsaicin. I'm just grateful the chili survived the deluge. #littletingly

Tuesday, January 19, 2016 at 7:16pm
Jan Becker likes How to Whistle.

Monday, January 18, 2016 at 8:52pm
For the first time in a very long while, I am experiencing the buzz that comes when I've written something new. What a sweet relapse.

Sunday, January 17, 2016 at 4:26pm
It just got all "Lord of the Flies" in my parking lot.
Conversation Between Three Children with Bicycles:
> Child #1: Rupert, come over here. I have an important announcement to make.
> Rupert: Yes, Leader?
> Child#1: I've decided that Dylan, and not you will be my second in command.

Rupert: Why? That's not fair (mumble, mumble...)
Child #1: You cannot question my decision. I'm the leader.
Dylan: Yeah, he's the leader.
Rupert: (hangs his head, kicks a stone) It's still not fair.
Child #1: When was anything ever fair?

Sigh.

Saturday, January 16, 2016 at 11:41pm
Something in South Florida has eaten my face.

Saturday, January 16, 2016 at 2:34pm
The Toddler's been expanding her use of the vernacular. I wish I knew
what she calls me when she pitches a fit at naptime, because it's much
filthier than anything I've ever said. I could use a few more words like
that in my vocabulary.

Saturday, January 16, 2016 at 1:17pm
The Toddler is bent on destruction today. She's learning the joy of
dumping her toys on the floor, which is cool. I get it, but then she calls
out, "Cheeeeee-ah, Cheeeeee-ah! (Tia, Tia)," like I'm going to pick them
up again. Yeah. She wins.

Friday, January 15, 2016 at 9:28pm
According to my ad preferences, Facebook believes I have an interest in
the large intestine. Oh, Facebook. You know me so well.

Friday, January 15, 2016 at 1:27pm
I am somewhat comforted knowing my (very far in the future) cause of
death will likely be compression injuries caused by being crushed under
an avalanche of books I keep stacked to my ceiling. Worse ways to go.

Thursday, January 14, 2016 at 12:28pm
The one good thing about having Creepy Maintenance Man replace the
hot water heater is that now our water is really "hot." #Creepy

Thursday, January 14, 2016 at 10:17am
The period between waking up and the first pot of coffee is the most perilous part of my day. Right now, for example, Creepy Maintenance Man is in the kitchen ripping out the fuse box to figure out why we have no hot water, and he's humming, and I need to poop (yes, this is TMI, but I haven't had coffee and we all do it), but can't with a humming creep in the kitchen. Even if the bathroom is on the other side of the apartment and has a door that locks. And aside from that situation, his activity is delaying my first brew. There may be blood.

Wednesday, January 13, 2016 at 8:45pm
Just me? Anyone else waiting (hoping) for the announcement tomorrow that, like Lazarus, David Bowie has been resurrected after four days?

Wednesday, January 13, 2016 at 12:05pm
Sometimes I want to just say the heck with society and go live out in the wilderness and rename myself Jan the Baptist and dunk anyone who trespasses in my vicinity. But then, I'm not sure I'd be comfortable eating grasshoppers and wearing a camel hair shirt.

Monday, January 11, 2016 at 3:41pm
It amazes me how in a day filled with Toddler snot and baby puke, one little thing can go graciously right for a change, and suddenly, I feel like dancing.

Monday, January 11, 2016 at 8:03am
I woke up this morning with the distinct feeling that today is the day Rumpelstiltskin is going to show up for my firstborn. It was probably wise of me not to bear children.

Saturday, January 9, 2016 at 11:11pm
"Horseradish is often used as a tonic for a tired or deranged system." This astounding quote has led me to the conclusion that I will write in horseradish on my ballot next election.

Friday, January 8, 2016 at 1:38pm
Once again, I am covered in Infant pee and Toddler goo. :P

Thursday, January 7, 2016 at 7:25pm
Now that the windows are open for winter, my evenings are filled with
sounds from the jail across the lake, and the intercom announcing lock-
down, ordering everyone back to their cells. I always take a moment to
wonder if they're talking about me too.

Thursday, January 7, 2016 at 1:29pm
I swear I'm not making this up.

> Creepy Maintenance Man: You're awful moist in there, but we
> don't think it's the hot water. Here's the plan, we're going to strip
> you down bare and suck up all that moisture. Then we're going
> to leave you bare for the weekend. I'll keep an eye on you to
> make sure there's no trouble. If you're still moist on Monday, I'm
> going to have to go in deeper.

Thursday, January 7, 2016 at 11:41am
Creepy Maintenance Man has assessed the damage, and believes, "You
need to spread your stuff out a little more" to prevent mold. Somehow I
think the leaky hot water heater and the rain are more of a causality than
whether I have spread my "stuff" adequately.

Thursday, January 7, 2016 at 8:51am
Before I make the call to Creepy Maintenance Man, I'm making eggs.
And I'm putting pikliz on them. By doing this, I hope to create a safe
zone around me.

Thursday, January 7, 2016 at 8:40am
I'm glad I'm not the only person who was disappointed when trying
Turkish Delight for the first time

Wednesday, January 6, 2016 at 11:19pm
I finally got up the nerve to empty out The Winemaker's Room (our utility closet) to find the source of the mold. I discovered he left us a box of Publix brand angel hair pasta in with the WD-40 and Rustoleum. Also, it appears we've sustained major water damage from the recent rains. This means that over the next week, Creepy Maintenance Man will be on extended visits in our apartment. Yay! 2016. #Winemakerchronicles

Wednesday, January 6, 2016 at 7:58pm
After splashing bleach on clothes that were not meant to be bleached, and inhaling the fumes from the oven while the peppers were roasting, and burning my arms and hands with capsaicin (AGAIN), one would think I'd know better than to turn on the garbage disposal to rinse away all the blistering parts of the peppers I didn't use with my face over the drain. Also, I have a bug in my ear. There's no other explanation.

Wednesday, January 6, 2016 at 3:33pm
Handling bleach and roasting hot peppers on the same day probably wasn't a great idea.

Wednesday, January 6, 2016 at 9:22am
In other news, last week when I was housesitting, an insect flew into my ear and stung me in my ear canal. For the past week, that ear's been swollen and clogged. Now the swelling is finally down and the block is trying to clear, I'm trying to convince myself that the bug is still not in there, doing whatever it is that bugs do when they are trapped in an ear canal. It's not that easy. I read a lot of Stephen King in middle school.

Wednesday, January 6, 2016 at 4:36am
Once again Janbecker found herself awake at 4:20 AM, researching how Vanna White stores her yarn. Here's the real question: How does one store one's yearn?

Tuesday, January 5, 2016 at 1:39pm
Conversation with The Shrink:

Shrink: Hi Jan Marie (No one calls me Jan Marie, unless I'm in trouble), how was your month? I tell him...
Shrink: Oh, shit.

Tuesday, January 5, 2016 at 9:44am
Fasting bloodwork then appointment with The Shrink. Happy Tuesday

Sunday, January 3, 2016 at 4:40pm
I'm spending the whole day in the Twilight Zone in my pajamas with the cat, a crochet hook and yarn, and a hot cup of something or other.

Thursday, December 31, 2015 at 6:57pm
Don't tell The Feline, but I may have wept just a little when I bid adieu to the Griffin - Wade hooligans and the whippet earlier this afternoon. In other news, it is my intention, now I'm back home, to subsist for the remaining entirety of 2015 solely on tabasco sauce, tomato juice. horseradish, celery, citrus juice (just a squirt), Worcestershire sauce, ground black pepper and mostly vodka. I might go a little wild and toss in a couple olives too, but only if there's enough room for the vodka.

Thursday, December 31, 2015 at 1:25pm
The end of The Twilight Zone episode "Time Enough at Last" makes me weep like a small child. Poor Henry Bemis.

Tuesday, December 29, 2015 at 2:50pm
I haven't mentioned this, but I've been walking around with the Jim Carroll Band in my head the past few weeks, and enumerating losses like the sad completed hit list of a master assassin (Michael, Tommy, Aunt Eunie, Diane, Grandma, Uncle Harry, Christopher, etc...). Today, I stopped at a Goodwill Superstore in Dania Beach that I always wanted to take my grandmother to, because I knew she'd love it, but never got around to going in. Her voice was in my head the whole time I was in the store ("Why don't they have prices on anything? How the hell am I supposed to know how much anything costs? What the fuck is wrong

with that guy? He looks scary. Jan Marie, your mother is going to kill me if I buy any more books."). I bought two Avenue cardigans, a pair of sandals with the original retail sales tags on them, the ugliest purse I've ever owned (sometimes this is the point), and books by Donna Tartt, Sherman Alexie, and Erin Morgenstern. I paid $19.76 for the whole haul with an over 55 discount. And I didn't protest when the sales clerk applied the extra 15% off, because Grandma whispered in my ear ("Keep quiet, Jan Marie. She doesn't need to know how old you are. Besides, you have all those wrinkles now, might as well use them for something.").

Tuesday, December 29, 2015 at 9:13am
I dreamt last night that I was locked in an epic wrestling match with a giant alligator, who was trying to pull me under to drown me and eat me. I woke this morning with a whippet sleeping atop my head.
Scorecard- Whippet: 1 Janbecker: 0

Monday, December 28, 2015 at 9:05am
I would have been perfectly content to live my entire life absent of the whippet licking my eyeball to wake me experience.

Sunday, December 27, 2015 at 9:53pm
Good god. You should never Google any combination of "William S. Burroughs and [possible sexual partner(s)]." JUST DO NOT.

Sunday, December 27, 2015 at 6:13pm
Charlie Parker has gotten loose and is running around downtown Hollywood. I suspect kitty is looking for some fried chicken (It's all your fault, Miles Davis and Quincy Troupe, that all I can think of when I think of Bird is fried chicken); she was spotted in the alley by some trash bins. Also, Jack Daniels made life easier for me earlier. This is rare for Jack, as he tends to complicate things.

Saturday, December 26, 2015 at 6:22pm
I'm pretty sure that to Alfie (the whippet), taking a piss on a royal palm feels similar to how I felt the first time I used a loo with a telephone extension right next to the toilet. #posh

Saturday, December 26, 2015 at 4:17pm
The hardest decision I need to make today is whether to go for a swim before or after I walk the dog. My kind of afternoon.

Friday, December 25, 2015 at 2:56pm
Merry Christmas. I am finally back in Hollywood with the whippet after a long morning of traveling home to see The Chef (who is working a double-shift) and The Feline (who gave me hell and demanded a half hour of petting). I then traveled to the two other housesits I'm doing where there are four cats, all who gave me hell. Got back here to Hollywood, and the whippet gave me hell. It's a full moon. I expect a lot of hell. But it's also good. The whippet calmed down and I called my Mom and talked to her while soaking my feet in the pool. Peace on earth. I think the animals are working on the goodwill to Jan.

Wednesday, December 23, 2015 at 4:35pm
I'm in Hollywood with a whippet for the next eight days. Whippets were bred to poach rabbits and other small game. Conveniently, there is a fat domesticated bunny poking around in the sweetgrasses with a smokey grey nose and a floppy tuft of white hair on her head. Unfortunately, she doesn't understand that it would be better to let me catch her than the dog. There may be blood. Om mani padme hum, I'm doing the best I can.

Tuesday, December 22, 2015 at 7:44pm
I'm not sure why, but I'm finding it harder to pack for eight days in Hollywood than a month in New York.

Tuesday, December 22, 2015 at 9:53am
I watched this show last night with The Chef, and thought my heart was going to fly out of my chest when The Roots came on. Holy hell, can Bilal sing. (stick with it through the rap intro).

Monday, December 21, 2015 at 9:04pm
Happy Solstice!

Monday, December 21, 2015 at 4:08pm EST
Something I just cannot reconcile: While thumbing through TV listings, I discovered that in the All in the Family "Archie Feels Left Out" episode, Archie Bunker was holding on fast to 49. That's only four years away for me. #cueanothermidlifecrisis

Sunday, December 20, 2015 at 4:07pm
Coincidence? The Chef received a call yesterday from The Winemaker. It was the first I recall receiving since summer. Last night, I entered The Winemaker's room (our utility closet), and discovered the walls and baseboards have become infested with black mold (our dryer vent opens to the elements. It's been rainy here in South Florida). I rarely enter that room because of the twisty mojo that lingers (it's quite similar to black mold). I believe the universe may be sending me a message. Sigh. #Winemakerchronicles

Sunday, December 20, 2015 at 1:40pm
I slept so hard last night, I squished my eyeball in my sleep and everything looks wonky today. I like it.

Saturday, December 19, 2015 at 8:40pm
It's 73°F in South Florida. Let the wearing of the winter parkas begin!

Saturday, December 19, 2015 at 5:58pm
Jan Becker added 2 new photos.
One of today's projects: I put Naked Allen back under glass in a shiny silver frame that will, I hope, keep him from jumping on my head in the

middle of the night. And then, because I don't have enough to scare the hell out of me at 2AM, I pulled Old Bull Lee out of the closet and stuck him in a frame too. #nightterrors

Saturday, December 19, 2015 at 4:27am
I am awake right now because Naked Allen Ginsberg fell out of his frame and landed on my head while I was sleeping. #igotbeat

Saturday, December 19, 2015 at 3:58am
Vikings wanted!! Volunteer crew needed for Expedition America 2016; no murder or pillage included

Friday, December 18, 2015 at 7:38pm
I was at the ocean today, and for a moment, in the midst of all the other things, it was everything.

Thursday, December 17, 2015 at 2:55pm
Sexy Australian handyman just said my name and it was like heaven landed in my lap. Sigh.

Wednesday, December 16, 2015 at 10:49am
I'm trying hard not to be maudlin about this, but since October we've had to say goodbye to four people dear to my family. It's like God (the universe, whatever it means to you) is taking all her best gifts back.

Tuesday, December 15, 2015 at 2:24pm
Giant penis christmas lights are well-hung but piss off neighbors via @HuffPostWeird

Monday, December 14, 2015 at 4:42pm
There is nothing so messy, nor so fun, as a Toddler double-fisting a plate of pasta with tomato sauce.

Monday, December 14, 2015 at 10:21am
Some lessons in retrospect: 1. Apparently, there is a very narrow margin between a therapeutic dose of Hennessy and a hangover. 2. It might be best to keep that margin in mind when the next day is scheduled to be full of an energetic Toddler who has learned it is good to holler when filled with joy and exuberance (For example: ELMO, ELMO! or OUTSIDE OUTSIDE!). 3. Whatever losses I am experiencing are more than mitigated by the abundance of affectionate, supportive, nurturing friendships I have been blessed with. <3

Sunday, December 13, 2015 at 11:47pm
Sometimes the best medicine is a break from the house, some curry, some poetry and a healthy dose of Hennessy.

Saturday, December 12, 2015 at 9:17pm
Tomorrow, there will be poetry and curry.

Saturday, December 12, 2015 at 4:51pm
I am learning today to mourn much more than is possible to understand. My mind can't wrap itself around the sudden loss of my cousin Christopher, just 17 years old, from a seizure in the middle of the night. I don't have words for this hurt. I don't think there is a lexicon that can contain them.

Saturday, December 12, 2015 at 8:59am
The nice thing about living on a lake used by a water ski academy is that I often witness spectacular wipeouts. The less than nice thing is that on weekends, there are boats running out there until 3AM (often playing Kool and the Gang on loudspeakers), and they start back up at 7AM. This adds exponential pleasure to witnessing spectacular wipeouts.

Friday, December 11, 2015 at 7:23pm
I keep thinking that Grandma's smile is about the prettiest thing I've ever seen. It's all in her eyes. I'm glad I took these photos. They make me giggle every time I look at them. :)

Friday, December 11, 2015 at 10:28am
Nothing says "Happy Friday, Janbecker," like a curdled quart of half &
half. Ugh.

Thursday, December 10, 2015 at 11:23am
Got this in my email late last night, and it makes no sense to me, because
I am certain the abstract I sent in was written in pure gobbledygook. Oh
well, first academic conference panel, check.: "Congratulations! We are
pleased to inform you that you have been selected to participate in the
Annual Graduate Student Conference of the Department of Modern
Languages and Literatures at the University of Miami, to be held on the
Coral Gables campus on February 12, 2016." God, help me.

Thursday, December 10, 2015 at 9:58am
Trump Campaign Officially Designated As Hate Group By Southern
Poverty Law Center https://t.co/gjwgpBoEJo via @FreeWoodPost

Wednesday, December 9, 2015 at 8:57pm
It turns out that urge I had at 3AM to make soup was a sensible one as I
am now spiking a high fever and just want soup, the cat and to sleep.
One should be wary of toddlers bearing sippy cups with fevers who
want to climb in one's lap during Sesame Street. One should be wary of
toddlers in general.

Tuesday, December 8, 2015 at 6:24pm
A Final #Grandmachronicle : I spoke to Grandma this morning. Since she
couldn't talk back, I read to her from the Tibetan Book of the Dead. The
section I read is a prayer from the appendix that I think of as the Tibetan
"calling all angels prayer." It's a plea for spiritual guides to lead
decedents to the next stage. I could hear Grandma breathing over the
phone, and thought how strong and clear her breath sounded, like it
would never cease. When I'd wished her a good journey, my mom told
me two crows had landed outside the hospital window. Just after 1PM
today, I was watching The Toddler when the call came that Grandma

passed. The baby isn't feeling well, and had climbed into my lap for comfort, and to drink her juice while we watched Elmo. I don't know if there is a word for a person who is orphaned of all their grandparents as I am now. I was fortunate to have been blessed so late into my life with this whacky Grandma, who loved drag queens, thrift stores, Burger King, her whole family--and me. When I got home this afternoon, I took a nap, and woke with what seems like the first shaft of sunlight hitting the lake after days of dark skies and rains, The Feline was curled against my belly, filling it with purrs, and I thought of Faulkner's Vardaman Bundren, and how he made sense of his loss. My grandmother is a fish now also. She is a pair of crows outside a hospital in Scranton, a shaft of sunlight through the window on a dark day. My grandmother is a constellation of unfettered atoms loose in infinite galaxies. She is home where she always has been--in heaven—because, after all, heaven is all around us if we choose to look at it that way, and I can't bear to see heaven as too far off if my grandmother must be there now. Thank you for all the prayers and good wishes this year for Grandma's health. It has meant a lot to me and my family to be bolstered by so much love.

Tuesday, December 8, 2015 at 1:15am
About this long week--It's not just Grandma in hospice that's making it seem so long. It's also that I can't sleep, so each day is at least 1/3 longer than usual, and filled with odd situations like this: The roofers show up to repair The Toddler's parents' leaky house. Their dog barks. The roofers are afraid. They step out of the doorway, leaving a handy exit for the dog, who sees two little hot shih-tzu bitches walking across the street, and goes over to lick their asses (this is what dogs do). The Toddler is barefoot, so I gather her up, chase the dog away from his bitch-ass love interests, and he runs up the street instead of heading towards his home. I give chase, catch the dog at end of the street, yell at him to sit, bend down and scoop him under one arm like a football (he is a medium sized dog, about 35-40 pounds). Just then, I feel something pull in my back, and burst a blood vessel in my hand. I don't waiver despite the injuries. I head back to The Toddler's house, dog under one arm, Toddler, chirping happily under the other because it's all so very

exciting to be out on a dog chase with Tia Juana in the middle of the day, especially when it feels like Tia is about to score a double touchdown after a 50-yard dash. Then, I start to feel both the kid AND the dog slipping from my grip. The child doesn't know yet not to run into traffic. The dog is an asshole (at least in this moment, I'll like him much more later in the day), I can't put him down either. I spot a roofer. I know from his reaction earlier I cannot pass the dog off to him, so I hand off the child and say, "Just for a moment, please, so I can get a stronger grip on the dog; I'm about to lose them both." He looks at me and says, "I am covered with tar." (How could this possibly matter to me?) I look at him and see that as scary as is the dog, the child terrifies this man even more. Nevertheless, I hand The Toddler off, and tell him she washes up nicely; it will all be over quickly, to please, bear with me. The Toddler is no longer happy, because she likes it better in my cozy armpit than being held at arms' length by a man she doesn't know--who is indeed covered in tar, and afraid of both her and her dog. She begins to whimper. The dog begins to whimper. The roofer has been whimpering since he first knocked on the door. This is five minutes' worth of my life today, and today has already been twenty hours long.

Monday, December 7, 2015 at 8:18pm
This is the longest week I've lived.

Monday, December 7, 2015 at 1:36pm
I was just changing The Toddler's cribsheets, she walked in the room, looked at what I was up to, walked back to the door, looked at me again, said, "Bye Felicia," and slammed the door shut.
#Whatsthematterwithallthesekidstoday

Monday, December 7, 2015 at 12:13pm
How much can one Jan bear?

Monday, December 7, 2015 at 1:02am
Eleanor Roosevelt sex scene in a poem. Genius.

Sunday, December 6, 2015 at 5:15pm
Chanukah is one of my favorite holidays, even though I didn't grow up
in a Jewish home. I rank it so highly, because it always seems to come at
the time of year when everything has become so desperately dark and
awful, and I've just reached the point where I need to feel things are
going to get better; along comes Chanukah with its lights to say "keep
going." Happy Chanukah. Grandma is slowly progressing towards her
disembarkment. Her breathing is becoming more shallow, her
temperature is rising, and her heart is starting to flutter a little. I just
spoke to her again, and even though she's non-responsive at this point, I
let her know we'll all muddle through without her just fine. My poor
Uncle flew in from Florida to see her, and while resting up at her
apartment, discovered the "toy" Grandma had me take her shopping for
a few years ago, so even in the middle of sadness, we're still getting gifts
of inappropriate delight and laughter from having known her. That's
probably more than many people get at a time like this.

Sunday, December 6, 2015
Nothing new to report on Grandma, other than that she's been moved
into hospice and is peaceful. I'm at a loss now that the soup's done, so
I'm planning to tear apart my bookshelves and reshelf them after curry
with The Chef this morning. The Feline has been keening in the middle
of the night. He sounds like his little heart is broken, but that might just
be because I took a shower and he hates it when I'm cleaned up (weirdo).

Saturday, December 5, 2015 at 8:47pm
Still no word on Grandma, and that's okay. She takes her time with
everything. I'm still making the soup. It's an Italian wedding soup
Michael taught me to make from his mom Rose's recipe. I apologize to
my vegetarian friends and the turkeys of the world, but after two trips to
the grocery store, I was able to find turkey necks, which are necessary for
this soup. There are hundreds of tiny meatballs in it. It's about the most
time-consuming thing I make. This is good. I washed 8 loads of laundry
also, which is a miracle given it is Saturday, and everyone in the building

is after the laundry room. The Chef will be home soon, and when he walks in, he'll inspect my meatballs and say they are too big (they are so tiny though). I will tell him, you're not the first fella who's said my balls are too big. I'll wager it is something I'll hear many more times in my life.

Saturday, December 5, 2015 at 6:14am
I received a message at 3AM that Grandma had a stroke last night, and was at the hospital. It was 3AM and I tried to go back to sleep, but had this mad urge to make a pot of soup. I didn't, because it was 3AM, and there is something profane about making soup at that hour. Instead I tossed around, wishing I was making soup, and that Grandma wasn't in the hospital. It's now 6AM, and there's a message that Grandma is waiting to let go, that she has a brain bleed and doesn't want surgery. Soup at 3AM makes no sense, but neither does anything else anymore. I should have made that pot of soup, dammit. #Grandmachronicles

Thursday, December 3, 2015 at 6:50am
Jan Becker likes Jerry Garcia.

Wednesday, December 2, 2015 at 2:03pm
I'm not sure my body will ever adjust to sweating in December because the temperature outside is in the 80s and the humidity is over 90%. My body says this is the time for twisted ankles on icy sidewalks, and shivering and snowbanks.

Wednesday, December 2, 2015 at 11:31am
Jan Becker and IPC Visual Lab are now friends.

Tuesday, December 1, 2015 at 9:01pm
I just had this interesting cellphone exchange with a random stranger:
      Unknown: Baby Daddy
      Unknown: You okay?
      Me: I think you have the wrong #
      Unknown: Twitch (I looked up twitch on urban dictionary. I'm not flattered)

Unknown: Sorry...try… Sigh.
I guess I should just be pleased to announce I'm a new father.

Monday, November 30, 2015 at 7:41pm
I've lived without a blowtorch for far too long.

Monday, November 30, 2015 at 2:56pm EST
Jan Becker feeling special.
God help me. It's naptime for The Toddler, so I took her sippy cup to fill
it, returned to give it to her, only to find the little demon guzzling my
coffee like she was competing in a beer-drinking contest at a frat house.

Monday, November 30, 2015 at 1:06pm
The only thing Cyber Monday means to me is that there are 3,000,000
extra junk emails in my inbox.

Monday, November 30, 2015 at 1:05pm
Jan Becker likes High Times.

Sunday, November 29, 2015 at 10:11pm
I am learning that writing requires almost super-human focus. For
example: I refuse to be distracted by The Chef in the bedroom vocalizing
in a manner that sounds like a mother humpback calling to her young. I
have no time to investigate. Prose before bros (and beaus).

Sunday, November 29, 2015 at 4:26pm
Facebook is suggesting that under films, I might like The Twilight Saga.
Facebook, what the hell is wrong with you?

Sunday, November 29, 2015 at 1:02am
Jan Becker is going to 2016 AWP Conference & Bookfair in Los Angeles.

Friday, November 27, 2015 at 4:13pm
All I want to do is sleep. This is normal for me post-Book Fair, but seems
a stronger urge this year. I received a call this morning that one of my

mother's neighbors, Diane, passed away. She was way too young, and died too quickly. I'll miss her—we all will. That's enough to wear me out, but every time I do wake up enough to look at the news, I just can't help thinking the safest place is hunkered under the covers with The Feline, who only poses a minimal scratching hazard, has no political affiliations, and is unconcerned with procuring anything other than a catnip mousie or a phallic-shaped object (he is fond of pens) for his stash under the bed.

Thursday, November 26, 2015 at 6:47pm
First, before anything else, I am thankful for all the love I receive, and the opportunities I must share my own little bit of love with the world. However, I am absolutely the WORST at Thanksgiving. Last year, I fell asleep while the bird was in the oven and wound up with an 8-pound brick I had to stuff down the garbage chute--and I'm an excellent cook (really, I am). This year, I forgot to pick up a roasting pan, and because Walmart and Target are the only places open on Thanksgiving, went to two of each searching for a pan RIGHT AT DOORBUSTER TIME. And of course, they were out. How the hell I wound up at Walmart on Thanksgiving when I make it a point to NEVER go there on a straight day is something I'll just blame on temporary psychosis. I jury-rigged a roasting pan, and have every alarm in the apartment set to wake me if I do fall asleep again. But this is it. No more cooking turkeys for me. I might not survive my next attempt, Happy Thanksgiving.

Thursday, November 26, 2015 at 1:11pm
I am thankful for The Chef most days, but today not thankful for this: He greets me with a full mouth kiss while getting ready for a double-shift at work and then asks, "Do you have any cold medicine? I think I'm coming down with something."

Wednesday, November 25, 2015 at 6:44pm
Note to Self- Two things: 1. Shopping at Publix on Thanksgiving Eve, not a good idea. 2. Neither is it wise to wipe the bloody gash you got from the lady in the motorized cart with a Puffs Plus with eucalyptus. Ouch.

Tuesday, November 24, 2015 at 4:39pm
Jan Becker added 2 new photos.
I found my phone buried under the front seat of the car. It had just enough juice in it left to take these. The prettiest thing I ever received in the mail. Also, HOLY SHIT. I'm in the Colorado Review!

Tuesday, November 24, 2015 at 3:13pm
It appears I've lost my phone, which is a shame, because I have photos to take of the prettiest thing I've ever gotten in the mail--and the phone is my only camera right now. Sigh.

Tuesday, November 24, 2015 at 9:50am
Nothing like a bad batch of coconut water to wake me up in the morn.

Monday, November 23, 2015 at 4:20pm
It seems the only way I am going to forge peace with The Feline after a 5-day absence is to suffer through a long afternoon nap. He's insistent.

Monday, November 23, 2015 at 2:33pm
Finally back home after The Miami Book Fair. Wow. What an amazing, eclectic, fun bunch of writers this year. Thank you. #MiamiBookFair2015

Sunday, November 22, 2015 at 5:22pm
My first Quinceañera! So excited!

Sunday, November 22, 2015 at 11:18am
The Rhythm Foundation is holding practice in the room with me. Dance party tonight at The Swamp! Dance party right now! #MiamiBookFair2015 #MiamiREADS (and dances)

Saturday, November 21, 2015 at 1:33pm
SUPER LOUD SHOUT OUT to the fabulous #MiamiBookFair2015 volunteers. Especially Ruth, who for two years has come when I needed her most, and runs for grande cappuccinos when I am about to fall over. You rock, Ruth! <3

Friday, November 20, 2015 at 12:22am
I'm trying to set the alarm on my phone to wake me early, and the choices are all like "Fairytale Rapture," "Mellow Sunday," and my personal favorite, "Broccoli Salad." I'm more in need of "Apocalyptic Death Metal Dirge" and "Slam your Face into Friday, Sleepyhead."

Thursday, November 19, 2015 at 11:57pm
Jan Becker added 3 new photos.
Beat poet good human hero man Gary Snyder. #MiamiBookFair2015

Thursday, November 19, 2015 at 6:01pm
Oh my God, front row for Gary Snyder!

Thursday, November 19, 2015 at 1:37pm
On my way out the door to Miami til Monday. I am certain I'm forgetting something essential--sanity perhaps.

Thursday, November 19, 2015 at 1:30pm
Viking.

Thursday, November 19, 2015 at 10:02am
Managed a full eight hours sleep last night. First time in about a month. It feels like I've been run over by semi with winter chains on its tires.

Wednesday, November 18, 2015 at 10:18pm
I am pleased to announce that I'm out of those effing Spanx. Holy important poetry, Reading Queer. Great reading!

Wednesday, November 18, 2015 at 1:57pm
If I were to film my struggle to get into Spanx and uploaded it to Youtube, I'd be a superstar.

Wednesday, November 18, 2015 at 11:21am
Jan Becker went to Paris is Still Burning.

Wednesday, November 18, 2015 at 10:50am
The Chef neglected to brew a pot this morning. Grr.

Wednesday, November 18, 2015 at 1:55am
My tactic for packing for the Book Fair (I'll be away Thursday - Monday) is to shove every piece of clothing I own into my bag and figure out the wardrobe when I get there.

Monday, November 16, 2015 at 7:18pm
Given the choice to put egg salad on bagel chips or elsewhere, The Toddler chose the floor--and Tia Juana. Egg salad in my hair, the protein is good for sheen, right?

Monday, November 16, 2015 at 3:27pm
We're approaching the tenth minute of silence during The Toddler's second attempt at a nap in her new home (the first was horrifically unsuccessful). This might mean she has actually fallen asleep, or it might mean she is in there plotting to overthrow her oppressor (that would be me). God, help me. #thestruggleisreal

Monday, November 16, 2015 at 11:57am
An Insomniac's Attempt at Punnery: I just found this recipe for Ernest Hemingway's burgers. I guess that would make them (wait for it) "HEMBURGERS." (HAHAHA)

Monday, November 16, 2015 at 2:15am EST
In South Florida, the power of small presses grows

Sunday, November 15, 2015 at 9:04am
Sunday Morning Reflection: I'm thankful this morning for the quiet. The Feline is curled next to me in his co-pilot seat. I've been thinking how much I envy him for his ignorance of the world around him. Last night

on the elevator, a group of kids were excitedly talking about the Broward County Sheriff that had been parked in the lot while the police looked through our bushes for what the kids say was a gun someone had discarded while running from them. That made me sad, because kids are so much better at finding dangerous things than even the best trained detectives, and I'd hate for something they found in our bushes to silence any of their laughter before the world steals it away from them with cynicism and age (even if at times they distract me from my work). The whole world is making me so fraught I've stopped looking at the updates from Lebanon and France, because for one morning, I want to be like The Feline and just embrace ignorance. On the upside, The Miami Book Fair opens this afternoon and I'll be there (5:30 PM at The Porch at The Swamp) with Leenie Moore and Michele Jessica Fievre, writing poems with the Miami Poetry Collective. I can think of no more effective antidote for the world's sickness than good books and poems. If I have to exit the peaceful zone of my apartment, there's no better place to be.

Sunday, November 15, 2015 at 3:02am
For some reason, I never became acquainted with Sun Tzu until recently. It seems the perfect time to give him a close reading.

Friday, November 13, 2015 at 7:05pm
I don't know how there could possibly be just one poet you won't want to miss at the Miami Book Fair this year. I can think of at least a dozen.

Thursday, November 12, 2015 at 11:52pm EST
Jan Becker likes December Boys: A Jay Porter Novel.

Thursday, November 12, 2015 at 10:09pm
I'm honored to have been selected as the 2015-2016 Writer in Residence at Girls' Club in Fort Lauderdale. This year's exhibit, "Self-Proliferation" opened earlier this evening. It's going to be an exciting year!

Thursday, November 12, 2015 at 11:46am
Occasionally, when I check the weather, my computer trips up and sends me the temperature in Lordville. It did that this morning where it will be 30° cooler than South Florida today. And Brucie, my friend Buck's dog died today. He was not an overly friendly dog, nor was he especially handsome, and when I gave him a bath this summer, it was worse than bathing a cat. He screamed and bit the walls. But there was one day, when out of all the dogs in Lordville, Brucie was the most well-behaved dog--the best dog. I'll miss him.

Thursday, November 12, 2015 at 7:04am
One of my best Miami Book Fair moments was when Iggy Pop called me "ma'am" as he signed my book.

Wednesday, November 11, 2015 at 10:02pm
Additional items on the list of things that make The Chef squirm when discussed: 1. Cervices 2. Mucous plugs 3. Pretty much anything labor and delivery related.

Wednesday, November 11, 2015 at 7:04pm EST
Donate your books to Read to Learn Books for Free with UberBOOKS:

Wednesday, November 11, 2015 at 6:10pm
Here's what I wish: If we want to honor veterans--really honor them-- let's take care of the homeless, traumatized and injured vets we have now--and their families. Then, maybe we can stop going to war. THAT would really be the best way to honor them.

Wednesday, November 11, 2015 at 11:48am
It's not the only thing I appreciate about him, but when sick, I especially love that The Chef knows where to find potent matzo ball soup.

Tuesday, November 10, 2015 at 7:37pm
The Chef came home I read him what I'd written, and he requested trigger warnings from now on. I call that a good day.

Tuesday, November 10, 2015 at 1:36pm
I should run a fever more often. 3,122 words so far today, and it's about to get bloody.

Tuesday, November 10, 2015 at 10:08am
Jan Becker and GirlsClub FortLauderdale are now friends.

Tuesday, November 10, 2015 at 9:44am
There's something Freudian in this scene: Creepy Maintenance Man, working the stump-grinder outside my bedroom window. #Creepy.

Tuesday, November 10, 2015 at 9:19am
Gargling every liquid in the house.

Monday, November 9, 2015 at 7:10pm
Train of Thought Wreck: 1. Summer colds are the worst. 2. It is always summer in Florida. 3. I have a cold again. 4. I decided that since I have a cold, it would be a good day to make tomato soup from scratch. 5. The Chef was at the knife sharpener yesterday, sharpening his chef knives (and the household knives as well). 6. Someone once told me he was impressed with my knife skills. 8. A side effect of the rhinovirus is dizzy-headedness and imbalance. I suspect fine-motor skills also compromised. 9. I loved the very tip of my thumb more than you can imagine.

Monday, November 9, 2015 at 5:28pm
Jan Becker likes John Lewis.

Monday, November 9, 2015 at 5:27pm
Jan Becker shared John Lewis's post.

Monday, November 9, 2015 at 10:55am
Jan Becker is going to Miami Book Fair.

Monday, November 9, 2015 at 10:24am
How Morning Proceeds Here on Crystal Lake: The alarm clock wakes
me with Pat Benatar's "Hit Me With Your Best Shot" as the chainsaw fires
up out by the lake. There, I spy not one, but TWO Creepy Maintenance
Men high in the branches of the dead live oak outside my bedroom
window, sawing off limbs. Double Creepy. Happy Monday.

Monday, November 9, 2015 at 5:12am
At least this time I had a good excuse for my sleepless night. I discovered
the Epilady is still on the market. It brought back 1986, and that was
scary enough when I was awake. I couldn't face it just yet in my dreams.

Sunday, November 8, 2015 at 8:24pm
I can only truly feel secure if I know where my hackle pliers are located.

Sunday, November 8, 2015 at 8:23pm
I can't believe it's only a week until the opening of 2015 Miami Book Fair!
I'll be making poems on the porch at The Swamp with Leenie Moore and
Michele Jessica Fievre. Pop in and say hi.

Sunday, November 8, 2015 at 2:23pm
I just submitted my first abstract for an academic conference, and I feel
like I broke something inside my brain. Ouch.

Sunday, November 8, 2015 at 4:03am
I'm going to have to figure out this sleep thing eventually.

Saturday, November 7, 2015 at 4:23am
5AM is lurking up on me again, and I am thinking of embossing,
debossing, deckle edges and elephant poo.

Saturday, November 7, 2015 at 12:31am
I found myself this morning at 5AM plotting a quest to encounter a tree
in Fort Lauderdale.

Thursday, November 5, 2015 at 4:19pm
On top of my wrist thing, The Toddler took a tumble, and it looks like she's going to have a shiner. The Kid's a trooper though. She's handling it better than I am. Bad day involving things with edges.

Thursday, November 5, 2015 at 10:21am
I think I might have broken it. Ouch.

Thursday, November 5, 2015 at 1:17am EST
Jan Becker likes Squatty Potty.

Wednesday, November 4, 2015 at 9:47am
This morning is no less strange than last night. Creepy Maintenance Man is here to repair the raining AC. The Chef is also present, but somehow the words, "I need to poke around inside your unit to see what you need" are no less creepy.

Tuesday, November 3, 2015 at 8:00pm
There is a bizarre scene here on Crystal Lake. More bizarre than usual. It involves a Chef, his former roommate (our dear friend Joe, who is here for an overnight visit), an air conditioning unit that has sprung a leak and is making it rain inside the apartment, and a misdelivered tome of questionable content, which will later (hopefully) lead to a visit from a neighbor to pick it up. Also, biting flies and an empty gallon-sized growler from the Salt Water Brewery. God help me.

Sunday, November 1, 2015 at 1:56am
I like staying up when the clocks go back. It's sort of like time traveling.

Saturday, October 31, 2015 at 2:49pm
Since it's Hallowe'en, it's only appropriate that I undertake the most horrific chore of the year--the cleaning of the funky Birkenstock footbeds.

Wednesday, October 28, 2015 at 12:29pm
Conversation with Creepy Maintenance Man #2:

(Elevator stops on my floor, arms laden with laundry, I enter, find
CMM#2 grinning wildly)
>Me: Oh, hey, how are you?
>CMM#2: Fantastic! I'm laying carpet! #Creepy

Wednesday, October 28, 2015 at 9:18am
Some life skills and wisdom I might not have learned had The Feline not
entered my life: 1. How to vigorously rub his rump while he's eating his
tinned food in the morning. Weird, I know, but he enjoys this, and
somehow I think it aids his digestion. 2. How to forget about wearing the
color black ever. 3. How to swallow back my disgust when he drops
assorted torsos on my pillow before I've had my coffee, and mutter,
"What a mighty hunter you are" instead of shrieking in terror.

Monday, October 26, 2015 at 7:17pm
Strange scene at Casa Crystal Lake (SNAFU): The Chef had a short day
today as he only had a meeting at work. I came home at 7PM to find him
passed out cold out on his back, suspiciously covered in glitter. Must
have been a helluva kitchen meeting.

Monday, October 26, 2015 at 8:44am
I had a terrible nightmare last night that I was locked in a sprawling
mansion with Kurt Vonnegut and Norman Mailer, and they weren't
getting along. That was bad enough, but then Buckley, Gore Vidal, and
Truman Capote showed up. I need dead white guys to leave me alone in
my dream space. That's not too much to ask, is it?

Sunday, October 25, 2015 at 2:55pm
I am happy to announce that after three days of lying about in my own
swill, feeling like a limpet, I have showered, and am on my way to the
grocery store to find something iron-rich to consume.

Saturday, October 24, 2015 at 12:36pm
Somehow, I lost the last 24 hours to a rager of a virus. I'm not sure where they went. All I do know for sure is that there was no coffee in them and therefore they were some of the most miserable 24 hours I've ever lost.

Wednesday, October 21, 2015 at 12:36pm
Good choice, #sexyjoebiden. The presidency is a thankless job, and you've earned a break from politics. Rock on.

Tuesday, October 20, 2015 at 2:36pm
The Chef is off work today. The toll of living with a writer is weighing heavily on him. After lunch at a fancy three-course Indian place in Boca Raton with pillows in the booths in case we needed to nap (Sapphire, it was good), we walked to The Funky Biscuit, which is The Winemaker's favorite haunt. I asked him a question about The Winemaker (which I will not repeat here). The Chef then asked, "Why do you want to know? Are you going to write about that too?" I wouldn't dare.

Tuesday, October 20, 2015 at 1:55am
Every noseeum in South Florida is in my bedroom biting me through the herbal bug spray. Apparently, that stuff is like truffle oil to gnats.

Sunday, October 18, 2015 at 3:28pm
If I could pick a perfect moment on a Sunday afternoon, it would be this: A sudden restful nap, cuddled belly-to-back with The Feline, our spines curled in harmony like an end quote.

Sunday, October 18, 2015 at 2:16am
Sometimes I forget about my Viking helmet. Note to self: Better remember that.

Saturday, October 17, 2015 at 2:14pm
Jan Becker went to Queer Quinceañera.

Saturday, October 17, 2015 at 12:55pm
I've been in some strange situations, but none are so fraught with sticky weirdness as Saturday in the laundry room.

Friday, October 16, 2015 at 2:11pm
Most satisfactory sound I've heard in the last six years: The impressive slap/thud my rough-drafted thesis makes when dropped on a table or desk. I've done this several times over the past few days, and by far, it was most sonically pleasing when dropped on the table in front of my thesis director. (Even if it needs major revisions). #wtfba

Wednesday, October 14, 2015 at 9:08am
The Feline ate my rough draft. Effing critics, man.

Tuesday, October 13, 2015 at 11:46am
What you are looking at here is a very preliminary, VERY ROUGH 149 page draft of my thesis. It is still far from finished. I should be ashamed even showing it to you. I feel like I'm announcing a pregnancy before the first trimester is over. It hasn't been poked over yet by the experts, and it's in all kinds of trouble, and right now, it's all kinds of ugly. BUT, it's mine. I did something something. Baby steps. #wtfba

Monday, October 12, 2015 at 6:53am
I just had a dream I was giving birth, and when the baby's head emerged, I looked down and it was Salvador Dali. Happy Monday.

Sunday, October 11, 2015 at 9:22pm
Tonight's Scorecard: Jan Becker: 1 Mealy bugs in the kitchen: 0

Saturday, October 10, 2015 at 8:18pm
I went to Wynwood tonight and saw the Miami Book Fair's Three Muses. They are BEAUTIFUL, these goddesses rising up out of the sea--and they aren't having any trouble keeping their books dry. When I leaned in close, they whispered in my ear, "go home and #wtfba Becker." And then

the cement told me to "protect your magic." And when the crossroads start speaking, it is good to practice listening.

Saturday, October 10, 2015 at 8:53am
Pick a Status Update: A. I had the kind of sleep one gets when one has a reaction to a bug bite annoying enough to send one to the Google at 4AM, where one discovers stories of spider bite reactions so severe they lead to gangrene OR B. If I must spend my Saturday morning with an ice pack on my head, I might as well be hungover.

Friday, October 9, 2015 at 11:39pm
I wish these creatures would stop gnawing at me. I have a lump the size of a quail's egg behind my ear where my spectacle stems rest against my skull. My craw is swollen enough without the extra help. #basta

Wednesday, October 7, 2015 at 1:38pm
Conversation With Creepy Maintenance Man (because my day is not strange enough already): (We both enter the elevator. I tear open a package and find the new Saul Williams poetry book. I've just come from the laundry room also, and the dryers are quite hot. I'm flushed, sweaty, and wearing the only clean shirt I have which has a tie at the neck to keep my lady bits from flopping out. The tie has come loose, but my hands are full, I can't fix it.)
> Me: Phew. Thank Goodness it'll be cooling down soon.
> CMM: (eyes on the prize, licks his lips. He is sweating also) It never cools off down here.
> Me: Sure it does, it'll be perfect come November.
> CMM: (eyes still at chest level) I can cool you off. I can cool you off REAL quick.
Oh My God. #Creepy.

Tuesday, October 6, 2015 at 2:44pm
Among the other strange things that have occurred today, I just discovered a tube of "peony pink" lipstick on my desk (I don't wear makeup). This better not be a hint.

Tuesday, October 6, 2015 at 8:10am
I have the flu. My Uncle Harry is in the ICU with Grandma and Mom, and it's looking like the prognosis isn't great for him (O ye buddhas and bodhisattvas, abiding in the ten directions, endowed with great compassion...). Another Uncle is in the hospital also. And of all days, today is the day I'm scheduled to see my shrink who thinks Jesus cured his asthma on the radio.

Tuesday, October 6, 2015 at 7:06am
Jan Becker shared Tommy Chong's photo.

Tuesday, October 6, 2015 at 12:46am
Apparently, another Jan Becker #wtfba. It was not this Jan Becker, and if I read it, I wouldn't understand a word of it. Still, for this Jan Becker, there is hope, that measly thing with wings. (file under things one should not Google when running a fever)

Monday, October 5, 2015 at 2:18pm
The only good thing about the flu is The Feline.

Monday, October 5, 2015 at 10:45am
Jan Becker feeling sick.
After six years in south Florida, I've finally figured out how to note the change of seasons. It's when the snowbirds arrive and infect me with their avian flu

Sunday, October 4, 2015 at 3:56pm
I just did the most unholy thing ever at my local Publix. If I wasn't so ashamed of myself, I'd tell you all about it. You'd be proud.

Thursday, October 1, 2015 at 7:31pm
For his 10th birthday The Feline received all his favorite things: 1. A new brush for his coat. 2. A package of special kitty formula duck sausages. 3. A can of catnip big enough to stick his whole head in. He's been brushed,

fed, and after burying his head in the catnip, is having visions while he munches on barley and alfalfa on the balcony. I love him way too much.

Wednesday, September 30, 2015 at 11:05am
Creepy Maintenance Man has come and gone. He always conveniently forgets that we have an electrostatic filter that doesn't get changed. He also informs me that for him, every day feels like Hump Day.

Monday, September 28, 2015 at 8:07pm
I normally find that taking delight in retail procurement is gauche. However, JAN BECKER-SIZED FUZZY SOCK MONKEY FOOTIE PAJAMAS! HELL YEAH!!!

Saturday, September 26, 2015 at 11:13pm
There was no coffee, so I just went Irish. Also, some folks are postulating that the full blood moon eclipse is a sign that the end is near. Whatever.

Saturday, September 26, 2015 at 8:44pm
Irish coffee.

Friday, September 25, 2015 at 7:43pm EDT
As punishment for jumping on my belly at 5AM and thwapping me in the face with his tail all night, The Feline is again feasting on snow crab.

Friday, September 25, 2015 at 4:26pm
Today has been a long-drawn-out exercise in handling frustration. Last night, The Feline slept with his tail in my face, and every time I changed position, he matched mine, so it was THWAP THWAP in the face with the tail all night. This morning he bounced up and down on my stomach until I got up and fed him. Today is laundry day also, and I went down to move the clothes from the washer to the dryer, and found my laundry basket thrown on the floor. The person who'd used the dryer before me left their clothes in the dryer after the cycle had finished, so I took their clothes out and neatly piled them on top of the dryer. I went back down to remove my clothes, and found them--STILL WET--strewn about the

laundry room. I give up. I'm just going to make a pot of tomato sauce and not leave the house the rest of the day.

Friday, September 25, 2015 at 12:43pm
I am officially in love with the pope. #popecrush

Thursday, September 24, 2015 at 11:35am
My favorite part of watching coverage of the pope's visit to Washington, DC has to be watching John Boehner cry when the pope addressed the crowd from the balcony. (also, #sexyjoebiden)

Monday, September 21, 2015 at 11:48pm
God help me. I've hit a honey-patch of depravity, a whole archive of Hunter S Thompson gonzo.

Monday, September 21, 2015 at 12:35pm
Funny how all my dirty words come out when I answer a call from Beverly Hills and it's a man claiming that he's from the IRS with a pending lawsuit for Mr. and Mrs. Chef, but doesn't know my first name (or that I'm not married and my last name is not the same as The Chef's), or my social ssecurity# or much of anything, including why he's wasting my time.

Monday, September 21, 2015 at 11:19am
Jan Becker shared Jan Becker's photo.
This is another Jan Becker (there are many). What I like about this one is the Donald Trumpish toupee on the horse.

Sunday, September 20, 2015 at 3:16pm
The Feline's reaction to my installation of a new and improved platform base for the bed is as I expected. He's pissed off and wary, even though the new bed is much higher and offers him easy access to the nether quarters where he typically hides phallic-shaped objects and himself from all maintenance men, Creepy and otherwise.

Saturday, September 19, 2015 at 11:41am
Nothing in my life is as amusing as watching the scramble when the
Fedex guy shows up and The Chef is still in his skivvies.

Thursday, September 17, 2015 at 3:54pm
A Sure Sign Mercury is in Retrograde, OR Conversation with Herbert the
Hippie Hermit Who lives Next Door:
> Me: (Walking down the hallway, I realize I left all my bras in the
> washer yesterday, and if I don't retrieve them the results might
> be scandalous. I spot Herbert jauntily striding towards me, and
> decide for once, I will not engage with him. I keep my head low)
> Herbert: (Giant smile on his face) Well, hello lovely neighbor,
> how are you today?
> Me: (I keep my head low, grimace.): Mostly good. How are you,
> Herbert? Herbert: I'm WONDERFUL. It's a beautiful day (I look
> at the grey skies, rain). AND, I HAVE LETTUCE.
> Me: Sigh.

Thursday, September 17, 2015 at 5:45am
A powerful thunder and lightning storm rolled through--when I say
powerful, imagine that sizzling noise you hear after lightning hits about
500 feet away--knocked out the power, sent the cat skittering under the
bed, startled me into dropping one of the containers of curry into the
sink (don't worry, there was plenty more), and then set off car alarms in
the parking lot, which woke up the mockingbirds and yeah, it's been like
that for hours. It is almost 6AM, and I am just getting to bed, because the
neighbors (and The Chef) sleep like Marcellus shale.

Tuesday, September 15, 2015 at 8:02pm
Can we get an ambivalent button too, Mr. Zuckerberg?

Monday, September 14, 2015 at 10:22pm
My cousin Amy just reminded me that today is my Grandma Becker's
birthday. I keep a framed photo of her on my writing desk. The last time
I saw her, I was six years old and we were moving to Hawai'i--and she

died while we were gone. Her and my grandfather were enormous influences on me when I was a wee Toddler. She taught me to read. I like to think I take after her in some ways. She crocheted. I learned that independent of her influence. She also had a great sense of humor: I was blessed to receive a copy of her chocolate cake recipe recently. The instructions say to stand back at one point during the mixing, because the batter erupts like Mt. Vesuvius. That's my gram. Happy birthday <3

Monday, September 14, 2015 at 5:58pm
Conversation with The Toddler:

> Me: C'mere Toddler. You're covered with pizza and peaches. Let's get you some clean clothes.
> Toddler: NO YUCKY. Me: (I catch the kid, strip her down. She runs behind Grandpa's bar, finds some booze.)

I get it, Toddler. I understand completely. Sigh.

Sunday, September 13, 2015 at 11:55am
Jan Becker shared Filming Cops's video.
I'll say it. Black lives matter.

Wednesday, September 9, 2015 at 2:20pm
Just so you know...If you see me out in public and it appears I don't have my Viking helmet on, don't worry. I am indeed still wearing it. It just becomes invisible when I'm trying not to intimidate people.

Tuesday, September 8, 2015 at 7:19pm
Humblemaking Conversation with The Toddler:

> Me: Toddler, can you say Viking?
> Toddler: (stretches her arms out looks really cute) UP, UP, JUICE, DANCE, DANCE.
> Me: (I pick her up) Toddler, can you say Viking? VIKING? Can you say VIKING?
> Toddler: (scowls) NO. POOPIE, YUCKY. POOPIE, POOPIE, YUCK.
> Me: (I realize she's not kidding) Sigh.

Monday, September 7, 2015 at 6:00pm
Between the booming of Thor's hammer as the afternoon thundershowers roared through, and semi-annual vacuuming of the carpets, The Feline is ready to swear off all things Viking, as that only seems to mean more noise.

Monday, September 7, 2015 at 11:31am
I can think of nothing more berserker than a Viking having hot flashes.

Sunday, September 6, 2015 at 10:47am
It's not easy to sleep with a Viking helmet on your head.

Sunday, September 6, 2015 at 1:57am
Conversation with The Chef:
> Me: Hi, Chef. How was your day?
> Chef: (appears alarmed) What are you wearing on your head?
> Me: A Viking helmet.
> Chef: WHY are you wearing a Viking helmet?
> Me: Because I'm a VIKING. Why else?

Saturday, September 5, 2015 at 11:01pm
I'm never taking my Viking helmet off. Ever.

Saturday, September 5, 2015 at 10:24pm
Someone should let these boxers know it's a violation of the flag code to wear those shorts.

Saturday, September 5, 2015 at 10:19pm
I would like it very much if someone would play theme music for me whenever I enter a room.

Saturday, September 5, 2015 at 9:59pm
That time Hunter S. Thompson went to Zaire, but missed the fight.

Saturday, September 5, 2015 at 9:18pm
Best night ever. Someone just gave me a Viking helmet.

Saturday, September 5, 2015 at 9:11pm
Singing Kumbaya at the boxing match is not a popular choice

Saturday, September 5, 2015 at 9:09pm
I'm not so sure that the women who hold up the round signs at boxing matches are meeting their potential.

Saturday, September 5, 2015 at 8:06pm
Boxing involves an awful lot of hugs, considering the objective.

Saturday, September 5, 2015 at 7:49pm
Here's something that doesn't happen everyday: "Boxing at the casino?" she asks. "Sure," I say. "That's the Lynne Barrett machine," they say. I sit down at the "femme fatale" machine. Drop in some change. JACKPOT. ALSO, I'm drinking bloody Marys and just saw some poor guy get knocked out. Pugilism, it's what's for dinner.

Saturday, September 5, 2015 at 3:34pm
Some psychedelic crocheted wool nests I threw together for the pelican rescue my friend Marina volunteers with. They use them for orphaned or abandoned baby birds. Those chicks will at least be stylish.

Friday, September 4, 2015 at 8:05pm
3rd eye chakra oil is not meant to be rubbed in 1st or 2nd eyes.

Thursday, September 3, 2015 at 5:28am
Jan Becker shared Mark Twain's photo.

Wednesday, September 2, 2015 at 9:35pm
I still don't know what was up with the car being pulled from the lake today. However, I found out about some interesting activity recently. I've seen these lights, but thought they were either helicopters or drones,

or smaller remote controlled flying things. Not sure about the Jesus Christ inquiry in this story. But really, could I live in a stranger neighborhood? Also, I found two more people (at least) have died in the lake over the past year. Weird.

Wednesday, September 2, 2015 at 10:41am
The Chef just informed me the Broward County Sheriffs just fished ANOTHER car out of Crystal Lake.

Wednesday, September 2, 2015 at 9:56am
Sometimes in my encounters with Creepy Maintenance Man, there are no words--only the awkward silence of the elevator. This morning, for example. He rode elevator down from the fourth to the first floor, where I boarded. He stayed in, and rode with me to my floor. No words. Only a piercing gaze, and a suspicious puddle on his end of the car. #Creepy.

Monday, August 31, 2015 at 9:06pm
The Feline reacted to watching Taylor Swift on Storytellers three times today with The Chef by vomiting kibble at my feet. It's okay, Feline. Let's hope this is just a phase.

Monday, August 31, 2015 at 10:44am
I woke up late this morning, stumbled to the kitchen for coffee, and found The Chef staring intently at the television. "I don't quite know how to tell you this," he said, "but I think I'm becoming a Taylor Swift fan." God help me.

Sunday, August 30, 2015 at 12:46pm
Curry consumed, coffee brewed, B-vitamins B-vitaminsB-vitamins-B-vitamins. Hammertime!

Sunday, August 30, 2015 at 10:42am
After a consultation with The Chef, we have reached the agreement that if I am to endure this day, I will need not only coffee, but also curry to fuel me. It is going to be fast and ugly at the Indian buffet this morning.

Saturday, August 29, 2015 at 4:24am
My horrorscope says that because of the Pisces supermoon I want to go off on a vision quest and make magic, and travel through space and time, but that there is just too much work to be done. Sigh. I'm a writer. I didn't realize these things were mutually exclusive.

Friday, August 28, 2015 at 12:59pm
I've discovered that a good, quick, legal way to catch a buzz in the middle of my day is to switch from my old single-vision glasses to the newer progressive bifocals. It's a little tricky, but there's this special zone on the lenses that makes everything feel like a funhouse.

Friday, August 28, 2015 at 2:56am
It probably was not a good idea to try out smoked oysters at 3AM.

Thursday, August 27, 2015 at 9:23am
I had the worst nightmare I've ever had last night. I woke up sweating, clutching the bedsheets, tears streaming down my face. It was so bad, I don't even want to say what happened, but this is the kind of terror one shouldn't keep to oneself. In my dream, Donald Trump got elected--and that was bad enough, but it got worse: Ann Coulter his running mate.

Wednesday, August 26, 2015 at 12:01pm
Despite the overcast conditions, and that it is not due for another three days, here on the lake, the supermoon is shining brightly, as it does whenever Creepy Maintenance Man climbs on the roof, and bends over to service the AC units.

Tuesday, August 25, 2015 at 10:04am
I'm not quite sure what to say when the mechanic calls about the beast and the cost of the repair is considerably lower than his initial quote. "Are you sure you dialed the right number?" doesn't seem too smart.

Monday, August 24, 2015 at 9:11pm
Jan Becker likes Wool and the Gang.

Monday, August 24, 2015 at 8:03am
Today is brought to you by the Letter M: It's back to school day! Time to MATRICULATE. I am going to the MECHANIC, to spend some MONEY. MY MECHANIC'S MATH MAKES ME MUMBLE! M!

Sunday, August 23, 2015 at 1:58pm
It's probably good practice for me to remember that when things seem at their crappiest (like the fact that if I don't want to die on I-95 in a flaming car wreck, I need to sink another $3-400 in a new pair of tie rods for the old beast which already cost me close to $700 I don't have to fix last week), random blessings seem to shower down on me from the Universe to give me a little hope. I can't say what just yet, but I received an inkling that a good thing is coming, and all I can say right now is: Thanks, Universe. It's time for something good.

Thursday, August 20, 2015 at 12:33pm
Ach. There is a good reason it took me two years to get my car fixed. Only in Jan Becker's world does a $35 repair multiply with the frequency of a tribble (x20 so far). Also, Note to Self: Beware The Toddler's water toys, unless you pack a change of clothing. #wetandbroke

Wednesday, August 19, 2015 at 5:01pm
TWO YEARS WITHOUT AC IN MY CAR IN SOUTH FLORIDA, AND ALL I NEEDED WAS A CRUMMY CLUTCH BOLT. F*%$#!

Wednesday, August 19, 2015 at 8:31am
The trouble with washing The Feline close to 11PM is not that it pisses him off, nor is it that he gets wet. Once pissed off and wet, it takes him hours to preen himself dry. Furthermore, being pissed off and wet doesn't prevent The Feline from bedding down in his preferred place, next to me in bed. This leaves me, this morning, barely rested, covered with the scent of wet, pissed off cat. I've been covered with worse.

Tuesday, August 18, 2015 at 3:06pm
Because my life is not daunting enough, nor filled with sufficient peril, I've decided that the time has come to bathe The Feline.

Monday, August 17, 2015 at 9:08pm
Conversation With The Chef (And Bill O'Reilly):
> Bill O'Reilly: Next up, I've got a story about a white band and a black band on tour together.
> Me: What the hell is he talking about? Why would he even say white or black? Who labels music by black or white?
> Chef: It's Bill O'Reilly. We're watching Fox News.
> Me: WHY ARE WE WATCHING FOX NEWS?
> Chef: I like to check in from time to time to see how close Donald Trump is to destroying our country.
> Me: Jesus Christ, Chef.

(The bands were Chicago and Earth, Wind and Fire. I repeat, Jesus Christ)

Monday, August 17, 2015 at 1:57am
See? We weren't all nuts thinking the government is in our vaginas.

Sunday, August 16, 2015 at 9:28pm
#sexyjoebiden

Saturday, August 15, 2015 at 11:25am
Conversation with Herbert the Hippie Hermit Who Lives Next Door: (I open my front door and see furniture piled outside along the walkway. Herbert, looking frantic pops his head out)

> Me: Oh No! Herbert, are you moving?
> Herbert: No, I got new furniture.
> Me: Oh, I'm so happy to hear this. I'd miss you terribly if you moved out.
> Herbert: I don't really care.

Friday, August 14, 2015 at 12:37pm
Conversation With The Chef:

> Chef: Did you see Blanco read?
> Me: Yes. Chef: What you think?
> Me: It made me cry. What you think?
> Chef: I liked it, but it did not make me cry.
> Me: What the hell's the matter with you?

Friday, August 14, 2015 at 9:16am
I'm having a hard time believing the American flag is going up in Cuba, somewhere besides Guantanamo Bay and Richard Blanco is reading.

Friday, August 14, 2015 at 6:02am
Inaugural poet to join U.S. Embassy ceremony in Cuba

Friday, August 14, 2015 at 1:02am
A sneak peek at the first line from poem Blanco's reading tomorrow at the reopening of the American embassy in Cuba, "The sea doesn't matter. What matters is this - that we all belong to the sea between us."

Thursday, August 13, 2015 at 10:20pm
Jan Becker was added to Books and Booze by Joseph Lapin.

Thursday, August 13, 2015 at 1:42pm
This is the kind of morning where my coffee is begging me to add some bourbon. And yes, I am aware it is nearly 2PM.

Wednesday, August 12, 2015 at 8:23pm
If, like me, you are in an area that is plagued with light pollution, or if you are experiencing overcast skies tonight, here's a link to catch the Perseids live tonight and tomorrow. These are some of the strongest meteor showers we'll get this year.

Wednesday, August 12, 2015 at 4:31pm
In a fit of unfettered disgust, The Feline has chewed up my Chicago Manual of Style, and spit the pages out on my office floor. Bravo, Feline! If it was not a necessary (though evil) tool, I would have done it myself.

Monday, August 10, 2015 at 7:03pm
An Observation on Swimming and Roberta Flack: I had to take a break from swimming recently (for reasons Megyn Kelly and most women would understand), but got back in the pool today. The water ski instruction boat was out on the lake with a student who was skiing great, right up until the boat's radio started in with "The First Time Ever I Saw Your Face," and then the student had the most spectacular wipeout I've ever seen. But not only that, when I got out of the pool, and looked out at where the rowboats are docked, three of them had capsized. The moral: Roberta Flack is a badass.

Monday, August 10, 2015 at 1:27pm
Sometimes, when I'm copywriting for the Miami Book Fair International, I come across a name on the list and worry I might just explode with glee..Sometimes? Hell, it happens about every 5 minutes.

Sunday, August 9, 2015 at 10:10am
Meanwhile, on Crystal Lake, we dance our Sunday morning dances.

Saturday, August 8, 2015 at 10:06pm
A surprise from The Chef on the sixth anniversary of our co-habitation:
In The Winemaker's room (our utility closet), I discovered where The
Chef hid things while I was away, including my yarn basket. In addition
to the yarn, it was filled with The Feline's penis-shaped catnip toys and
his wild turkey feathers. #thankshoney

Saturday, August 8, 2015 at 10:09am
My first date with The Chef was to visit Mark Twain's grave and writing
studio in Elmira, NY. Someone had stolen his pipe from the studio years
before (Duh, I told the guide, it never should have been left out to begin
with.). I was allowed to sit in his writing chair (stiff, but functional), so I
think I have Twain's energy in my bum--I probably should have rested
my head on the seat instead. We planted edelweiss at his grave. 6
months seems short for a theft of this magnitude.

Friday, August 7, 2015 at 10:25pm
Six years ago tonight, I crossed the border to Florida from Georgia on my
move south from Binghamton. I lost my wallet at the first rest area in
Jacksonville with half a tank of gas and the rest of Florida to get through.
In Port St. Lucie, I stopped at a gas station and handed the cashier about
$2.00 in change, and she pitched in another $3.00 someone had
fortuitously left on one of the pumps, and it was enough to coast into
Pompano Beach on fumes at about 3AM, where I was greeted by The
Chef, who'd stayed up to cook me a meal and welcome me home. Bon
Anniversaire, Florida. You've taught me so much over the past six years.

Friday, August 7, 2015 at 11:06am
Morning-after-GOP-debate-thought-while-reading-political-analyses:
When are the American people going to win a political debate?

Friday, August 7, 2015 at 2:47am
Jan Becker shared Bernie Sanders's post.

Thursday, August 6, 2015 at 10:37am
The Chef is a little skittish, and startles easily. I took advantage of this tendency just now. We'd both been waiting anxiously for the coffee to finish brewing (we use a French Press, and time the brew to four minutes before pressing). But when it was ready, he moved towards the pot, as if it was his turn to lower the press. I sidled up beside him and in my best Joe Friday voice ordered him to: STEP AWAY FROM THE COFFEE POT. Poor guy jumped out of his boxer briefs. But I got the first cup, so it was worth inflicting upon him a few moments of arrhythmia. The moral of this tale: Never stand between a Jan and her brew.

Wednesday, August 5, 2015 at 9:32pm
I was in 6th grade when I read John Hersey's book Hiroshima, and I remember how terrified I was then that people were capable of such terrible harm. We were still in the middle of the Cold War. Reagan was in office, and the entire eight years of his presidency were one long panic attack for me. It's been 70 years since we dropped the bomb, and much of the time, I'm not sure that we haven't exchanged the Cold War for a war even colder and more deadly, more insidious, because it's amorphous and the sides aren't as clearly defined as Axis and Allies. If there is one thing that gives me hope for the future though, it's that human imagination can work miracles. Happy Universal Peace Day.

Wednesday, August 5, 2015 at 1:02pm
Meanwhile, here in Pompano Beach, I still have no air conditioning in my car. The "feel Real" temp is currently 101°F. But I'm not complaining one bit, because the car isn't starting anyway. #blessings

Tuesday, August 4, 2015 at 12:45am
Sometimes the best way to deal with Venus is to take a hot shower, put on a clean pair of sock monkey pajamas, and say goodnight to the moon.

Monday, August 3, 2015 at 5:34pm
I'm still voting for Bernie, but #sexyjoebiden

Monday, August 3, 2015 at 10:47am
Strange dreams featuring priests and potatoes. Not sure about that.

Sunday, August 2, 2015 at 9:52am
Swimming, Day 3: I think something is working with this swimming thing. I woke up today without feeling there was a vise clamped down on my spine for the first time in awhile. Sometimes I find it hard to concentrate when I'm swimming laps though, because foxtail palms are way too pretty when they are swaying in the breeze as they do, and god help me if I catch sight of a live oak when I'm on a backstroke lap. Live oaks require a few moments of reverence at least.

Saturday, August 1, 2015 at 12:54pm
Conversation with Herbert, the Hippie Hermit who lives next door:
 Me: Hi Herbert! How are you?
 Herbert: (Frowns) I thought you'd moved out.
 Me: No, I just went north for a month.
 Herbert: (still frowning) Oh, I'm sorry to hear that.

Saturday, August 1, 2015 at 11:35am
I just realized that it was a week ago today I left Lordville. Well, most of me left. I think there's still some integral piece of me there.

Saturday, August 1, 2015 at 9:50am
Day 2 of swimming regimen: I was not pooped on. The ducks out back were rather intense, all chuffing and demonstrating how tough and territorial they are, but I ain't afraid of no ducks.

Friday, July 31, 2015 at 11:31am
Some random thoughts on swimming and 3AM messages from my Muse: 1. Today's 3AM message from The Muse-- Lemon Curd. WTF, Muse? I've never had lemon curd. It sounds disgusting. 2. It is absolutely logical that the day I begin a swimming regimen is the day Creepy Maintenance Man stations himself in the pool area. I'm not sure what his

purpose was out there, but it involved ogling. 3. 3rd lap in, a crow shat on my head. I kept going. 4. My back feels looser after the dunk.

Thursday, July 30, 2015 at 9:55pm
Bizarre bit of trivia that reveals way too much about The Chef: He is using The Feline's nail clippers to trim his toenails. He claims it is the only suitable tool in the world for this chore.

Thursday, July 30, 2015 at 5:50pm
Since there are only so many days I can spend with a heating pad, I'm getting back into the daily swim thing starting tomorrow.

Thursday, July 30, 2015 at 12:09pm
If he is a Feline, why is his favorite position downward dog?

Thursday, July 30, 2015 at 4:23am
John Dufresne says we should write about the thing that wakes us up at 3AM. Dammit. The muse sent me this.

Thursday, July 30, 2015 at 4:17am
I never thought I'd say this, but #sexydicknixon

Wednesday, July 29, 2015 at 4:39am
I woke just now and expected that when I opened my eyes I'd be in my room in Lordville with children's shoes hanging off the brass headboard and the possibility of a bat to dodge. Instead, I was greeted by Naked Allen Ginsberg and a nearly full moon. Also, I've got a raspy voiced cat still yelling at me for leaving him nearly a month. At least he's losing his voice with all the yelling he's done over the past two days.

Tuesday, July 28, 2015 at 2:28pm
A Confession: I am terrified of things The Chef has left in the refrigerator over the past month. I thought I saw a strawberry in there, but on closer inspection, it appears to be a mutating life form. God Help Me.

Tuesday, July 28, 2015 at 12:52pm
In the past twelve hours since I've been home, The Feline has done nothing but follow me around the house, griping that I left him for a month. Last night, every time I fell asleep, he bit me and yelled at me. Apparently, I am not allowed to leave the house. Ever.

Saturday, July 25, 2015 at 7:53am
It is morning in Lordville. My last for a while. The morning glories are glorious. In the Lordville Living Flower Museum, the purple coneflowers and poppies have begun to bloom. The birds are feasting as they do every day, like it's Thanksgiving. There is a fog nestled along the river and down by the railroad tracks. And the creek that runs down to the river is making its soft noise. I was reminded yesterday of the folk lore about the magical villages of Germelshausen and Brigadoon that pop up rarely and then disappear as quickly as they are found. It has been like that here, and I am blessed and thankful I have friends like Buck and Callie, and Aunt Esther, who opened their beautiful, wild (did I mention there is a polar bear in the hotel?) home for me to find respite from the concrete and mayhem of South Florida. Thank you. <3

Friday, July 24, 2015 at 3:24pm
These are my last 24 hours in Lordville (this year). As usual, everything here is quiet. Like most things about here, I will miss that.

Wednesday, July 22, 2015 at 8:41am
It's hard to describe, but here in Lordville, the way the sun comes up, it's easy to forget how dark was the night. If I could give an approximation, it would be the light streaming through a spider web in the maple tree, a doe startled on the creek bank across from the old hotel, birds out for breakfast, and the floppy ears of an injured mutt on my lap as I drink my coffee. It would be like opening my chest up and handing you my heart.

Tuesday, July 21, 2015 at 5:16pm
I don't believe this. More paparazzi! And this time The Chef has my camera, so no evidence. And there's a whole bunch of them. Weird.

Monday, July 20, 2015 at 10:32pm
It occurred to me about an hour ago that I'd drunk two cups of coffee today, neither made by me, and while it's not completely an anomaly, most days I take care of the chore. The first cup came this morning when I was all clenched up with back spasms on Buck's back porch, and the brew knocked the fog right out of me. The second came tonight after dinner, when Buck had made himself a cup of coffee, and spontaneously poured half the cup into a mug for me. That's a good friend. I'm nowhere near that good.

Sunday, July 19, 2015 at 12:41pm
I slept until 10 this morning. In Lordville, that's like sleeping a whole day. Yesterday was good. Lunch with Mary (THANK YOU, MARY <3), and another kayak ride down the Delaware yesterday afternoon. Even waking so late, today has already been full. Lordville Presbyterian Church had me in a pew for service, then Caterina came by for coffee and to dress the mannequin, who was still in her 4th of July garb. It's going to be hot today, so we put her in shorts, a white sleeveless shirt and a cowboy hat. The Chef has my camera, or I'd take a picture. You'll just have to trust me; she looks fabulous.

Friday, July 17, 2015 at 11:31pm
I really miss the naked folks here at Yasgur's Farm.

Friday, July 17, 2015 at 8:23pm
Bethel looks a little different without all the naked folks.

Friday, July 17, 2015 at 2:14pm
When I grow up, I'd like to live in a house like this, with a rocking chair in every room.

Thursday, July 16, 2015 at 11:35pm
In the absence of a moon, there is plenty of light left in Lordville. Across the road, in a field, someone will sleep in a tent tonight. Right now, they

are roasting marshmallows over a fire. On the hill the stained glass is gleaming. There is a freight train passing right now, and the hotel is rumbling. The tracks are lit up from the engine and the crossing lights. Earlier I went out to the middle of the bridge and looked at the sky, and I wish I could have taken a picture of it to give you. With all those stars, it would have been your best baby photo ever.

Thursday, July 16, 2015 at 10:36am
Meanwhile in Lordville, we are dancing in the solar disco

Wednesday, July 15, 2015 at 9:52pm
1. The temperature is dropping to 49 degrees tonight. I might die. 2. Why is it that the claws only start scuttling in dark corners when I am alone?

Tuesday, July 14, 2015 at 11:24am EDT
One of the beautiful things I remember about Chenjerai Hove is how he spoke of a house being on fire as a metaphor for how he felt about the situation in Zimbabwe and his own exile. He said to see the fire and understand it, one must travel away to have a clear idea of how destructive the fire is. Thank you, Chenjerai Hove. I'll remember you.

Tuesday, July 14, 2015 at 11:18am
The Chef has arrived in Binghamton. This means somewhere in town, they are roasting a fatted pig and preparing libations that would blind a mere mortal. I'll see him later tonight. Meanwhile, here in Lordville, the stream continues its path to the river, the kitchen smells like a night of curry and friends, and I am washing a truckload of filthy clothes.

Monday, July 13, 2015 at 2:08am
THE SAGA CONTINUES: In Lordville, it seems I have many encounters with wildlife close to bedtime. Tonight, for instance--I was out looking at the stars, and thought I heard a metallic clang in the yard across the road that just might be a black bear, and since I decided long ago that there is absolutely no practical reason for me to be close to a black bear, I came in and went up to go to sleep. Guess who was back? Yeah. THERE. WAS.

A. BAT FLYING AROUND IN THE BEDROOM. A BAT. Guess whose friend, Buck (superfriend) gave her a badminton racquet to sleep with? Yeah, that would be me. The only problem was that the racquet was on the other side of the room, in the bed, where I want to go. Still. I want to be in that bed right now. Anyhow, I grabbed a towel, some holy medals and took a few light swings to distract him while I moved in for the racquet. Which I grabbed, it was a tight match. I clipped him a few times, but on, or about the tenth swing, I nailed him hard. Right in that sweet spot on the racquet head, you know, the spongy spot. The birdie went sailing across the room, and slammed into first the wall, and then the floor, where he lay there looking like he was dead with his wings all folded up and pathetic. I grabbed a bathrobe from the back of the door and tossed it over him. He started squealing as soon as the cloth touched him, so he was just stunned. So, I take him outside and shake out the bathrobe, AND OF COURSE HE GETS STUCK IN THE DAMNED SLEEVES. HE'S. A. BAT. I was just freaked out thinking the bear might come over and kick my ass for bullying the bat. Finally, I got him loose from the bathrobe. He was pissed. He was yelling at me as he was flapping off to bug someone else in need of a good night's sleep. He says: "Write the fucking book already, Becker."

Sunday, July 12, 2015 at 10:19pm EDT
I like to walk up the hill at night in Lordville and stand in front of the church, because they keep it lit, even when no one's around, but tonight as oft happens, I was there, admiring the glass when something started getting killed in the woods and ruined my reverie with its death shrieks. (Also, I held a rattlesnake rattle today).

Sunday, July 12, 2015 at 4:48pm
Sometimes you must haul a bucket of rocks up from the river for the dog to chase, and rip out a bunch of Japanese bindweed blocking your friend's view of the creek, and then maybe roll around in the stream a little and call out to the dog, "Oh, Chika, Chika, this is cold." Sometimes it helps. You don't know exactly how, but it helps.
#writethefuckingbookalreadyBecker

Sunday, July 12, 2015 at 2:36am
I was just standing on the front steps of the hotel, trying to look at the stars before I climb into bed (it's overcast), and a PORCUPINE swaggered up like he'd just hit last call over in Equinunk. So I asked him, "What's a spiky haired dude like you doing in a town like this?" I guess it wasn't the sight of me in my fuzzy Cookie Monster PJs that lured him to the hotel, because my voice startled the critter, who squealed, and in turn startled me. I might have woken Aunt Esther. Drunken porcupines are a menace, man. Good night, Facebook.

Sunday, July 12, 2015 at 11:16am
After he left here last night, the porcupine ate Jakob's apple tree. Also, I get all the news I need for the day from Aunt Esther, who likes to rock on her front porch.

Saturday, July 11, 2015 at 10:32am
For the next 17 days, please feel free to randomly interject with: "Write the fucking book already, Becker."

Saturday, July 11, 2015 at 4:04am
The good news is that I managed to lock the bat out of the room tonight. The bad news is that for the past three hours, he's been hurling himself at the door in an effort to come in. Weird little bat.

Friday, July 10, 2015 at 6:36pm
Hear ye, hear ye, hear ye! Let it be known that Robert J. Bullock climbed to the top of the Lordville water tower on July 5, 2015. And it was amazing.

Friday, July 10, 2015 at 8:24am
In an effort to come to peace with this bat, I've been researching its symbolism as an animal sign. It appears to be connected to intuition and rebirth. These are good things. Last night, I closed off the back half of the hotel to keep the bat from buzzing me as I slept. It didn't work, because

all I managed to do was lock the bat in the room with me. I still got a good night's sleep, despite the echo-location squeaks all night long. And I felt safer with the badminton racquet, but I couldn't bring myself to swing at the poor creature when it was flapping around over my head. He's just trying to make a living. As far as I know, the bat is still upstairs in the bedroom. I'm going to sleep tonight with a badminton racquet.

Thursday, July 9, 2015 at 3:31am
THERE IS A BAT IN MY BEDROOM. RIGHT NOW. A BAT. EEK!

Tuesday, July 7, 2015 at 4:06pm
I am trying to pretend there are no wasps in the kitchen. It's not working. There is still a wasp in the kitchen.

Monday, July 6, 2015 at 11:53am
All of Lordville is filled with Buck's laughter,

Sunday, July 5, 2015 at 7:46pm
Finally fulfilled my lifelong secret dream to drive a golf cart. It was badass.

Sunday, July 5, 2015 at 6:34am
I should probably take the scissors off my neck before I fall to sleep.

Saturday, July 4, 2015 at 11:11pm
My bedroom in Lordville has a Murphy bed.

Saturday, July 4, 2015 at 9:55pm EDT
In case you were wondering, they banned Bob Denver from the Great American. Not really fair, the monkey was the menace.

Saturday, July 4, 2015 at 9:05pm
We're sitting around the rhubarb, talking about the time Bob Denver let his monkey loose in the Great American Fair.

Saturday, July 4, 2015 at 10:36am
I like being in a place where people wave when they drive by.

Saturday, July 4, 2015 at 9:33am
Good morning, America. How are you?

Tuesday, June 30, 2015 at 9:37pm EDT
I have arrived in Philly. Headed to the bar!

Tuesday, June 30, 2015 at 5:58pm
On the tarmac. On the tarmac. I'm stuck on this plane on the tarmac.
#imtoosexyforthisplane

Tuesday, June 30, 2015 at 5:48pm
Jan Becker at Hartsfield-Jackson Atlanta International Airport.
I'm stuck sitting on the tarmac on Atlanta, because of storms in PA.
When I boarded the plane, my seatmates had swiped my window seat.
They are from Pakistan. "Asalaam aleukam," I told them, "you're in my
seat." "No fights today," the man told me. "No fights any day." I
answered, "especially during Ramadan." His wife is reading her Quran
aloud. I like it. It's peaceful. Who knows how long we'll be sitting here?
At least another hour, they say. I'll just relax and listen to some prayers.

Tuesday, June 30, 2015 at 4:23pm
I'm not sure why they needed me to sit through six body scans. #dirtytsa

Tuesday, June 30, 2015 at 3:49pm
The TSA felt me up.

Tuesday, June 30, 2015 at 8:53am
My body knows how much I love traveling. Cue the gastric distress.
Also, The Feline is extra cute this morning. Surely emotional blackmail.

Monday, June 29, 2015 at 8:20am
It is not wise to snort cayenne pepper (even accidentally) before 9AM.

Sunday, June 28, 2015 at 7:11pm
I bought socks. This is something I haven't done (or worn) in six years.

Sunday, June 28, 2015 at 11:47am
In about 48 hours, I'm leaving on a jet plane for Philadelphia, then going on a road trip to Lordville, NY, where I plan to hole myself up and write (thank you Feed Buck for the quiet space).

Sunday, June 28, 2015 at 9:41am EDT
Another Weird Scene out on the Lake: Again, I let The Feline out this morning, because his attitude was like, "Bitch, please, you are only here to feed me and let me outside. And maybe stroke my belly from time to time." Again, the squawking commenced out on the balcony. Again, I went out to investigate. Today, a murder of crows has teamed up with the scrub jays harassing The Feline. What is next, I wonder? A flock of mockingbirds? I don't get it. I see crows harassing scrub jays often out there. The crazy nastyass Feline don't care. He just does what he wants (licks his butt and yawns).

Saturday, June 27, 2015 at 11:12am
Weird Nature Scene on the Lake: I put The Feline outside as I do every morning, and heard a commotion of squawking coming from the balcony. I went outside to see what was going on and there was a gaggle of pissed off scrub jays on the railing, harassing poor kitty. He seemed unfazed, sprawled out on his back, belly up, enjoying a cat nap.

Saturday, June 27, 2015 at 10:45am
Yesterday was auspicious. In addition to all the big things happening in the country, it was the 27th anniversary of my graduation from high school. I had to use my calculator to figure that out.

Friday, June 26, 2015 at 11:14am
I'm probably premenstrual, because after my rant this morning, I went to the chiropractor, and on the way home started weeping openly when I

heard NPR announce the Supreme Court decision on marriage equality. Maybe it's not the female thing. Maybe it's because despite how screwed up it is, I love my country and have been wanting to feel there is some measure of justice and equality in the land of the free and the brave. Over the past few years, I've watched my LGBTQ friends fighting the classiest fight ever for their civil liberties, and I'm proud of how so many of them held out through it all. LOVE WINS. LOVE WINS. LOVE WINS. I am going to go crawl back in bed with The Feline now and weep. <3

Friday, June 26, 2015 at 8:01am
I cannot for the life of me understand why friends I thought I knew are defending the Confederate flag. Especially friends who live North of the Mason-Dixon. I don't need a rehashing of the Civil War. This flag wasn't solely flown as some nostalgic vestige hearkening back to the Civil War. It was resurrected as a symbol of the Confederacy in the 50s and 60s when the Klan was rising in popularity and the civil rights movement had begun to pick up steam. It means "sit down and shut up" to a large segment of the population. I don't care what the "facts" are about Abraham Lincoln's record regarding the emancipation of enslaved people--BECAUSE A WHITE SUPREMACIST SHOT HIM DEAD TOO. And for the love of all things holy and sane, reposting Ted Nugent quotes as a defense of the flag isn't going to win you any debates.

Thursday, June 25, 2015 at 7:49am
A Baker's Dozen Random thoughts: 1. I'm leaving this atrocious South Florida heat for almost a month in five days! 2. The Feline is going to be lost without me. 3. Coffee? 4. I miss thick deep woods with moss and mushrooms, and ferns. 5. and horse flies. Dammit. 6. The Feline is going to be pissed when I get back. 7. Coffee. Go get your coffee. 8. Why are there no clovers in South Florida? 9. I am going to freeze my ass off up there, better pack the winter clothing. 10. FIREFLIES 11. See #6, See #6, forget #6. See # 3 & 7. 12. Better pack the curry too. 13. Repeat #s 1-12.

Wednesday, June 24, 2015 at 3:42pm
Best and worst words of day: BEST--Chiropractor- Your spine is
behaving, I'm giving you day off. See me Friday. Worst: Feels like 103° F.

Wednesday, June 24, 2015 at 8:25am
Random thoughts this morning: 1. Teaching makes me happy. 2. I love
The Chef for many reasons, one of which is how unfazed he was when I
told him, "Honey, I need you to stay home this afternoon. We are
expecting a tiara delivery." 3. Horrible thing the chiropractor told me
yesterday that I was able to put out of my head until just now, and may
finally break me (or at least my spine) "I want you in here every day this
week." 4. If Jan Becker whimpers in the chiropractor's office and no one
hears her, she IS really whimpering. The tree does make a sound when it
falls. 5. Dear South Beach eateries: Enough with the bacon and truffle oil.

Tuesday, June 23, 2015 at 6:36pm
Bacon-infused bourbon. It's a thing. <hiccup>

Tuesday, June 23, 2015 at 10:53am
Conversation with Creepy Maintenance Man:
> Me: (Carrying groceries up the walkway. I pause to adjust the
> bags. I see CMM, he's smiling. turns on the sprinklers and soaks
> me) HEY! You just soaked me. That was not nice!
> CMM: You looked hot. #Creepy

Monday, June 22, 2015 at 11:58am
Jan Becker feeling twisted.
If this writing thing doesn't work out, I want to go back to school and
become a chiropractor, so I can beat the crap out of people every day.

Sunday, June 21, 2015 at 3:42pm
The Feline has a new oddly creepy, yet endearing game he likes to play:
push penis shaped objects (pens and pencils) under the bathroom door
when Jan is trying to find five minutes of peace.

Sunday, June 21, 2015 at 10:29am
Happy Summer!

Friday, June 19, 2015 at 8:22pm
Wisdom from Dr. Seuss on the boob tube tonight (THE LORAX) when the rest of the crap on TV is making me want to eat too much chocolate and lock myself up for the foreseeable future: "Unless someone like you cares a whole awful lot, Nothing is going to get better. It's not."

Friday, June 19, 2015 at 4:13pm
Less than 24 hours! Shuckers is ready for us. It's going to be hot!

Thursday, June 18, 2015 at 6:50pm
A thing that hardly seems to matter, given the heartbreak in South Carolina and the Dominican Republic, and reminds me that there are much worse things in life (it still sucks, but at least there's perspective): Some asshat broke into my car AGAIN and stole my GPS AGAIN. I hope whoever stole it gets to where he's going, you asshat.

Thursday, June 18, 2015 at 12:59pm
One of those odd (when taken out of context) things I say that bears repeating: After today, I'll stay on my side of the alphabet.

Thursday, June 18, 2015 at 9:21am
Jesus. Charleston. <3

Thursday, June 18, 2015 at 2:20am
I'm trying to sleep on my back because the chiropractor suggested a different position. This is infuriating to The Feline, who is accustomed to spooning. I finally got to sleep, and woke to find him eating my thesis draft. Again. #littleshit

Wednesday, June 17, 2015 at 1:30pm
I miss the 70s.

Tuesday, June 16, 2015 at 8:36pm
The chiropractor confirmed what many have been saying for years. Jan Becker is twisted and crooked...and now cracked out and adjusted.

Monday, June 15, 2015 at 6:31pm
Jan Becker added 2 new photos.
Several reasons I may have a headache: 1. Booking plane tickets is painful. 2. The Chef has reconfigured our living room, so he has easier access to his stereo equipment. This means half my living room is now a stereo, and another quarter of the living room is filled with vinyl. 3. Since The Chef can access his LPs, I am listening to loud techno, currently, The Disposable Heroes of Hypocrisy. 4. He's got PURPLE STROBE LIGHTS.

Monday, June 15, 2015 at 2:36pm
Flights are booked. Only took me three hours to figure that out.

Sunday, June 14, 2015 at 9:31pm EDT
A disturbing (yet satisfying) discovery in which I place The Chef's metaphorical shit in the street by oversharing on social media: While looking in the freezer for a container of tomato sauce I'd frozen, I discovered, in the rear corner, tucked safely away, a lone cup sized portion of frozen curry sauce I thought had been reheated already. When I opened the lid, it became evident that someone attacked the frozen curry as though it was a pint of Ben & Jerry's. Unless I have been sleep craving frozen curry, we all know who the culprit is in this situation.

Sunday, June 14, 2015 at 3:22pm
The rodents and reptiles are teaming up down here. Be afraid.

Sunday, June 14, 2015 at 11:30am
The diplomatic situation with The Feline is continuing to decline. After 36 hours of little to no sleep, I found myself in deep slumber last night. It didn't last. Every time I hit NREM 3 stage, he chomped on my hand, demanding I pet him. And goddess help me if he sniffs out the wiener dog scent on my pillow. I may never rest again ever in that eventuality.

Saturday, June 13, 2015 at 7:27pm
I'm home from the weekend road trip. The Feline is giving me stinkeye, and chewing me out for leaving him alone with The Chef for three days. I am taking the longest shower in history, which will not improve the diplomatic situation at home, but is necessary for the greater good.

Saturday, June 13, 2015 at 7:03pm
Jan Becker added a new photo to the album: Rolling Stones Road trip. Sympathy for the Devil

Saturday, June 13, 2015 at 7:03pm
Jan Becker added a new photo to the album: Rolling Stones Road trip. Only in Florida would the flushing of Depends undergarments be an issue at the gas station potty.

Friday, June 12, 2015 at 6:51pm
Sign I may be growing old. A man in the crowd approaches me and asks for drugs: "Got any Tylenol?" Sigh.

Friday, June 12, 2015 at 6:01pm
What the hell is molested sauce?

Friday, June 12, 2015 at 5:29pm
The walls in the hotel room are purple and textured. Even the ceilings are textured. The elevator is completely lined with woodgrain. We are in an uber lift right now. On the car radio, Frankie says "relax." This is a good idea. Orlando is full of giant churches. We're heading to the parking lot. And on the radio, "Start Me Up."

Friday, June 12, 2015 at 9:27am
Holy cow, Rolling Stones tonight.

Thursday, June 11, 2015 at 7:24am
ELEVEN HOURS, TEN MINUTES...Eleven Hours, Nine Minutes...

Tuesday, June 9, 2015 at 1:13pm
I gave in and put Facebook on the new phone. Dammit.

Sunday, June 7, 2015 at 12:23pm
The Chef is in the living room listening to Hootie and the Blowfish. That just ain't right.

Saturday, June 6, 2015 at 1:20pm
Turns out there is something to saying a stoned person is spaced out.

Saturday, June 6, 2015 at 1:16pm
As predicted, I plan to spend the afternoon elbow deep in mangos and curry powder. Chutney day has arrived!

Friday, June 5, 2015 at 1:17pm EDT
Apparently, pie is a great peace broker. It's in the oven and the smell is wafting. I went out to switch my laundry around and ran into my neighbor, Herbert the hermit hippie, sniffing at my door. He said, "hi."

Friday, June 5, 2015 at 10:19am
She can bake a cherry (/apple/rhubarb) pie...Just pitted about 3 pounds of cherries in 15 minutes. Odd, the feeling of accomplishment I'm experiencing at that.

Thursday, June 4, 2015 at 10:07am
The problem with The Chef playing "Stone Soul Picnic" is it takes at least a week to vacate my head, and I'm only two days into the damned week.

Wednesday, June 3, 2015 at 12:12pm
Happy Birthday, Allen Ginsberg.

Tuesday, June 2, 2015 at 6:40pm
Two things today which fill me with unreasonable terror: 1. The sight of Creepy Maintenance Man on the roof, dancing all by himself. 2. Waking

from a nap with a headache to hear The Chef dropping the needle on Stone Soul Picnic by the Fifth Dimension.

Saturday, May 30, 2015 at 8:37pm
The rent's too damn high.

Friday, May 29, 2015 at 7:36pm
Where I cracked inside today: I-95 Northbound Sample Rd. Exit, in the mangroves lining the ramp. Here is what I saw: A Broward County Sheriff supervising a crane that was ripping out a tent village whose residents include an amputee who relies on his wheelchair to get around and a gaunt woman whose sign reads, "God Bless." They were scooping everything into a large dump truck that will carry it to the top of the landfill I watch the sun set over in the evening.

Friday, May 29, 2015 at 1:12am
I'm rereading Oliver Sacks' Hallucinations right now. Interesting stuff.

Thursday, May 28, 2015 at 6:05pm
I finally received my replacement phone today. It's going to take me about a month to figure out how to use it, and all my contacts have been wiped out. If I am in your phone with my old cell#, and didn't send you text messages after I'd drunk too many bourbons (which I do very occasionally) my number's still the same, and it would be helpful if you'd send me a text to that number so I can add you back into my contacts. If you weren't in my phone, but want to be, you can send me a DM on Facebook, and I'll add you--unless you're Mike Huckabee. And if you are none of the above, then you can look at the first picture I snapped on the new phone. I think it is some sort of requirement that one must take a photo of the cat as soon as one gets a phone. Anyhow, he's handsome, The Feline.

Wednesday, May 27, 2015 at 4:12pm
In other news, I've received my official Mike Huckabee for president 2016 membership card. I'd be annoyed and call campaign headquarters

to let them know I'm voting for Bernie Sanders (no matter who gets the official nomination), but I'm happy they are wasting the postage on me.

Wednesday, May 27, 2015 at 2:20pm
The Chef brought home a pen from his new credit union with a cushion grip, a stylus tip, and even more wondrous, a flashlight. And I am not at all ashamed of this, but I stole it. He didn't even bother to put up a fight.

Wednesday, May 27, 2015 at 12:16am
Sexy Joey Biden...

Sunday, May 24, 2015 at 9:15pm
When I first came to visit The Chef in 2000, he pointed out a house just around the corner from here where Geraldo Rivera, along with the Broward County Sheriff's Office busted a crack dealer in the 80s. Tonight, when I drove by, there was a man on the roof of the house dangling a minion piñata into a crowd of about 35 screaming children. There goes the neighborhood...

Saturday, May 23, 2015 at 12:02pm
Let's hypothetically say The Chef needs a day off from work to attend a show he bought tickets for months ago, but the show falls on a holiday weekend, and he can't get the day off through a normal request. In that event, let's say, the process of calling off is so unfamiliar that he spends weeks practicing what to say and who to call and at what time, and when the day he needs off comes, he finally just calls and says, "I'm sick," blowing his elaborate narrative. He might also then pout for hours in the living room before the show, and worry how his coworkers are managing without him--and give me extremely detailed instructions on how to answer the phone should work call looking for him while he's out at let's say, Todd Rundgren. Poor Chef. If any of this is more than hypothetical, let's hope the show is worth all this anxiety.

Friday, May 22, 2015 at 2:44pm
This continues to disturb me. There's only one yarn color.

Friday, May 22, 2015 at 2:11pm
Another day in paradise...

Thursday, May 21, 2015 at 1:20am
I was alone with Edwidge Danticat in an elevator and managed to speak proper English and not gush too much the whole ride. There was also a reading, and a baby. A bourbon later, I'm still in the elevator with Danticat. Part of me will always be in the elevator with Danticat.

Wednesday, May 20, 2015 at 6:16pm
I live within an hour's drive of my favorite living writer, and I'll see her tonight. Things could be much worse.

Wednesday, May 20, 2015 at 10:31am
Words from the numinous, bass-toned voice outside my bathroom window this morning that I am adopting for my mantra for the day: "Things could be much worse."

Tuesday, May 19, 2015 at 10:42pm
Jan Becker shared Miami Book Fair's photo.

Tuesday, May 19, 2015 at 8:20pm
I've subscribed to the Old Farmer's Almanac Companion because they inform me of things like when the best days are to plant second season crops, the best days for fishing, and the best days to castrate a bull. These are all very important things to know.

Tuesday, May 19, 2015 at 4:59pm
Returning home this afternoon, I happened on a convergence of Creepy Maintenance Man #1 and #2 with a big industrial looking wet-vac between them. I just kept my mouth shut and kept walking. That moment was too ripe to comment.

Tuesday, May 19, 2015 at 8:22am
Morning. All is quiet here on Crystal Lake. Even the birds are making no noises. It is so quiet, all I can hear is the hum of the turnpike as morning traffic slogs past the towering landfill. But then, as to that lark at break of day that Shakespeare was so fond of, I hear a voice entering my windows, gliding across the floor, and slipping into my bed to tickle at my ears under the sheets. Lo, it is Creepy Maintenance Man, in the yard, cackling.
WHEREFORE ART THOU, CREEPY MAINTENANCE MAN

Monday, May 18, 2015 at 1:15pm
The planet mercury is once again behaving like a miserable gremlin. I'm ignoring it. I have revisions to work on. #suckmybuttlittleplanet

Sunday, May 17, 2015 at 1:28pm
A Lesson Learned: Before giving oneself a Splendor in the Grass haircut, it's wise to make sure one's Chef is up to shaving one's neck. Mine is not.

Saturday, May 16, 2015 at 10:19pm
They don't make shows like HR Pufnstuf anymore.

Saturday, May 16, 2015 at 6:55pm
All The Winemaker's wine made the trip to North Miami today for the Gulf Stream Magazine launch party without detonating. It's a good day.

Friday, May 15, 2015 at 2:48pm
Random Encounter with Herbert, the Hippie Hermit who lives next door: : (returning from pharmacy, arms laden with bags. I stop at my door, turn the key. I hear Herbert's door open slightly. I look over, and see just the tip of his nose and an eye)
    Me: Herbert! Wonderful to see you again!
    Herbert: (slams door shut) ...

Wednesday, May 13, 2015 at 9:21pm
Jan Becker likes Bernie Sanders.

Wednesday, May 13, 2015 at 6:52pm
Conversation with Herbert, the Hippie Hermit who lives next door:
> Me: Herbert! I haven't seen you in forever! How are you? I just want you to know, you're my favorite next door neighbor ever.
> Herbert: (raises his eyebrow): Really? Why is that?
> Me: You never make any noise. You never bother me. You're just nice and quiet.
> Herbert: (Looks down, scowls) Well, let's just say maybe you are not my favorite neighbor ever.

Wednesday, May 13, 2015 at 1:16pm
The sporadic habit of occasionally staying up all night to write, and then sleeping until noon has odd effects on my body. I woke up feeling I'd consumed several quarts of rotgut. But then I had coffee, and my brain is starting to clear, and there's this weird endorphin rush going on inside. All this for five sentences. And yes, I could focus on the fact that I spent all night writing five sentences, but those were some perfectly constructed sentences. Stanley Fish would be proud.

Tuesday, May 12, 2015 at 11:08pm
Frustrated Grammar Confession: I just spent 20 minutes trying to figure out if the sentence I am writing is supposed to read "one another" or "each other." I'm still not positive I got it right.

Tuesday, May 12, 2015 at 7:35pm
There are Brussels sprouts almost ready to roast in the kitchen, because I am craving cruciferous vegetables, and children are out on the walkway screaming their little throats raw and running and twisting ankles. This may be related to the vegetables, but that should have no effect on them, because I'm not sharing. The Feline is freaked out, because he does not enjoy children (especially those who scream), nor does he appreciate cruciferous vegetables. The catnip is tall in its pot and he has cat grass aplenty. That's all he cares about as far as greens are concerned.

Monday, May 11, 2015 at 8:45pm
It wasn't so bad. They didn't take the cheese grater to my feet.

Monday, May 11, 2015 at 10:36am
I'm getting a mani/pedi this evening. It's a gift from Laura and Walter. I have never had a mani/pedi, nor have I ever even been in a nail salon. This is terrifying on so many levels, but probably less frightening than it is for anyone who has seen my feet in their current state.

Sunday, May 10, 2015 at 9:10pm
The good thing about cleaning is that I was finally able to get the storage bin of rough drafts out of my bathtub (we have two bathrooms. I'm not that disgusting). They are now more readily accessible for revision work. Also, I found two tins of smoked oysters. I have no idea why I have smoked oysters, but I have two tins. How does one eat smoked oysters?

Sunday, May 10, 2015 at 12:35pm
Perhaps because it is Mother's Day, I am spending the day cleaning my office. If mother could see the state of the room, she'd likely have a grand mal. Since I spent most of my childhood avoiding cracks in the sidewalk to prevent spinal fractures, I often consider how my actions (or in this case, inactions) could cause bodily harm. I'm even dusting, Mom. <3

Saturday, May 9, 2015 at 7:16pm
It's that time of year up North when the coltsfoot has started growing leaves after popping up all ragged and yellow-headed. The black flies are hatching, which means the fish are hopping around in the streams trying to catch them. And the ramps. I've never smelled anything so simultaneously god-awful and amazing. They've got their bunny ears out now in culverts along the Lackawanna. But what I miss most is that the spring mushrooms are probably starting to come up too, especially the oysters. I wouldn't mind all of this, except so far, on any foraging ventures I've been on in Florida, the only mushrooms I've seen look like poison, or more of a good time than I can handle right at that moment.

Friday, May 8, 2015 at 9:02am
A request for advice and a short list of home remedies that have not stopped my leg cramps, which are so bad, I've popped blood vessels in ankles and the tops of my feet. If you have an additional remedy, please share, because my next option is a muscle relaxer, and that will leave me very happy, but non-productive: 1. A gallon of Pedialyte over two days + LOTS OF WATER. 2. Pickle juice 3. V8 4. Calcium / Magnesium / Potassium supplements. 4. Hot epsom salt soaks. 5. Cold soaks. 6. Walking it off. 7. Bananas. I'd try tonic water, but I can't tolerate it.

Thursday, May 7, 2015 at 5:51pm
Today while watching the Toddler, I'd slipped off my slimy Birkenstocks, and turned away from her for a quick moment. This was just enough time for her to pick one up and stick it in her gob. I'm certain she has now reached the stage of development where she actually understands the new sounds she's adding to her vocabulary, because before I could reach her to take the sandal away, she threw it at the dog and yelled out, "YUCKY." Sorry, Kid. In other news, I'm feeling better.

Tuesday, May 5, 2015 at 1:41pm
This bug is robbing me of my ability to send emails without grammatical errors, missing words and misspellings. I can take the rampaging sinuses, clogged ears, sore throat, aches, raging fevers/sweats and chills, but dammit, leave my language alone, you miserable virus from hell.

Monday, May 4, 2015 at 8:25pm
Oh, Christ. I think I accidentally took a double dose of flu meds. Everything is suddenly so very pretty. That incident at CVS yesterday now has contextual significance. I will be lying down until the room stops its spinning.

Monday, May 4, 2015 at 2:56pm
I asked The Chef to bring me Pho. He came home with Jewish penicillin. Logically I know this is equivalent, but I'm too cranky not to dicker with him over the distinction.

Monday, May 4, 2015 at 12:05pm
The world looks so very different when the fever spikes to 102° F.

Sunday, May 3, 2015 at 7:17pm
There is no logic behind my decision to cook several gallons of tomato sauce today. I'm too stuffed up to taste or smell it. I have a ton of other things waiting to be done, no appetite, and I'm tired. But there's an Italian grandmother in me who's saying it's only right to have a full pot simmering on the stove, on a Sunday afternoon with a Flower Moon rising. And there's a witch in me too, who wants to fill a cauldron with healing things like garlic and pepper near Beltane. So I'm listening, because the wise women in my belly say this is how it should be.

Sunday, May 3, 2015 at 6:23pm
Jan Becker likes Earth Porn.

Sunday, May 3, 2015 at 2:25pm
There is a jet ski out on the lake that sounds like one of those very long Tibetan horns (a dungchen, or a dharma trumpet, they're called). It's making my chest rattle. This is not entirely unpleasant.

Sunday, May 3, 2015 at 10:05am
My nursemaid (The Feline) is on strike, and is demanding better pay.

Saturday, May 2, 2015 at 10:00pm
In other news, I managed to crawl to the pharmacy for Dayquil today, and while my order was being tallied, a receipt popped up that said, "Potential cough syrup abuse." It wasn't even a formula with Sudafed in it, just regular generic daytime cold stuff, and I think it was the first box I've bought this year. I asked the clerk what would happen if I took the medicine home and flogged it. So 1984 at CVS this week.

Saturday, May 2, 2015 at 2:00pm
Damn. Experiencing that moment when a student writes a damn letter that makes you cry, because they say things that make you think, "Maybe I got through to a few of them." But then, you don't know if it's that your cardiac muscle is just functioning properly, or the fact that you're running a damn fever. You just have to stop everything and curl up with The Feline and have a good cry for a little bit. #iheartundergradssometimes

Saturday, May 2, 2015 at 8:50am
Quarter to 9 AM: I am feverish and ask The Chef to make sure I'm up later this morning to grade. He assents. I give him the Vulcan salute. He fails to reciprocate. I prompt him again. He tries, but cannot. Poor fellow is now seeking absolution by offering prayers to his autographed photos of Grace Lee Whitney and Michael Dorn.

Saturday, May 2, 2015 at 4:25am
4:20 AM: I wake up for middle of the night wanderings and find that the Duchess of Cambridge is in labor, and not only that, but there are live-bloggers, blogging this. I have a commentary in me somewhere about priorities and the media, but I might as well go back to my wandering.

Friday, May 1, 2015 at 6:49pm
Jan Becker likes World Naked Gardening Day.

Friday, May 1, 2015 at 4:26pm
Portfolios were due today at 4PM. Right now, it's 4:25, and I have about 11 emails from panicked students...Sigh.

Thursday, April 30, 2015 at 3:49am
Close to 4AM mysteries: 1. Why is the shoe shine brush in the middle of the bathroom floor? 2. How many skeins of yarn would it take to cover the Freedom Tower in crocheted glory? 3. Where did my purse walk off to? 4. What EXACTLY was Garcia Lorca doing down by the watermelons? <---This last one haunts me so.

Wednesday, April 29, 2015 at 6:51pm
THEY HAVE GRAVY FRIES?!? ARE YOU EFFING KIDDING ME?!?
GRAVY FRIES?!? I AM NEVER LEAVING.

Wednesday, April 29, 2015 at 6:50pm
Jan Becker likes Eat Your Poem.

Wednesday, April 29, 2015 at 6:45pm
Oh, eff you, Blackboard, for hiding a whole slew of ungraded work from
me until just before student portfolios with revisions are due. Sigh.

Wednesday, April 29, 2015 at 12:23am
I'm experiencing conflicting emotions. I found out in the past couple of
years that Henry Norris, who was Henry VIII's Groom of the Stool (and
lost his head for schtupping Anne Boleyn) is my 15th (or so) great
grandfather (on my maternal grandfather's side). So I've been watching
Wolf Hall to see what that was all about. Only, here's the rub. The actor
they picked to play my grand daddy is hot. And that's just not right.

Tuesday, April 28, 2015 at 10:16pm
I just ate a German pickle so good it was like a religious experience.

Tuesday, April 28, 2015 at 4:07pm
There will be more later in the week, and I realize my Facebook break
wasn't much of a break, but for me, it was a big step away from the
vitriol. Anyhow, I'm back to let you know, I can really shake it down.
Done grading all the things--until the final things come in. I can say this,
now that I can dance. Watch me now!

Tuesday, April 28, 2015 at 10:06am
Once again, I fell asleep on the toilet in the middle of the night, which is
not good for my back. This means I woke up in a foul mood, which is
currently compounded by some of the racist/classist rhetoric

surrounding the protests in Baltimore. I'm checking out of Facebook land today, because it's probably not healthy for me to be this pissed off at people I respect most of the time. I will just say this: We (the People of the United States of America) have been severing the spines of our citizens for centuries. This is nothing new. We (the People--of the planet Earth) have been operating under an unofficial state of emergency for eons. This is also nothing new. Maybe I'm getting too old for all this crap, but I don't have time for anyone who can't acknowledge that every person on the planet belongs to the same human family, and that all this fighting is just one enormous family feud.

Sunday, April 26, 2015 at 7:01am
I'm off to the swamp with Love the Everglades Movement and Orange Island Arts Foundation for a day full of poetry. The forecast is calling for a 96° high, record breaking temperatures. I'm anticipating ecstatic visions and heat-induced hallucinations. Should be fun.

Saturday, April 25, 2015 at 7:27pm
I'm not sure what it is about finishing up the semester. I just want to sleep for about 600 years.

Friday, April 24, 2015 at 10:16am
Today is my last day teaching this semester. I am taking delight in the small things this morning, like stealing The Chef's banana from his cereal bowl. Funny how something so small can bring me such joy.

Thursday, April 23, 2015 at 9:58pm
This is from an earlier thread. It's a comment on a student poem. I normally do not repeat things. However, I have been repeating it for most of the day, to every student who ambiguously referred to love in their poems, so once more won't hurt: "Here you mention 'Love'. What is love exactly? Can you be more concrete? Love means different things to different people. A proctologist, for example, probably loves diseased colons. I do not think that is what you mean, so it might be best to be more specific..."

Thursday, April 23, 2015 at 1:37pm
Stack of grading, allergies acting up, I searching for a decongestant and find the Mexican Valium instead. Oh, Universe, you temptress.

Wednesday, April 22, 2015 at 8:19am
The thing that makes me most happy this morning, even before I've brewed a pot of coffee and given The Feline his early dish of fish, is to look out the window over the lake and see the sky coated with light grey clouds. The water level on the lake is very low for this time of year and it seems to me there are fewer birds fishing out back lately, especially brown pelicans. The pelicans are always good for a laugh when they fish. It's like watching awkward teenagers smash themselves into walls the way they free fall into the water when they see their breakfast shimmer just under the meniscus, and often, they pop back up with a fish in their bill, toss back their heads and swallow in a great gulp. And while the pelicans have the sense to not dive into a shallow lake, it doesn't seem to deter the water skiers, who offer me no moments of humor at all, not even when they crash.

Tuesday, April 21, 2015 at 1:24pm
4/21/15, 1300 hrs: I just woke up after a long night of poetry and chocolate and an impressive buffet of all the things. For a change, The Chef had coffee ready for me. This is good, because when I looked out on the balcony, I discovered that during yesterday's storms, my aloes grew wings and took flight, and are now strewn about. Shattered terra cotta shards everywhere. If I listen hard, I think the aloes are crying out to be repotted, but this may just be what's going on inside my skull. My brain feels like a swamp and cane field fire, heavy and thick, and a bit syrupy. "I grow old, I grow old. I shall wear my trousers rolled."

Monday, April 20, 2015 at 3:39pm
Random blessings and peeves: 1. Class was surprisingly lucid today. 2. My mailbox at the south campus thinks I am Jan Baker. This isn't so bad, I know some fabulous Baker boys. However, 3. On top of the misnomer

from the department, Einstein Bagels thinks my first name is Yania. 4. It should be illegal to sell anyone a bagel with cream cheese that isn't toasted unless the customer specifically requests a cold lump of dough. (I hardly ever eat bagels). 5. Tornado warning?

Monday, April 20, 2015 at 7:37am
I have a feeling that many of my students are under the impression that today is a federal holiday.

Sunday, April 19, 2015 at 7:56pm
Random Confession: There is a knight anole living in the tree right outside our front door. It's close to two feet long, and hangs out on the railing during the daytime. Sometimes, even if I don't have to, I like to walk out the front door and have a showdown with it where we give each other the stink eye, and it shuffles to the other side of the railing to see if I'm really a threat. Here's why. After the stink eye, if I approach it very deliberately, the anole does an amazing jump from the railing (we're on the third floor) into the tree. This gives me an excuse to yell out, "leaping lizard!" and I have always wanted to say that.

Sunday, April 19, 2015 at 11:57am
Grading, grading, grading...

Sunday, April 19, 2015 at 9:13am
I'm looking for my cleanest dirty shirt. Happy Sunday.

Saturday, April 18, 2015 at 8:54pm
When Jan Becker has a plumbing emergency (kitchen sink clog/overflow), it is not a measly pathetic half-assed clog. It's a clog so big the plunger mutilates itself, and a deluge so deep Noah's flood looks like a treacly little rain creek in the desert. Victory will be mine, Mighty Clog!

Saturday, April 18, 2015 at 6:25pm
Comcast Guy shows up to figure out my connectivity issues, looks over
the equipment, says everything's fine. He walks out the door, and the
internet goes down again.

Friday, April 17, 2015 at 9:26am
Today should be interesting. I have a particularly gruesome mosquito (or
other noxious insect) bite in a particularly tender and personal spot, and
an inability not to scratch until I'm raw. I will likely be at it all day. My
poor students.

Thursday, April 16, 2015 at 11:55pm EDT
When I was a kid, we had this volume of American folk tales I used to
read all the time. I remember reading Rip Van Winkle over and over, and
thinking, "Wow, it would be great to fall asleep and wake up in 20
years." These days, I'm happy if I can get in 20 minutes.

Thursday, April 16, 2015 at 4:38pm
Conversation with The Toddler:

> Toddler's Mom: Look! Your Tia Juana's here ! Say "hi! Hi, Tia
> Juana, HI!"
> Me: Hi kiddo, hi, hi!
> Toddler: (smiles, stretches out her arms) DIE! DI-EEE! DIE!

Everyone's a critic.

Thursday, April 16, 2015 at 9:06am
I am praying that the Universe grants me the patience required to deal
with the Post Office. The good news is that it does not appear that my
mail has been re-routed, nor my identity stolen. This is a relief. It took
me a long time to get this identity in (dis) order, and I'd hate it if
someone swiped it on me when I'm finally becoming comfortable with it.

Wednesday, April 15, 2015 at 3:50pm
God Bless the woman selling frozen water on Calle Ocho. And thank you Cindy for a sandwich and a chocolate chip cookie. Thank you, Universe for putting chocolate in my gullet today.

Wednesday, April 15, 2015 at 8:39am
So, it's not the end of March, but the roach inspector will be driving up in his truck tomorrow morning, and I do believe the tax collector wants me to cut my wrists. I also don't live in Johnson City, but I've been there-- and God help me, miss the "Home of the Square Deal." There is no snow here to turn sour, and the sun is always shining, and perhaps that is even worse than clouds sometimes. I miss the color grey. Anyhow, Facebook should stop asking what's on my mind, because you get this for an answer. And I'm not a professor, but I play one on television. Dear Ruth Stone, I hope you have reached the next galaxy, because I think sometimes this one feels like a black hole. And I'm okay, this is just me before coffee, contemplating a shower and a drive to Miami through the Everglades, with no AC on Tax Day when I still have not filed and didn't get quite enough sleep last night.

Tuesday, April 14, 2015 at 10:37pm
Sometimes the student typos are fortunate: "I love all of your quarks." That's some serious sub-atomic love right there.

Tuesday, April 14, 2015 at 7:21pm
Love the Everglades Movement is doing it right.

Tuesday, April 14, 2015 at 4:36pm
Unfortunate student typo of the day: "She stroked my gentiles lightly."

Tuesday, April 14, 2015 at 3:20pm
219 girls are still missing in Nigeria, and it's been a year today. 365 days of hoping and praying. As long as it takes, I'll keep those girls in my prayers. <3

Tuesday, April 14, 2015 at 11:59am
It appears that the gecko survived the night, and The Feline let me sleep in till 11:30. This morning The Chef and I are arguing over the definition of a particularly unkind Creole profanity, but this is what happens when there is no coffee waiting for me when I sleep in.

Tuesday, April 14, 2015 at 1:41am
I have a situation. A gecko in the living room. This means either I will get no sleep tonight, because The Feline will be up hunting and howling or, it means I will finally get to sleep and wake up with an armless, legless, tailless, but still alive and squirming gecko stump on my pillow.

Monday, April 13, 2015 at 3:22pm
Unprecedented teaching moment: Class is over at 1:50. At 1:49, I say, "Okay, class. You are free to go." No one moves. I say, "Really, you're free, you can go off into the world." No one moves. A student raises her hand, "Can't we just stay here? Maybe forever?" Weird.

Monday, April 13, 2015 at 11:12am
Jan Becker feeling sparkly.
Thank you Miami Beach Gay Pride for covering me in so much second-hand glitter it will take several showers to wash off.

Monday, April 13, 2015 at 12:14am
Nothing smells as pretty as milkweed in bloom.

Sunday, April 12, 2015 at 8:53am
Facebook is asking what's on my mind again. I'm a weird combination of so happy to be here and homesick for the woods.

Saturday, April 11, 2015 at 8:01pm
I received the first piece of mail I've gotten in about two weeks today. It was a Victoria's Secret flyer addressed to Janaina R Becker. WTF?

Saturday, April 11, 2015 at 1:15pm
I'm trying to understand the logic of living with The Chef, and being requested to bake cookies for him. Of course I am doing this, but he's the professional here.

Saturday, April 11, 2015 at 11:43am
If you are in the area, my (long-suffering--sorry, Les ;)) thesis director Les Standiford will be reading from his new book Water to the Angels tonight at 6PM at Murder on the Beach in Delray Beach. And if you're not in the area, you might want to check out the book anyway, because it is highly relevant these days--and history, that's a fairly important thing.

Friday, April 10, 2015 at 4:48pm
Conversation with a shrieking 6- year- old in the library tower at FIU:
> Child: LALALALA LOUD NOISES
> Me: (after an hour of this while I am trying to grade, I have had enough. I hear the child approach and step out into the hallway) Hey. This is a whisper floor. I am having a hard time working because of all the noise you are making. I realize you are small and that someone probably gave you too much sugar (I look at his father--he looks down at the floor like he's done something wrong), but people are trying to work.
> Child: Why don't you go back to FIU?
> Me: You are in FIU. I work here. I teach. I am trying to work right now, and I can't because you've been yelling. It would be helpful if you piped down. I know it's not easy, but this is the library. There are people here trying to study.
> Child: Where's your dad?
> Me: I'm a grownup, I don't bring dad to work. I don't bring kids to work either. I know people are trying to study and need it to be quiet. (I look at his father, who is extremely interested in his shoelaces...No eye contact).
> Child (whispers) I have to pee now.
> Me: Good. That is something you can do very quietly right?
> Child: (nods) Unless I poop. That can get a little noisy.

Friday, April 10, 2015 at 3:19pm
Holy hell: Power goes out in the library tower, and for some reason, today is the day everyone brought their kids to work--and the kids are all terrified of the dark and shriek like little banshees in the halls. If it happens again, I might have to growl at them from the dark pocket of the office, so they have a story to tell their grandkids one day about the dragon in the library tower. RAWR!

Friday, April 10, 2015 at 10:59am
It appears that the on-going identity theft/ mail hijacking scheme has recurred. This is just a theory at this point, but I've not gotten any mail for about two weeks. I figure the best way to know if we've had our address changed through the post office again is to send myself some mail, but that would be too simple. So, I'm spending some time today writing myself a love letter. Also, in case it has been stolen, I'm going to send myself a card that looks like it could contain money and write a note to the mail thieves, letting them know how stealing a writer's mail is one of the lowest things one human can do to another. I receive pay through the postal system. I could get a PO Box, but c'mon, I'm a writer. Ain't no money for that, especially if my pay has been rerouted and cashed in someone else's account.

Friday, April 10, 2015 at 9:20am
I want to do all the don'ts.

Friday, April 10, 2015 at 1:22am
Jan Becker went to Poetry in the Park.

Friday, April 10, 2015 at 12:15am
If I were a practicing fiction writer, I could have great fun with headlines.

Thursday, April 9, 2015 at 10:42pm
Holy Poetry Party, South Florida. I just got back from a bar in Miami packed with poets, stopped at the grocery store to pick up a tomato, and there were poems wiggling their fingers at me in the dairy aisle, yawping their little hearts out from the deli case. The clerk at the checkout is writing poems. One cannot walk five feet without tripping over a poem down here. (Also, two bloody Marys <hiccup>)

Thursday, April 9, 2015 at 2:35pm
Facebook is asking what's on my mind. Here is a random list: 1. If it weren't for The Feline's calming presence, I'd likely be in the Puzzle Haus. 2. Only in South Florida must one budget 3 hours for a 45-minute drive. 3. Really, Jan Becker, you don't have leprosy, it's hives. 4. Why does Hawai'i have an interstate highway? 5. What EXACTLY was Garcia Lorca doing down by the watermelons? 6. Yes, good idea to take shower.

Thursday, April 9, 2015 at 12:33pm
There's a lot going on in Miami this month for writers, but if your dance card is free tonight, I'll be at The Annex in Wynwood tonight from 6:30 to 8:30 PM, leading tonight's First Draft, sponsored by The Center at MDC. First drink is on the house. And if you can't make it tonight, the link below has their upcoming schedule.

Thursday, April 9, 2015 at 11:58am
Kind of morning where even my "things to do" have things to do.

Wednesday, April 8, 2015 at 4:59pm
Conversation with a student who did not at all like Pablo Neruda's "Ode to Bees":
>   Student: What the hell was that about?
>   Me: Honeybees
>   Student: What's all that other stuff? What's he got the ocean in there for? Who wrote this? Is he dead?

Me: Pablo Neruda (This led to a brief discussion of Neruda's biography, his communist beliefs, collective work ethics as exemplified by the honeybees, a brief discussion on bee sexuality, the collective unconscious, the political strife in Chile and the Nobel Peace Prize, continue verbatim). Some people think Neruda may have been poisoned.

Student: Shit, they should have poisoned him for this poem.

An Instructor weeps.

Wednesday, April 8, 2015 at 8:03am

Morning Conversation Between two guys named Al and George outside my bathroom window:

George: Good Morning, Al! Welcome to Paradise!

Al: Mornin', George. But this ain't Paradise.

George: Whaddaya mean? Sunshine, beaches, girls in bikinis. We can have a drink in the pool.

Al: This ain't paradise, George.

George: Well then, Mr. Bright and Cheery, where exactly is Paradise?

Al: Massachusetts, George.

George: You high buddy? I've been to Massachusetts.

Wednesday, April 8, 2015 at 12:39am

A Random Confession: I forgot to buy The Feline his treats today, so I'm slipping him kibble and pretending it's special. I'm not sure he believes it, but so far he's not marching against me, or putting up picket signs.

Tuesday, April 7, 2015 at 1:41pm

Today's daunting task: I need to figure out how to get past Creepy Maintenance Man, who is armed with a pressure sprayer, to get to the laundry room to wash my clothes. I should probably change out of the white t-shirt too, just in case.

Tuesday, April 7, 2015 at 8:21am

Jan Becker likes Cheech Marin.

Sunday, April 5, 2015 at 9:25pm
There is a man in the backyard whistling very loudly, and making strange grunting noises out by the lake. I find this oddly comforting. Occasionally he shouts out words, but they're in Portuguese, so I can't understand them, but they sound like they're harmless. I hope, anyway.

Saturday, April 4, 2015 at 12:39am
This is a little weird (what else is new?), but I am so happy to have gotten a real rejection letter today. Above all other parts of this crazy writing life/job, I hate being rejected or passed over for a contest, and hearing nothing from the journal. It's like getting the silent treatment from the snotty kids in junior high.

Friday, April 3, 2015 at 8:42am
I wonder if Jesus would think "Good Friday" is an oxymoronic name for the day too?

Thursday, April 2, 2015 at 5:04pm
The Chef's sister and family survived the visit. The Feline even came out and let the kids pet him (which never happens). Tia and The Chef are going down for a long nap. Zzzzzzzzzzz

Thursday, April 2, 2015 at 1:05pm
So far, the visit is going well. They are all out on a nature walk. I'm here, sick with a cold, answering student emails. I probably should not answer student emails on dextromethorphan, because I find myself wanting to ask questions like Ginsberg: "Which way does your beard point tonight? Who killed the pork chops? What price bananas?" I find these questions are somewhat more logical than the emails they answer.

Thursday, April 2, 2015 at 9:21am
I've known The Chef for sixteen years, and have lived with him almost six years. I've known his brother, The Winemaker for slightly longer, and one of his sisters for probably about ten years. There are two more sisters

I have yet to meet. The Chef is in the kitchen tossing pizza dough right now in preparation for one of those sisters who is in town on vacation. I already like her slightly more than The Winemaker, because she was decent enough to book a hotel room. Estoy nervioso. The Chef only pulls out the pizza dough for VIPs.

Wednesday, April 1, 2015 at 10:30pm
It's even worse when I say I'm going to trim his nails, then I neglect to do so, and The Feline taps again for a treat, snags a nipple (happens every damn time. Ouch).

Wednesday, April 1, 2015 at 7:29pm
I know it's time to trim The Feline's nails when he draws blood tapping at my arm for a treat.

Monday, March 30, 2015 at 9:45am
Woke up this morning to news that wine I took to a friend from The Winemaker's batch he left behind has spontaneously exploded all over the friend's kitchen. He left two cases here. I am nervous. (Julio and Erica your bottle should be fine, that came from a different Winemaker in the same family). Also, if a houseguest leaves potentially explosive booze in your house, that's a declaration of war, isn't it? #Winemakerchronicles

Sunday, March 29, 2015 at 10:36pm
Facebook wants to know what's on my mind. Bed. Also, I had a fantastic weekend, met BRAVE EDGY WRITERS, got over my fear of Easter bunnies, and survived South Beach on a busy weekend.

Sunday, March 29, 2015 at 9:53pm
Jan Becker likes Free Mali the Elephant.

Sunday, March 29, 2015 at 4:28pm
Survived my first Miami car accident. Nothing major, just a busted headlight. It only took me six years to have one, and this time, it was not

my fault. Folks are here writing up a storm! But still, we miss you. Wish you were here.

Sunday, March 29, 2015 at 7:56am
Today in 1958, Elvis Presley entered boot camp.

Saturday, March 28, 2015 at 8:50am
Thank you pernicious Everglades varmint who found my face so pretty you felt the need to suck blood from my lower eyelid, and left it swollen and weepy. I will see the day much differently because of you.

Friday, March 27, 2015 at 10:33pm
On the Marine Corps air station where I lived in Hawai'i, the bugle sounds Reveille at 0445 hrs (no wonder Marines are cranky). I'm sleeping in til at least 0500. Then I'm taking a shower, putting final coat of polish on the boots, spit shining them til they gleam, and heading to the Hotel Gaythering on Lincoln Road in Miami Beach for writing boot camp with Reading Queer at 1400hrs sharp. I wish you all pleasant dreams (and/or ecstatic visions) and a lovely weekend. I know mine will be. Good night.

Friday, March 27, 2015 at 2:49pm
There is a high-pitched sound coming from something in the adjunct/TA office. I'm not sure where, but I would like to kill it. I tried turning off all the lights, and the computer equipment, anything electronic, and it's not working. It's painful to sit in here. (Where I will be for the next 3 1/2 hours). In other news, the watermelon Greek life event was back on again. Today there was a melon eating contest. Food contests and undergrads together should not mix. I managed to get sprayed with watermelon juice and saliva from 25 feet. Yuck.

Friday, March 27, 2015 at 9:30am
I am dealing with the world's most elusive, yet vicious mosquito ever.

Thursday, March 26, 2015 at 11:09am
The Universe delivered an unexpected gift for me yesterday. Creepy Maintenance Man #2!

Here is our first conversation: (Scene, I have just arrived home from my long drive with no AC through the Everglades. Temperature is about 85, but very humid. I have 17 new bug bites on my driver's side arm, bugs in my hair, and am dehydrated. I run into the new maintenance man, who is like our more familiar character, but with a handlebar moustache)

> Creepy Maintenance Man #2: Phew, it's hot!
>
> Me: grumble, grumble. I noticed. I just drove from South Miami with no AC.
>
> Creepy Maintenance Man #2: I wouldn't bother to get that fixed if I were you. I never use the AC in my truck. Not even in the summer. I LOVE the heat. The way it feels when your pores cleanse themselves. (looks me up and down) It's good for you to be that hot from time to time. Makes your skin look wet. #Creepy.

Wednesday, March 25, 2015 at 4:36pm
Thank you everyone for birthday wishes! Three things, and a resolution: 1. A tip: It's not a good idea to run across Interstate 75 (5 lanes). I'm glad I missed the fella who darted on foot across the far-left lane as I was zipping along to work. 2. The presence of a Baby on Board sign in your window does not mean it is okay to drive like an asshole (I saw two of these today). 3. My favorite interaction with an undergrad this semester. Quite possibly ever. Here's the scene. There's some sort of Greek life event going on out on one of the quads and there are like 500 watermelons out, and these undergrads are bowling across the lawn with them, or carving them. It's like watermelon mecca. I walk over to one who is plucking one off the lawn and I bark at him in my best drill sergeant voice: You! Garcia Lorca! What are you doing down by the watermelons?!? I swear, I've always wanted to say that. Resolution: I will not subject myself to another summer with no AC in the car.

Tuesday, March 24, 2015 at 11:51pm
I keep trying to hit reset on a New Year, and failing miserably. I tried on January 1st, January 21st, February 19th, even on March 21st, which are all new years for someone somewhere. I think tomorrow's a good day to try again. March 25th, along with being the birthday of Aretha Franklin and King Kamehameha (yes, and Jan Becker too), is New Year's Day on the old Roman calendar. So, one more time, when the clock hits midnight. Happy New Year! <3

Tuesday, March 24, 2015 at 7:18pm
This is just getting ridiculous now. Grandma has the shingles. Everything else is progressing as it should be (for the most part, she has an infection). Ouch, Grandma. Jeeze. #Grandmachronicles

Tuesday, March 24, 2015 at 2:17pm
The only rooms in the apartment I can freely occupy are the kitchen and the bathrooms. Everything else is soaking wet from Carpet Guy. My wifi connection keeps going down, making it impossible to grade. I think when life hands Jan Becker wet carpets and shoddy wifi, the only logical move is to make curry.

Tuesday, March 24, 2015 at 10:26am
I'm stuck outside with The Feline until the rugs dry from Carpet Guy's visit. He has given us clear orders. Nothing on the rugs until they dry. I think he managed to get most of the sand out. Carpet Guy is concerned with his aura. His wife works at a spiritual wellness center, and they've banned him, because his aura is bad. I dunno. He seems like a nice guy. I didn't notice anything off with his sparklies.

Tuesday, March 24, 2015 at 6:40am
I'm grinding my beans at 6:30 AM with no grievances, and let The Feline out for his morning hunt flat-footed instead of on tiptoe. This is all it takes for me to have a good morning. #Winemakerchronicles

Monday, March 23, 2015 at 7:46pm
I've got a bonfire going in the apartment fueled by mountain and white sage, yerba Santa, and sweetgrass. A St. Michael novena is burning, and there's a candle glowing in George Clinton's wineglass. It's quiet. The Feline is out hunting, and in about 30 minutes, when he comes in, I'm climbing into a hot bubble bath with a shot of bourbon and a washcloth. Perfect evening.

Monday, March 23, 2015 at 3:21pm
Just when I thought I could relax, I got word that my brother, who drives a big rig, was in a head-on collision with another tractor trailer. Thankfully, he has a very hard head and is okay, but please, knock it off. No more scares.

Monday, March 23, 2015 at 11:26am
Ladies and Gentlemen, and anyone who may identify somewhere outside that oppressive binary of gender construction, The Winemaker has packed his possessions and has left the apartment! He left two cases of wine, but took all the Riesling. Pity, because the Riesling is actually good this year. He also left three pounds of sand in the kitchen, and spread throughout the apartment on the floors, walls, couch, anywhere sand will stick. My fridge smells like sweat socks. The Feline has PTSD and gecko hunting separation anxiety. But, it is finally quiet here. There will be no more requests for help with the lotion, no more tip-toeing in the kitchen in the morning when I brew my coffee. No more long-term houseguests, for this year at least.
Here is our "Final" Conversation:

> Winemaker: Becker, I'm leaving now. I'll be out of your hair for good.
> Me: Well, you're not going far, right? You'll be in the area for a little while.
> Winemaker: Right.
> Me: Call if you need bail money. Be careful. Godspeed, Winemaker. Safe journeys.

Winemaker: Thanks, Becker, I had a good visit. I'm going now. I'll be out of your hair for good. (Comes in for a big hug)
Me: (I hug him back with vigor and glee) Winemaker, we both know that's not true. You'll be back in my hair in no time at all.
Winemaker: This is true, Becker, but I wanted to leave you with a happy thought.
Becker's happy. Winemaker, out. #Winemakerchronicles

Sunday, March 22, 2015 at 11:47pm
These are strange days. Today was a constant battle with the internet, and not enough accomplished. I did, however, talk to Grandma, who was yawping up a nor'easter and is looking forward to all the new foods she's going to try on her heart healthy diet, like "that funny bread." She means bread that is not white. I let her know everyone had been praying for her and wishing her well, and she is thankful for that. Says she has a lot of adventures left and can't wait to come back for another visit. Universe, not just yet, please. I need to get a good night's rest. Every night for at least the next three months.#Grandmachronicles

Sunday, March 22, 2015 at 7:09pm
The Chef just announced to me that The Winemaker is leaving tomorrow. Not to return home yet, but to stay with his friend Chuck for a few days. Good luck, Chuck! #Winemakerchronicles

Sunday, March 22, 2015 at 2:28pm
My cell phone is broken. Comcast is giving me trouble too with internet, phone and cable all at once. This just means that all the plotting I did to get The Winemaker and The Chef out of the house for the day by making them breakfast is for naught, because I can't grade when the internet keeps going out every five minutes. If you've been trying to reach me on my cell, it's dead, and will remain so for the next week or so, until I can scrape together enough to buy a new one. You don't want to talk to me right now anyway. Trust me. #Winemakerchronicles

Sunday, March 22, 2015 at 12:11pm
While we are on the subject of CLIMATE CHANGE and GLOBAL
WARMING, The Winemaker is much happier this morning eating his
home fries and eggs. "Becker," he told me, "you ought to be canonized
for these potatoes." I'm not sure we're thinking of the same canons, but
that's all right. I can handle this variety of CLIMATE CHANGE and
GLOBAL WARMING. #Winemakerchronicles

Sunday, March 22, 2015 at 10:17am
Since FIU is a state school, and the state has banned the words CLIMATE
CHANGE and GLOBAL WARMING from the acceptable lexicon of state
employees, if I use the terms CLIMATE CHANGE or GLOBAL
WARMING in class, am I subjecting myself to censure? Does this
oversight of language extend to social media? Will posting words like
CLIMATE CHANGE or GLOBAL WARMING send me in for an official
psych evaluation? That would be okay. I think the shrink believes in
CLIMATE CHANGE and GLOBAL WARMING. My shrink already tells
me how Jesus cured his asthma on the radio (I swear this is true). He's a
state employee too. If I ask him about his opinions on CLIMATE
CHANGE or GLOBAL WARMING, and he answers using the words
CLIMATE CHANGE or GLOBAL WARMING, who will evaluate the
shrink? And what of the science students in my classes? What if they
want to write about CLIMATE CHANGE or GLOBAL WARNING? Can
I comment on enjambment in a poem if the line breaks on words like
CLIMATE CHANGE or GLOBAL WARMING? Because we could
certainly use a line break. CLIMATE CHANGE or GLOBAL WARNING
CLIMATE CHANGE or GLOBAL WARNING CLIMATE CHANGE or
GLOBAL WARNING

Saturday, March 21, 2015 at 8:18pm
Saturday Afternoon was spent with The Winemaker in relative peace. I
had a good hour long nap with The Feline. The Winemaker is all about
the March madness nonsense. I'm making he and The Chef breakfast
tomorrow and then kicking them out of the apartment so I can grade in
quiet. Apparently, The Winemaker's disposition is largely improved by

promises of eggs and homefries. 'Twould have been nice to know this before now. #Winemakerchronicles

Saturday, March 21, 2015 at 5:37pm
I am so tired; the walls are breathing. The Winemaker is watching television. I've left him instructions to wake me up before he goes out tonight. I have a feeling I won't see anyone until tomorrow. #Winemakerchronicles

Saturday, March 21, 2015 at 7:22am
My Aunt Wendy is one of my favorite people. She's a hard worker. She likes her word find and crossword puzzles, and has exacting standards when it comes to washing dishes. She prefers the water to be blisteringly hot. She has one of the prettiest smiles I've ever seen, and gives great hugs. She also has Down Syndrome, which is usually one of the last things that comes to mind when I think of her, though it's an important part of her identity. Wendy is fortunate that her family and community loves her exactly as she is, which is not the case for many others born with trisomy 21. Today is World Down Syndrome Day. I'm observing it as a day of thanks that I am blessed to know Wendy, and of hope for other people with Down Syndrome who don't have support. I'd say for "people like Wendy," but she's too unique for me to say that <3

Saturday, March 21, 2015 at 12:08am
Three things: 1. I am exhausted and am going to sleep hard shortly, because I'll be up at 6AM tomorrow to start all over. 2. I love my drive to the South campus through the Everglades. I love how big the swamp is and how small I feel driving through it. I do not love the absence of air conditioning on the first day of Spring in the Everglades. (To give you an idea of that, if you are not in South Florida, it will be 88° tomorrow + humidity). My driver's side arm is suffering. I have so many deep blistered bites I can't count them. And I can't take a picture to show them, because my phone is broken. If I could, you'd be that word which is a weird combination of disgusted and amazed. 3. It took Grandma less time to go into the hospital with congestive heart failure, two strains of

the flu, pneumonia--and then have a heart attack and kidney failure--and then recover enough to go back home than it is taking The Winemaker's visit to end. #Grandmachronicles -1 #Winemakerchronicles -0

Friday, March 20, 2015 at 3:47pm
Although I can't speak to her directly right now, because my cell phone died, I hear Grandma is on her way home (to my mother's house, with visiting health care to assist). Her kidneys are much better, and though her heart is damaged, she's ready to get the heck out of there and is reportedly back to "normal," at least in terms of chattering to herself. Thank You, Universe/God/PositiveEnergy/Jah/All-is-One/WhateverYouCallIt. <3 #Grandmachronicles

Friday, March 20, 2015 at 12:26am
Late night Conversation with The Winemaker (who just walked in the door as I was making coffee, inflated his air mattress and laid down):
Winemaker:
> Becker, I'm going to bed, Me: I have some work left tonight. I'm going to be up a few hours. I just let the cat out. I'll need to walk by you to let him in in a little while.
> Winemaker: Becker, that is unacceptable. Normal people sleep.
> Me: I'm not a normal person, I'm a grad student. The cat just went out. He'll be up all night howling if I try to let him in now.
> Winemaker: You treat that cat better than you treat me. What do I need to do to get a good night's rest?
> Me: The cat is easier to live with. You could book a hotel room.
> Winemaker: Becker, that's cold. You're new on the scene. You dance in here, keep me up all night, make noise...that cat.
> Me: Winemaker, you've known me sixteen years.
> Winemaker: Becker, you're new on the scene.
> #Winemakerchronicles

Thursday, March 19, 2015 at 10:25pm
Seriously the weirdest month ever. My cell phone is acting strange, so I can't access any numbers or messages on it. Grandma's going home from

the hospital tomorrow, and I won an AWP Intro Journals Award, and found out about it on Facebook. I'm only mentioning it here, because the essay started with my phone being rerouted and a friend, Robbie Abrams ' death, and then another friend Christie Casher's death back to back during two days. And I've gone through a few of those just recently again. I'm happy it's going in the Colorado Review, and that people will get to read about Christie and Robbie. I miss them. I'd rather have them back than a hundred awards, but I can't have that, so I'll take this minor consolation. <3

Thursday, March 19, 2015 at 5:56pm
Got some unexpectedly wonderful news. They're springing Grandma from the hospital tomorrow. I'd be surprised, but it's Grandma we're talking about. She's still in rough shape, but I think she'll be more comfortable at home with my mother. #Grandmachronicles

Thursday, March 19, 2015 at 10:07am
Two things I find puzzling: 1. Why is there sand in my bedsheets? (please, do not answer. The implications are way too frightening). 2. Why have my tomato plants doubled in size since The Winemaker started hanging his sweatsocks on the tomato cages? (I just want to know if they are safe to eat) #Winemakerchronicles

Thursday, March 19, 2015 at 8:21am
Late night Conversation with The Chef:
> Me: I had a good day. It involved good friends, a new baby, combat boots, and creative writing, and The Winemaker leaves Sunday. I'm all tuckered out. Goodnight. (I lean in to give him a kiss)
> Chef: (turns his head to the side, then looks down, like he's guilty of something) The Winemaker's not leaving Sunday.
> Me: What do you mean?
> Chef: Yeah, he's not going Sunday.
> Me: When is he going home?

Chef: I'm not sure, but not Sunday. You know The Winemaker doesn't go by the same rules of propriety as the typical mortal. Me: F&%@, %$#* ...I had a good day... (shake my head, walk off to bed. No kiss for The Chef--traitor) #Winemakerchronicles

Wednesday, March 18, 2015 at 10:28pm
I had a good day, it involved good friends, a new baby, combat boots and creative writing. It was so good, I'm all worn out. Good night now.

Wednesday, March 18, 2015 at 8:28am
I have learned that there is a time to be loud and obnoxious and a time to tiptoe in the kitchen in the morning. Despite my threat to brew my coffee with a roar this morning, when I saw The Winemaker sleeping peacefully in the living room, I realized that peace is more precious than vendetta, and made my cup in silence. Lest this be construed as a concession, I must point out that I have too much work to do to also deal with cranky post-Paddy's Day Winemaker. My coffee tastes better having been brewed in peace--relative peace, that is. The Feline still roared to be let out, but he has work to do outside, which involves hunting for geckos and eating kitty greens, and no Winemaker can put him asunder from that noble quest. #Winemakerchronicles

Wednesday, March 18, 2015 at 1:33am
Conversation With The Winemaker and The Chef:
> Winemaker (in livingroom with Chef, while I am trying to sleep in the bedroom): SOMETHING REALLY LOUD, CHEF, WHYN'T YOU RETIRE AND GO ON THE FESTIVAL CIRCUIT WITH ME..WE'LL HIT BONNAROO AND SLEEP IN A TENT FOR FOUR DAYS.... (CONTINUES VERY LOUD ABOUT WHEN HIS BROTHER WILL RETIRE AND GO OFF WITH HIM ON GRAND ADVENTURES).
> Chef: Ha ha ha ha, yeah. Me in a tent for four days...
> Me: (from bedroom where I am trying to sleep/have been trying to sleep/work/think/etc since his visit began) Winemaker, in five hours, when I get up for the day and start working, I am going to

make the loudest cup of coffee you've ever heard in your life. A jackhammer in your ear would ring dulcet compared to what I'm fixin' to brew.

Winemaker:(dead serious) Becker, it's just courtesy not to make coffee that early in the morning. People need to sleep.

Chef: Me in a tent for four days. Hahahaha

#Winemakerchronicles

Tuesday, March 17, 2015 at 7:55pm

Grandma Update: So far today, Grandma is still feeling much better, though her kidneys are still in trouble, and she'll be penned up in the hospital for some time to come. Still no word on her ticker either. But here is a positive sign: Mom went home. She'll be back to see Grandma tomorrow, but for now, she's stable, and that's a relief. For now. #Grandmachronicles

Tuesday, March 17, 2015 at 3:53pm

Sometimes in the middle of your day something so wonderful happens, it feels like your chest might split open cause your heart is suddenly so happy it's doing a jig. Then you might realize it's not your story to share, so you have to keep the happy to yourself for just a little while. This is where I am. So happy, but not my story to share. <3

Tuesday, March 17, 2015 at 11:11am

This is my 6th St. Patrick's Day in Florida with The Winemaker. I can be assured of two things: 1. This is the one day of the year I will be reminded frequently that The Winemaker and The Chef are half-Irish (this goes unsaid 364 days of the year). 2. There will be beer in The Winemaker's belly. (let us all hope it stays there). #Winemakerchronicles

Tuesday, March 17, 2015 at 9:31am

Leave it to Grandma: Apparently all it took for her to start looking better and ready to fight was some heartburn medication and a (potent) painkiller. Mom is reporting she had a better night, and may not be ready to turn in her dance card just yet. This is Grandma's 4th day in the hospital, and my mother has been there the whole time (except for a quick trip to Walmart for clean underwear and clothes). Part of the reason I am posting these updates is that she might not be able to call out with information regularly. Let's hope Grandma has a good day today. My Mom needs a break. (The rest of us too. Worrying is tiresome). Keep it up, Grandma! Way to rally! Thank you all for your good wishes and prayers <3 #Grandmachronicles

Monday, March 16, 2015 at 10:18pm
The inside of my refrigerator is filled with sand, and smells like sweaty socks. #Winemakerchronicles

Monday, March 16, 2015 at 7:50pm
The upside to all of the drama surrounding me right now is that The Winemaker has stayed away from me with his bottle of lotion. Little blessings. #Winemakerchronicles

Monday, March 16, 2015 at 7:28pm
Update on Grandma: Still no exact numbers on heart function, but the doctors are saying she "is in a very weakened state." Her lungs are sounding a little better, but her kidneys are crapping out, so they're calling in a kidney doctor to figure that out. She's still not eating (3 Days now), and is dreaming of taking a cruise on a ship that has lamps on the deck railings. If there is one in Grandma's dream, I'm not liking that metaphor one bit, but then, I'm no captain here. #Grandmachronicles

Sunday, March 15, 2015 at 6:02pm
A Sad Update: Grandma's not doing well. I got a call from my mother that she's had a heart attack and her heart function is compromised. To complicate things, she has pneumonia, and is so sick with the flu, they can't really treat anything related to the heart problem right now or get accurate measures of where her health really is at the moment. It's okay, Universe. I changed my mind. I can handle whatever you toss my way. (I'll update when I know more). #Grandmachronicles

Sunday, March 15, 2015 at 12:41am
In an epic music video duel game of The Winemaker's invention, he fired off Faith Hill. I volleyed with Puddles the Clown, He is walking around humming "Royals." I am going to sleep. Becker 1 - Winemaker 0. #Winemakerchronicles

Saturday, March 14, 2015 at 2:18pm
The Winemaker is taking a break from his normal agenda of beach/pool/home/shower/pasta/nightlife to sit in the living room watching sports commentary. I am unsettled by how comfortable with his routine I have allowed myself to become. #Winemakerchronicles

Saturday, March 14, 2015 at 10:20am
Conversation with Grandma (who lost 12 pounds of water weight overnight, and is doing better):

> Grandma: The doctor says I can't eat anything fun anymore or my lungs will fill back up. You know what they gave me for breakfast? Oatmeal. I have a whole freezer full of hot dogs and kielbasi. What am I going to do with all that?
> Me: You need to listen to your doctor, Grandma, and behave yourself. You're not allowed to scare the hell out of us like this.
> Grandma: You know what I'd like? I'd like more of those hats you make. Can you send me another hat?
> Me: I'm only going to send you a hat if you get better. Otherwise, a hat will do you no good.
> Grandma: I'll tell your Mom to leave a little hole in my grave so you can drop it in. Me: If you die, I'm going to write about you. So you'd better recover.
> Grandma: (sigh) I'll do my best, Jan-Marie, but you shouldn't threaten me like that. #Grandmachronicles

Saturday, March 14, 2015 at 1:27am
Thoughts after two-fingers of bourbon with The Winemaker on a Friday the 13th of hell on Crystal Lake: My cat loves me. And somehow, that is enough until morning #Winemakerchronicles.

Friday, March 13, 2015 at 7:52pm
I just received a call from my mother that Grandma is in the hospital
with congestive heart failure, but is improving, and if she continues to
improve, is expected to go home on Monday. I would like to make it
abundantly clear to the Universe that now is absolutely not the right
time for Grandma to go off on her next adventure. Yes, she is 82 years
old, and that's probably longer than most people can expect to live, but
there is a limit to how much loss I can endure in one year, and I have
already reached my quota for this year. So, if you pray or throw off
energies or light candles or whatever to whatever deity or entity you
think might have some authority in matters like life and death, please
pass along: Jan Becker has had quite enough grief this year. Leave
Grandma alone, Mr. Reaper Man. #Grandmachronicles

Friday, March 13, 2015 at 6:27pm
In other news, if a student makes me throw up while reading a draft of a
short story, that student might get an A on their rough draft.

Friday, March 13, 2015 at 3:42pm
Oh, jeeze Louise. Undergrads, I've read A Picture of Dorian Gray. You
can't swipe Oscar Wilde and expect me not to notice. Sigh. (Not a full
case of plagiarism, but a very subtle theft of descriptions and dialogue.
Sigh.). I HATE PLAGIARISM. GAH!

Friday, March 13, 2015 at 12:33pm
Mid-morning Conversation with the Winemaker who woke me up
clanging things in the kitchen (the satisfying reversal):

> Me: Winemaker! Do you have to make so much noise in the
> morning?
> Winemaker: Touché, Becker. Touché. #Winemakerchronicles

Thursday, March 12, 2015 at 4:51pm
Conversation with The Winemaker which supports my theory that
peacemaking requires grunt work:

Winemaker: (at my office door, knock, knock, knock) Becker.
Me: Yes? Winemaker: Do you remember yesterday?
Me: Sort of, can you be more specific? Winemaker: You did that
thing, that miraculous thing, where you laid your hands on me...
Me: You need lotion applied to your back?
Winemaker: Yeah, could you? I'm telling you, it was a miracle,
Becker. Me: I hear that pretty often, Winemaker. (I grab the
lotion, start applying)
Winemaker: Oh, thanks, Becker. One more thing. About your
cat. Can you do something to keep him out of my socks? Why's
he in my socks?
Me: I'm not sure. What did you do in your socks?
Winemaker: Becker, you ask too many questions.
#Winemakerchronicles

Thursday, March 12, 2015 at 12:35pm
This year, The Winemaker has been given an additional restriction on his
visit. Because the downstairs neighbors complain if anything drips onto
their balcony from ours, we've picked up a laundry rack for him to hang
his wet clothing on. He is currently employing it to dry his wet gym
socks. I can't keep The Feline away from them. He's out there right now,
muzzle-deep in funky Winemaker foot swill. The catnip is feeling
neglected, but from my observation of The Feline, it appears he's found a
better buzz. #Winemakerchronicles

Thursday, March 12, 2015 at 11:50am
Somehow, I've managed to sleep past The Winemaker. I'm surprised at
how ambivalent I feel at realizing that there is no need to pussyfoot
about the kitchen and keep my voice low. Maybe I'll be quiet anyway.
#Winemakerchronicles

Wednesday, March 11, 2015 at 7:49pm
O ye Buddhas and Bodhisattvas, abiding in the Ten Directions, endowed
with great compassion, endowed with foreknowledge, endowed with
the divine eye, endowed with love, affording protection to sentient

beings, condescend through the power of your great compassion to come hither...O ye Compassionate Ones, Aunt Eunie is passing from this world to the world beyond. She is leaving this world. She is taking a great leap...O ye Compassionate Ones, defend Aunt Eunie who is defenseless. Protect her who is unprotected. Be her forces and her kinsmen. Protect her from the great gloom of the Bardo. <3

Wednesday, March 11, 2015 at 4:36pm
It occurs to me that waging peace sometimes involves concessions and/or gestures of goodwill; often these can be uncomfortable things. I was overly crabby last night when The Winemaker interrupted my television time, and I've been feeling guilty since. So, when I saw him just now in the living room, trying to reach the one spot on his back that defies lotion application, I, Jan Becker, Peacemaker (in training), stepped up, and rubbed the poor sot's back with moisturizer. He was happy with this. The Buddha path is endless. #Winemakerchronicles

Wednesday, March 11, 2015 at 1:55pm
My days seem to be filled with awkward in-between moments during The Winemaker's stay. For example, right this minute. I have a 1-hour window between when I need to be right here, and when I need to be there (sitting The Toddler). There is no shortage of things I should be doing in that hour, but I'm stuck, because I know as soon as I start anything, the door will fly open, in The Winemaker will pop with his sand and lotion and showers and calculations about the base tan he's trying to build for summer, and any project I have my hands in will be interrupted. Perhaps the lesson here is to learn to live with this brief period of liminality and stare out the window at the clouds and pelicans over the lake. #Winemakerchronicles

Tuesday, March 10, 2015 at 11:25pm
Telephone Conversation with The Winemaker from his position out on the town:

      Winemaker: Becker, where's The Chef?
      Me: He went right to bed after work, Winemaker.

Winemaker: What's going on there?
Me: I am taking the rare opportunity to watch television in the living room and relax after a long day in my office grading.
Winemaker: Great! I'll be there in five minutes. (He took five minutes). #Winemakerchronicles

Tuesday, March 10, 2015 at 7:44pm
#sexyjoebiden <3

Tuesday, March 10, 2015 at 5:45pm
The Winemaker is sitting in the living room on the leather couch, mostly naked, covered in moisturizer. Sigh. #Winemakerchronicles

Tuesday, March 10, 2015 at 3:53pm
I was pondering the number of bad serial killers in my students' short stories (WHY?) when The Winemaker walked in. #Winemakerchronicles

Tuesday, March 10, 2015 at 9:29am
Morning conversation with The Winemaker as he was preparing his breakfast:

Winemaker: Becker, I'd like to salute you for your silence this morning.
Me: You're welcome, Winemaker, I endeavor to make your experience here a pleasant one. Wait! Is that Trix cereal? Damn, Winemaker, that's some very colorful breakfast food. How can you eat that so early in the morning?
Winemaker: (low, growly, morning warning voice) You wouldn't understand. Silly Becker. Trix are for kids.

(I think The Winemaker is 62 years old, but who's counting?)
#Winemakerchronicles

Tuesday, March 10, 2015 at 2:10am
Jan Becker shared a video on YouTube.
Why must I always run into Bukowski at bedtime?

Monday, March 9, 2015 at 11:25pm
Conversation with The Winemaker (as I was posing for this photo):
    Me: Winemaker, what do you think? It's my fifth coat of parade gloss.
    Winemaker: You know, Becker, nobody looks.
    Me: Maybe not, but it's a matter of pride, Winemaker.
    Winemaker: I'm just giving you the layman's perspective, Becker. Nobody looks.
    Sigh. #Winemakerchronicles

Monday, March 9, 2015 at 5:21pm
It is important to warn The Winemaker when one is returning home after an afternoon with The Toddler (formerly known as The Infant), lest one run smack into a butt-naked Winemaker changing after a swim in the Atlantic. I'll remember this next time. Also, he has been here more than 24 hours and is just now bringing in the wine. Apparently, The Winemaker has never spent 24 hours locked in a trunk in the Florida sunshine. I might be able to remedy that. #Winemakerchronicles

Monday, March 9, 2015 at 3:46pm
Another observation that may or may not have anything to do with The Winemaker's arrival: My fingers have broken out in tiny painful blisters since he got here. Perhaps tis an autoimmune response? He might be an allergen. Further inquiry is needed. #Winemakerchronicles.

Monday, March 9, 2015 at 9:10am
Less than 24 hours into his visit, the first skirmish of contention has occurred between The Winemaker and The Feline, who likes to go outside and hunt for geckos while his Uncle Winemaker sleeps peacefully. Who could blame The Feline for wanting to be out in the world, where the pelicans are dive-bombing into the lake, and the ducks are doing their mating dances on its shores? I cannot find fault with this. However, I will have to teach him that it is best not to sing loudly in his Uncle Winemaker's ears to get the point across. Or, just let this continue and nod emphatically while The Winemaker scolds me on my lack of

courtesy for responding to The Feline by opening the door and setting him free. Either way, someone will label me discourteous. There are worse things I could be. #Winemakerchronicles

Sunday, March 8, 2015 at 10:07pm
Conversation with The Winemaker (who does not eat vegetables, but was found consuming a large bowl of my curried chickpeas The Chef heated for him and tossed with pasta):

> Me: Winemaker, do I see you eating a bowl of curried chickpeas? You're eating curry? You'e eating vegetables?
> Winemaker: Becker, don't ruin my dinner by telling me what I'm eating.
> #Winemakerchronicles

Sunday, March 8, 2015 at 4:01pm
The Winemaker has now been here roughly three hours and already I am swallowing a muscle relaxer. Whether this is correlative is yet to be determined, but my back is in spasm and begging for mercy. #Winemakerchronicles

Sunday, March 8, 2015 at 12:12pm
And so, it begins. The Winemaker has arrived. The Feline has retreated to his spot under the bed. I am joining him. #Winemakerchronicles

Sunday, March 8, 2015 at 10:46am
I somehow forgot how much elbow work goes into getting a decent base of parade gloss spit-shined into combat boots (working on the fourth coat today). On the upside, I also forgot how fond I am of the smell of vigorously worked leather and wax.

Sunday, March 8, 2015 at 10:38am
Jan Becker likes Florida Native Plant Society.

Saturday, March 7, 2015 at 11:36pm
Conversation with a cagey Chef on the eve of The Winemaker's visit:

Chef: Jan, I'm distressed by something you said earlier.

Me: (confused) To what do you refer?

Chef: (somber) You seemed to indicate that you were concerned The Winemaker might overstay the two week limit we've imposed.

Me: Your brother never comes for just two weeks.

Chef: He bought you out, didn't he?!?

Me: What are you talking about?

Chef: He paid you some kind of bribe, and he's going to be here for a month, isn't he? You've sold out.

Me: No, I haven't spoken at all to The Winemaker. I swear, scout's honor (I was a conscientious objector from the Girl Scouts, so this is not a valid affirmation).

Chef: (looks worried, stressed) Well, what do we do if he does try to stay?

Me: (Sigh, I throw my arm around The Chef for comfort) We do what we do every year; we muddle through.

Chef: He totally bought you out. Damn.

(He did not buy me out. I swear. The Winekmaker is too tight with a buck for bribes.) #Winemakerchronicles

Saturday, March 7, 2015 at 3:06pm

The Universe has showered me with fortune! I went to the grocery store, and saw one of the workers cleaning out the change machine. She had a pile of coins that had been rejected. I asked her what they do with them, and she said they throw them out. I asked her if I could have them. They are mostly foreign coins, but from everywhere! Centavos from Cuba, the Dominican Republic, Ecuador, and Brasil, pence from Great Britain, bolivares from Venezuela, piastres from Jordan, something from Mexico, a dollar from Jamaica, a euro, twenty-five cents from the Bahamas, 10 cents from the Dutch Antilles, 100 pesos from Chile, the requisite Canadian coins, and then mystery money with Cyrillic characters and Asian ideograms I can't read to say where it's from. I'm rich somewhere.

Saturday, March 7, 2015 at 1:34pm
Jan Becker likes The Sacred Science.

Saturday, March 7, 2015 at 10:05am
With 24 hours or less until The Winemaker's arrival, I am not (as I would prefer) naked and drinking bourbon. However, I am granting myself the concession of no pants on spring break (Thank you, Julie, for the reminder), while I grade student assignments completely sober and catch up on all the things I have neglected since the beginning of January. I'm declaring this a new start, since India just celebrated Holi and the lunar Spring. This 2015 Roman calendar year has been wretched and filled with more stress and grief than is manageable. I'm hitting the reset button. This will give me a brief window to celebrate something. Happy New Year, again and again--until the redux shifts this rotten paradigm. #Winemakerchronicles

Friday, March 6, 2015 at 4:22pm
Conversation with an undergrad that affirms I have officially accepted I am now a middle-aged woman (I concede, Nicholas Garnett, you win):
            Undergrad: Thank you, and have a good spring break.
            Me: You too. Stay safe. (My ovaries are protesting)

Friday, March 6, 2015 at 12:47pm
The one good thing about the new parking change is that watching him bent over painting numbers on the parking spots affords me the opportunity to reflect on how apparent it is that Creepy Maintenance Man should have been a plumber.

Friday, March 6, 2015 at 8:58am
The parking spot wars have commenced here on Crystal Lake well ahead of the implementation date of Monday. Under the new regulations, each apartment gets one spot in the lot in front of our building, any second drivers must park across the street in a dark, scary parking lot. I have informed The Chef that he is the second driver. He is balking at this designation. I'm an English major, I've told him, and that

means heft. You carry just a knife, which is handy if you're jumped in that scary lot late at night. Aside from this mini-skirmish, per the new regulations, if someone parks in a first-driver's designated space, we are to call the tow trucks on the interlopers. And though these regulations do not start until Monday, there are nasty signs across the windshields of folks already, demanding people move their vehicles. Sigh. I just want to park in peace.

Thursday, March 5, 2015 at 8:19pm
Last night The Chef and I cleaned out the walk-in closet where The Winemaker stores his clothes during his migration. It's about the size of a decent New York City apartment in there. We hardly ever open the door. Last night, there was a strange occurrence that may be of import for the observation log. A terrible fetor was wafting out of the corners of the room, but no matter how hard we looked, we could not determine the source. And then it was suddenly gone. We have a theory that it may be sewer gas, as Roto Rooter had been to the building with their big industrial equipment earlier. I think that, should it recur, the fetor may be quite useful. If the stench swaddles in The Winemaker's clothing, we will be able to smell him well ahead of visual contact...Oh, wait. I forgot about his cologne habit. Nevermind. #Winemakerchronicles

Thursday, March 5, 2015 at 2:25pm
The combat boots have arrived! I'm not home to see them yet, but they're waiting for me.

Wednesday, March 4, 2015 at 10:21pm
The Winemaker is on the phone with The Chef right now. I suspect he may be renegotiating the length of his stay. We whittled him down to two weeks from a marathon visit of six weeks last migration...I just heard The Chef say, "Weeeeelllll, Okaaayy." Be strong, Chef. Be strong. #Winemakerchronicles

Wednesday, March 4, 2015 at 12:39pm
The cleaning woman in my building has a crush on The Chef. She waylays him in the hallway with talk of a high school love who made her baked Alaska long ago, and flutters her eyelashes at him and talks sweetly. The Chef always returns from his encounters with her, cheeks flushed, slightly out of breath. When I run into her, it's a different story. She's a little more brusque with me, unless she is talking about The Chef. Then, she gets all soft-tongued and sweet. In relation to me, she calls him, "your friend" or "your roommate." I don't bother correcting that to "domestic partner." There's no need for catfights here.

Wednesday, March 4, 2015 at 9:24am
Today, we are Winemaker-proofing the apartment. This is similar to baby proofing... I was going to qualify that first statement, but really, same thing, different kind of baby. #Winemakerchronicles

Tuesday, March 3, 2015 at 8:41pm
This was today: Drove to Miami to see my sad shrink. Realized I left The Feline outside on the balcony. Called The Chef, no answer. Left a message. No response. Drove all the way back to Pompano Beach. The Feline was curled up on the bed. The Chef was playing Depeche Mode " VIOLATOR" on the hi-fi and missed my call, but let The Feline in. Drove right back to Miami for a second time in my car which still has no air-conditioning. So now I am sunburnt and tired and hungry enough that the cat looks appetizing.

Tuesday, March 3, 2015 at 1:00pm
The kind of day where even The Shrink is in tears.

Monday, March 2, 2015 at 11:36pm
As I was heading off to bed, The Chef informed me that The Winemaker is en route and can be expected here on Thursday, two days ahead of our previous prediction. This does not bode well for my planned beauty rest. #Winemakerchronicles

Monday, March 2, 2015 at 5:12pm
Two things I received in the mail today that have me vexed: 1. New, exhaustive parking regulations from Building management. Also, they assigned us spot #68 (like it would kill them to bump us up one more slot and make parking fun). 2. A Birthday card that reads, "HAPPY BIRTHDAY! You should stop by our offices soon to discuss the procedures we offer." This was from a plastic surgeon. Jesus.

Saturday, February 28, 2015 at 11:12am
While not exactly certain of his arrival date, The Chef seems convinced The Winemaker will be arriving next weekend, which will coincide with FIU's Spring Break. I am prepping the Spare Bed of Broken Backs. Goddess, grant me serenity. #norestforthewicked #Winemakerchronicles

Sunday, February 22, 2015 at 3:28pm
Jan Becker shared her photo.
It's fitting that I decided yesterday I'd try believing that we've been tricked into thinking we aren't already in Heaven. My friend Michael Davis passed away this morning. I can't put into a Facebook post how much Michael means to me. As a child, I always wanted a big brother, and the universe sent Michael when I needed one. When going through the scariest time of my life, he was there, and told me to get my shit together, get my ass to college, and write. He taught me about reggae music, and Rastafari, and OneLove. When I set his house on fire, he took me to Panama and Costa Rica and Mexico (it was an accident). He introduced me to The Chef and taught me where to find mushrooms. I am who I am largely because of this man. I'm glad Heaven isn't another place, that we're already here, because the world without Michael, isn't one I want to live in. And Michael, I know I can't see you anymore, but you can nudge me the next time I'm in the woods if you see any papinkis. <3

Sunday, February 22, 2015 at 10:05am
It's Sunday, Chef's day off. This means CURRY for breakfast. Yay!

Sunday, February 22, 2015 at 1:23am
I had a good day. I played with words and people I love and who love me. I determined that any boundary between Earth and Heaven is probably just another political manipulation, but if it's not, I also survived South Beach traffic during the Wine and Food Festival, so for now, I don't have to worry that my theory is wrong, and can continue living here in heaven peaceably for the foreseeable future. <3

Friday, February 20, 2015 at 4:29pm
Dear FIU undergrads who are still under the age of 25, just two things: 1. If you are an off-key soprano, please do not under any circumstances attempt to sing anything recorded by The Psychedelic Furs in a public hallway, especially if the hall has very high ceilings. 2. "The Robot" is an inadequate medium to utilize when getting on one's groove, unless you are double-jointed and dancing to Lipps, Inc. If you couple the robot with Taylor Swift (as I just witnessed), you'll likely only succeed in becoming a source of nausea and rampant confusion.

Friday, February 20, 2015 at 10:34am
It is much too early in the morning for me to concern myself with participles and gerunds, and other grammatical conundrums. Also, I need to brush up on my parts of speech. But, not before coffee. Never before coffee. It is also too early in the morning for me to figure out where in my schedule I can fit carpet cleaners. Or even talk to The Chef about carpets or cleaning--or when in all this chaos The Winemaker will arrive and wreck both our carpets and my grammar with his sand dune relocation project. I do not want to talk to anyone until I have had at least three fingers of very strong coffee. Make that a double.

Thursday, February 19, 2015 at 3:47pm
If there is an upside to this cold snap (beyond having the opportunity to bundle myself in layers of warm things), The Feline has found one. Because the temps are dropping into the high 30s tonight, I brought the potted plants. This means his catnip is in the house. This also means The Feline is in full-on space kitty cowboy mode, chasing the psychedelic

spiders that only he can see climbing the walls. He has declared his intention to disenfranchise himself from all establishment ties and relocate to a kitty cat commune somewhere in the Pacific Northwest.

Thursday, February 19, 2015 at 2:44am
The problem with sleeping til nearly noon is that I may not go back to sleep til noon the next day. I also can't find the cord to my electric blanket, and it's dropping into the 40s tonight. I know to you Northerners this sounds whiny, but my blood approves and electric blanket cords are a better fate than wisdom tonight (since feeling is first).

Wednesday, February 18, 2015 at 11:53am
Something about the world just doesn't seem right when I sleep until nearly noon. The Feline is satisfied with this arrangement though, so maybe it's all right.

Wednesday, February 18, 2015 at 2:26am
Jan Becker likes Mother Jones.

Tuesday, February 17, 2015 at 8:50pm
#sexyjoebiden

Tuesday, February 17, 2015 at 5:33pm
From a student email (posted with permission): "Just so you are aware I'm probably going to be heavily inebriated with a horde of hippies in the middle of the forest come class time this week..." I was beginning to worry about this class. They all seemed so studious. And sober.

Tuesday, February 17, 2015 at 10:01am
The strawberry jam incident appears to be over, but replaced with The Infant's case of the sniffles and sneezes. I woke with miraculously clear ears. Therein lies my focal point for the day. I can hear again, and suddenly the world is no longer a giant whirl-a-gig. This is no small gift. Beethoven and Goya might agree if they could hear me ask.

Monday, February 16, 2015 at 10:11pm
An equation: The strawberry fruit leather in my ear canal + hydrogen peroxide (Jan Becker - common sense) = strawberry jam in my ear canal

Monday, February 16, 2015 at 8:56pm
One of the many professions I worked in prior to college was as a residential program director at a group home for dually diagnosed adults with mental illness and developmental disabilities. Several of these people had intermittent explosive disorders. Not once in all the years I worked in that field, or the years before, when I worked security at a hospital in Boston, did I find it necessary to pull out a gun and shoot someone dead, and I've been attacked with items much more intimidating than a broomstick. Medical restraint methods are easy to learn. Easier than this.

Monday, February 16, 2015 at 8:12pm
Tonight's agenda involves hydrogen peroxide and a strawberry fruit leather-filled ear canal. Draw conclusions as to where this will lead me.

Monday, February 16, 2015 at 11:38am
File under "Things you did not want to know:" I pulled something resembling a strawberry fruit roll up from my ear last night, and now my hearing is all off-balance. I guess the ear is like the rest of me now.

Saturday, February 14, 2015 at 7:26pm
In case you're wondering, I got The Chef a Valentine's Day gift, despite my general dislike for the holiday. It's a deluxe nose hair trimmer. Ahhh, romance.

Saturday, February 14, 2015 at 9:36am
Happy Valentine's Day. Also, Happy Birthday, Dad. RIP

Saturday, February 14, 2015 at 12:17am
A Tale of Love (and of Confusion): The Chef came home tonight, and said that he'd brought me a bottle of small batch bourbon for Valentine's

Day, but that he'd dropped it when he was checking the mail, and it smashed. He said I needed to smell this bourbon, so we went back down to the mailbox together. The smell had all evaporated from the walkway, but he had me sniff the trash can, because he'd picked up the broken bottle and tossed it. That is the love part of the tale. I sniffed a trashcan full of small-batch bourbon for Valentine's Day. This sign was in the elevator. That's the confusion part.

Friday, February 13, 2015 at 10:33am
Sometimes I go back through my notebooks and look over notes I've taken in class and wonder what I was thinking. Today's intriguing entry: "Grilled slug." What the heck was that about?

Thursday, February 12, 2015 at 10:52pm
A wonderful thing about The Chef: He is always warm, even when it's so cold that my fingers are numb. And if he doesn't always like to share his heat? That's okay too. I move faster than he does, and have no trouble catching him.

Thursday, February 12, 2015 at 4:21pm
Note to self: Oh, Jan Becker. Read the labels before you pop anything into your gob. Pharmaceutical companies do not care that your allergy pill looks EXACTLY like your muscle relaxers.

Wednesday, February 11, 2015 at 8:38am
Everything seems to be working a little better as far as universal machinations go. The Sheriff is mailing me police reports, and the parking people will take proof the plate was stolen by email once it arrives. I am filling the tub with hot water and bubbles and preparing my one shot of bourbon for the mercury-is-direct-bite-my-butt-crummy-planet it's writing day ritual.

Wednesday, February 11, 2015 at 1:48am
An executive decision: I had written "writing day" on my calendar for tomorrow. And despite the need to run around Fort Lauderdale tracking

down police reports and visiting the courthouse, I am going to honor the obligation I planned. I'm calling it a religious observance. I can deal with the other stuff another time. And bourbon at 9:51. One shot. Naked.

Tuesday, February 10, 2015 at 6:32pm
Strange thing that makes me giggle with delight after an afternoon in South Florida rush hour traffic (I only almost died four times on an easy commute): I received a parking citation from the city of Fort Lauderdale today from January 19th. The reason I am happy: I have an alibi. I was watching The Infant that day. Also, this ticket is from the license plate that was stolen. I'm not sure why that makes me happy, but it does.

Tuesday, February 10, 2015 at 9:56am
23 hours and and 55 minutes til mercury goes direct. At 9:51 AM tomorrow, I will be naked somewhere, with a glass of bourbon in hand.

Monday, February 9, 2015 at 10:33pm
I miss Douglas Adams at times like this.

Monday, February 9, 2015 at 4:29pm
Is it just me, or do baby food combinations seem like they were created by desperate potheads with a mad case of munchies?

Monday, February 9, 2015 at 3:06pm
It appears that I shall have to design a line of edible jewelry if I'm to decorate myself while in the company of infants.

Sunday, February 8, 2015 at 5:05pm
Note to Self: When applying aphid repellent to your habanero plant (a toxic mixture of pulverized garlic, onion, dish soap and cayenne that has been fermenting in a spray bottle on the porch in the sun for a week), it is wise to pay attention to where the breeze blows, lest you repel your face.

Sunday, February 8, 2015 at 3:50pm
Jan Becker likes Marriage Equality in Florida.

Sunday, February 8, 2015 at 9:48am
Waiting for The Chef to wake up so we can venture out for curry is like waiting for the sun to poke its nose above the horizon on Christmas morning when you're six years old.

Saturday, February 7, 2015 at 3:47pm
I have THE MOST UNBELIEVABLE GROUP OF STUDENTS this semester. 1. They come to class. 2. They do their homework. 3. They come to my office hours to talk about writing. 4. Class meets Friday evenings (6:25- 9:05PM), so none of them have social lives. 5. They ask me where literary events are occurring because they want to roll around in words, even on weekends (see #4). 6. They pay attention to their grammar! 7. THEY READ PRIDE AND PREJUDICE FOR FUN. I think I took the wrong turn at that signpost up ahead and have entered the fifth dimension beyond that which is known to Jan. It is a dimension as vast as space and as timeless as infinity. It is the middle ground between light and shadow, between science and superstition, and it lies between the pit of Jan's fears, and the summit of her knowledge. This is the dimension of imagination.

Saturday, February 7, 2015 at 2:08am
In an effort to weigh my school bag to see if it could be contributing to my head/back aches, I broke the damn scale. Back to the wheelie bag.

Friday, February 6, 2015 at 10:38am
On this lovely Friday morning, I find myself shopping for combat boots.

Friday, February 6, 2015 at 1:04am
Lord Voldemort is fulfilling all his campaign promises.

Friday, February 6, 2015 at 12:07am
I just read something that a student wrote that was so incredibly good, other than a couple of minor suggestions for revision, all I could say was, "Damn." It was about curry.

Monday, February 2, 2015 at 4:19pm
On days like this, when the last thing I want is another headache, the wise thing to do is to stay away from anything connected to my bank account. Wisdom is the one trait I've yet to develop. Dammit.

Monday, February 2, 2015 at 12:36pm
It appears that the headache from hell has finally exited my skull. I am saying this with trepidation, and in fear I may just be jinxing myself. There is, after all, about 600 pages waiting to be read and commented on.

Monday, February 2, 2015 at 9:15am
Phil has made his official proclamation! Six more weeks of winter!

Sunday, February 1, 2015 at 3:29pm
I went to The Infant's church dedication with a migraine, and started hallucinating when they brought out the electric guitars. OUCH.

Sunday, February 1, 2015 at 11:07am
I just realized tomorrow is my favorite holiday.

Saturday, January 31, 2015 at 4:39pm
The Feline's curative powers are limited. The headache has rebounded again, coupled now with gastric distress. I am researching plans for a DIY guillotine, which should solve at least one of these problems.

Saturday, January 31, 2015 at 10:43am
I have a headache the size of Siberia.

Friday, January 30, 2015 at 10:21pm
A moving van unloading at my building always means something new here. Tonight, it was a couple and their son who was holding a giant grass-green roll of bubble wrap and looked like he was fixing to pop the whole roll, maybe roll around in it and become Bubble Wrap Man. His parents looked exhausted. I told them, "Welcome Home." That was fun.

Friday, January 30, 2015 at 5:55pm
I attend college at an institution that (I hear) has excellent programs in both architecture and engineering. This is not evident in the adjunct office, which has ONE electrical outlet for the whole office, and two computers and a printer hooked up and running already.

Friday, January 30, 2015 at 9:29am
I thought of my grandmother this morning when I woke up in my own bed, which I'd piled high with woolen blankets (two), a thick comforter, and three pillows positioned to cushion the few pointy parts I possess (knees and elbows). I found on waking that my fingers were buried deep in the softest parts of The Feline's belly, where they belong. I only allow him to live with me because he keeps my fingers warm while I dream. It's been twenty-three days since Grandma slept in her own bed. I went only two weeks out of mine, and it felt like years. I hope she appreciates being back in her own sack as much as I do. #Grandmachronicles

Thursday, January 29, 2015 at 3:56pm
My mother called from a McDonald's in Scranton. United Airlines is holding her luggage hostage in Newark. She rented a car to get Grandma home. They are at my grandmother's favorite restaurant. #Grandmachronicles

Thursday, January 29, 2015 at 11:04am
An update: My mother and Grandma's flight from Newark to Scranton was cancelled. Not delayed, cancelled. The possibilities of how the Garden State could mess with the matriarchs of my clan are endless. #Grandmachronicles

Thursday, January 29, 2015 at 9:48am
Grandma has officially left the state of Florida. Godspeed, Granny and Mom. #Grandmachronicles

Wednesday, January 28, 2015 at 10:48am
The Bull rang this morning at 8AM sharp, and spoke to The Chef. I am not sure what was said, but The Chef was out the door within five minutes of hanging up, and I haven't seen him since. One does not argue with a postal cop called Taurus.

Tuesday, January 27, 2015 at 10:29pm
In other news, there was a message on our machine from the law enforcement person handling the hijacking of our mail to Hialeah. Apparently, the identity of everyone in my household relies on the whims of a man named Taurus. We are calling him "The Bull."

Tuesday, January 27, 2015 at 7:51pm
I am tired. I have a busted thumb knuckle and a pissed-off neglected Feline. Worried about my grandmother who is having issues with vertigo on the opposite end of the state. I owe everybody everything, and all I want is to stick things in my face and then climb into my pajamas. #Grandmachronicles

Monday, January 26, 2015 at 11:39pm
Hey you, friends up north. I hope you are all hunkered down and warm. I hope you all stay that way until it passes. ♡♥♡

Monday, January 26, 2015 at 11:57am
Mom and Grandma are holed up outside of Tampa. They were due to fly out tomorrow, but are held up by this giant Juno thing, with no idea of when they'll be able to go home. Grandma is sleeping peacefully. Mom is freaked out because she can't reach anyone to rebook her flight. Sigh. Maybe she should crawl in bed with Grandma and follow her example. #Grandmachronicles

Sunday, January 25, 2015 at 7:24pm
Jan Becker likes Sayings of the Buddha.

Saturday, January 24, 2015 at 5:17pm
Not 48 hours, but a nap until 4PM is respectable enough a starting
slumber point. Also, in other news, we may have figured out where the
mail has been going, since it has not been coming here. Apparently, our
address was changed to a shady corner of Hialeah. Sigh.

Saturday, January 24, 2015 at 10:11am
Grandma and Mom are on their way to the west coast of Florida. The
apartment seems barren and quiet. My plans for the day involve a
muscle relaxer for my broken back and 48 hours of slumber. Bon
Voyage, Mom and Grandma. And Goodnight night, Mrs. Calabash
where ever you are. #Grandmachronicles

Friday, January 23, 2015 at 11:06pm
Grandma and Mom are leaving tomorrow for the last leg of their
vacation. Grandma wanted to know if there were any thrift stores in the
area around their hotel. I did a quick search and came up with 142 in a
ten-mile radius of where I booked their room. I may be sending my
grandmother to the promised land. #Grandmachronicles

Friday, January 23, 2015 at 12:38pm
No shoeless, tattoo-faced white guy in a hospital gown, who is
considered dangerous is going to keep me from teaching tonight. (FIU
ALERTS)

Friday, January 23, 2015 at 9:20am
This morning, I had not one, but two alarms fail to go off at 5:30. The
Feline was left out on the balcony all night, and is pissed at me. I never
lock him out, so I'm not sure what happened there, but I went to sleep
early to be up on time. Here's what I don't get: God is not awake at 6:30
in the morning, and yet, on the drive over to babysit, I saw people
putting their children on school buses. This seems like institutional
cruelty to me.

Thursday, January 22, 2015 at 10:25pm
I have George Jones all up in my face here in the spare bed. This may
have something to do with why I can't sleep. #Grandmachronicles

Thursday, January 22, 2015 at 4:19pm
Some random observations and a confession: 1. The more colorful The
Infant's mashed foodstuff, the funkier her diaper. Today, she is eating
orange. 2. Teething biscuits taste like styrofoam...and ass. 3. A
confession: Sometimes, the noises The Infant makes when she's waking
from a nap scare the bejeezus out of me. I approach the nursery door
more than half-expecting Linda Blair to be waiting to attack.

Thursday, January 22, 2015 at 12:19pm
One of The Winemaker's secret powers is his ability to know when he is
being spoken about. He rang today with declarations of filling our living
room for the entirety of March. I wasn't home to put the kibosh on his
plans, but The Chef must have sensed my hackles are up about the
impending visit and lay down a cap of two weeks. I think that's about
two weeks too long, but much better than the six weeks of suffering I
went through last year. #Winemakerchronicles

Thursday, January 22, 2015 at 8:50am
My battle with the Spare Bed of Broken Backs continues. Last night I had
the brilliant idea of trying the old air mattress on top of the futon to see if
that would be any better. Apparently, The Winemaker poked a tiny hole
in it sometime before he left after his last visit. The damned thing leaked
all night, and I woke up unable to crawl out of bed on my own. My
mother was there to hand me a boost up. Grandma is snoring peacefully
in the comfort of my sack. When they leave Saturday, I am going to build
a great bonfire to destroy the spare beds. I may even strip down naked
and dance around the fire out by the lake. It will be a gruesome scene.
#Grandmachronicles

Wednesday, January 21, 2015 at 4:11pm
So far, The Infant has eaten a plateful of assorted mashed things in purple and green, two mum-mum rice husks and drank a full bottle of formula. This wore her out, so I changed her diaper (Remember that 80s song "There's a Monster in My Pants?") and put her down for a nap. After ten minutes, I heard noises broadcasting over the loudspeaker, went in to check on her, and she was trying to eat the baby monitor.

Wednesday, January 21, 2015 at 10:11am
It started last night when they got home from the botanical gardens.
> Grandma: YOU KNOW WHAT TOMORROW IS, DON'T YOU JAN-MARIE?
> Me: Yes, how could I forget?
> Grandma: WHACKY WEDNESDAY! WHACKY WEDNESDAY! WHACKY WEDNESDAY! This continued until she left for the Salvation Army this morning. Sigh. #Grandmachronicles

Tuesday, January 20, 2015 at 7:16pm
I sent Mom and Grandma to the Fairchild Botanical Gardens today while I was away. The Chef had the day off, and last I heard was doing his taxes. I am home now, and nobody else is, except The Feline who is purring very loudly beside me. His purrs are just putting a bumper cushion on the peace of the apartment. I'm not sure what to do with all this quiet. #Grandmachronicles

Tuesday, January 20, 2015 at 9:28am
In an effort to get a few hours' sleep after reading Pride and Prejudice till 4AM, I pulled the cushions off the couch and managed 4 hours of solid slumber. Bonus: I found 16 pounds of sand (I suspect The Winemaker) and $50,000 in pennies. I'm plotting my escape--or, at least a decent spare bed. #Grandmachronicles #Winemakerchronicles

Monday, January 19, 2015 at 7:45pm
Word has come that my uncle's wife is still not well, and it's not safe for my mom and gram to visit them yet. Grandma will be here. probably

until Saturday. The Feline is thrilled. He loves her so (traitor).
#Grandmachronicles

Monday, January 19, 2015 at 2:24pm
Grandma has vertigo and a craving for peanut butter and Ritz crackers.
They may be leaving tomorrow for my uncle's place near Tampa. We're
waiting to hear what the doctor says about my aunt's flu. It occurs to me
that at 82-years of age, there are too many things waiting to snuff you.
My mum ran out to the store, so I'm Grandma-sitting. I'm terrified.
#Grandmachronicles

Sunday, January 18, 2015 at 11:35am
Grandma's review of the September/October 2014 American Poetry
Review: She likes Sandman Simonds' poem (IT HAS ALLIGATORS), but
not "THAT POEM WITH THE HORSESHIT. WHAT THE HELL IS
THAT???" Everyone's a critic. #Grandmachronicles

Saturday, January 17, 2015 at 6:48pm
My grandmother is a lot like Ma Barker in that she has led me into a life
of larceny. Only instead of stickups, Grandma's got me swiping Splenda
from every dinner joint in South Florida. #Grandmachronicles

Saturday, January 17, 2015 at 1:49pm
Sit right back, and you'll hear a tale....

Saturday, January 17, 2015 at 11:42am
My mother booked us on a 3-hour riverboat tour with a stop on an island
with alligators and birds of prey. The possible outcomes of this
adventure are intriguing. #Grandmachronicles

Saturday, January 17, 2015 at 9:38am
It appears my email has been hacked again. Sorry if you received a weird
email. I'm convinced it has to do with my cell phone. I knew I shouldn't
have bought one of these damned things.

Friday, January 16, 2015 at 4:33pm
Pride and Prejudice (the book) may put me into a coma. What is this fresh hell I am trying to read?? Why?

Friday, January 16, 2015 at 11:23am
I'm teaching a class this semester, my first since last spring. I'm excited to get back in a classroom; I've missed teaching. I'd love to bring Grandma to sit in tonight, but the class doesn't end until 9:05 PM, and that's past Grandma's bedtime. I couldn't possibly speak over her snores. But I can dream. I'll just pretend she's there. #Grandmachronicles

Friday, January 16, 2015 at 12:21am
Grandma is up wandering through the witching hour. I am going to sleep before she discovers me. I have a feeling my mother is in for a long night of elbows in ribs and prodding from Gram. Best to retreat to slumberland. 7AM wake-up here in the Puzzle Haus. #Grandmachronicles

Thursday, January 15, 2015 at 3:25pm
Every time that area is flooded, I get the heebie jeebies. In addition to the wastewater, a big part of that area is built on top of a superfund site, including FIU's Biscayne Bay Campus. Who knows what the hell that could be doing to the bay?

Thursday, January 15, 2015 at 12:59pm
I sent my mother and grandmother to a nature center in West Palm Beach so I could get my materials ready for the class I'm teaching tomorrow night. When I mentioned that there were gator feeding sessions at the nature center, my mother asked, "Grandma?" "Yes,"I responded, "Grandma can feed a gator too." My mother looked at me quizzically, "That's not really what I meant." "Oh, no," I answered, "You cannot feed my grandmother to the alligators." #Grandmachronicles

Wednesday, January 14, 2015 at 10:35pm
Scholars have argued for years about what exactly it was Paul of Tarsus saw on the road to Damascus that rendered him temporarily blind. Some say it was a vision of Christ. Others say it was a giant ball of light. The medics claim it may have been heat stroke, or botanists, a hallucinogenic plant, and meteorologists have hypothesized that it was lightning. I have my own theory. I think it was a terrible angelic being. And I think it looked like my naked Grandma. #Grandmachronicles

Wednesday, January 14, 2015 at 1:32pm
Grandma has a problem my mom just doesn't understand. She has so many books, she had to commandeer an extra storage unit in her senior citizen high-rise in Scranton. But now there's a new problem. Her bff, Sonny, a drag queen who lives next door put a couple of boxes in the storage space (which belongs to someone else entirely). Grandma says this means war! I completely get where she's coming from. #Grandmachronicles

Wednesday, January 14, 2015 at 8:49am
I was up at 3:30 this morning, and it was so quiet and peaceful, I just wanted to stay up forever listening to the silence, but I thought to myself, "You better go to bed, Jan Becker." Here is why I had that thought: At 7:00 this morning, I knew I'd hear Grandma in the living room (I'm sleeping on the living room floor--The Chef is working double shifts these days). And I was right. First I heard "MARGARET ANN [my mother], JAN-MARIE'S STILL SLEEPING!?! WOW, SHE SURE SLEEPS LATE!!" Then, reading the crawl on Good Morning America, "A MAN AND HIS WIFE WERE KILLED YESTERDAY WHILE DRIVING ON THE INTERNETS [interstate]" and then "WHAT TIME ARE WE GOING TO THE SALVATION ARMY?" God help me. If I'd remembered it was whacky Wednesday, I'd have gone to bed much earlier. I still need coffee. #Grandmachronicles

Monday, January 12, 2015 at 4:12pm
Unexpectedly, my mother and grandmother will be extending their visit.
They were going to head to the West coast tomorrow to visit my uncle,
but his wife has the flu. This morning, my mother bought me some evil
eye protection, which was a necessity I don't want to explain. On a
lighter note, Grandma found a mannequin whose dress had slipped,
"Cover up your boobies!" she said and provided the dummy with some
modesty by straightening her dress. #Grandmachronicles

Monday, January 12, 2015 at 12:14am
Jan Becker added 2 new photos.
Regarding that parallel narrative: There is always a chance that when
one hears a call that everything's freaky, a response to it might not be
greeted with kindness. In the second grade, there was a girl named
Sharon Van Patten. She had kidney problems, and was always at the
nurse's office getting a clean pair of pants. While out doing that one day,
the teacher gathered us, and said she wanted us to be kinder to Sharon.
She said the kids bullying her were hurting her terribly. At recess that
day, I went up to Sharon, and told her I was sad to hear kids picked on
her, that I would be her friend. Sharon looked me in the eye and
responded, "You leave me alone," in a cold, dead voice. And it hurt. It
hurt then. It hurts today to get those same words from someone else, but
I get it. Sometimes it feels more secure down in a deep hollow than on a
hilltop where one is vulnerable and exposed to the expanse of the
heavens. If you've been stuck in a small dark space, that much space and
light can be intimidating. Not everyone is ready to come out of that. But I
am out. I spend a long time climbing up the hill, and I'll be up here doing
other things--like making hats. Nothing in the world is better than a
good hat that feels like a hug around your head. There are plenty of
people with fine heads that appreciate a good "Love you. Welcome
Home." And sometimes, one just needs to be one's own friend, and give
oneself a hug around the head. I'm keeping this one exactly for that
purpose, though it's impractical in the tropics.

Sunday, January 11, 2015 at 5:29pm
Jan Becker added 2 new photos.
Grandma has stolen The Feline's affections (floozy). He hasn't slept with me since she landed. He curls up next to her every chance he gets. She says she doesn't like cats, but I caught her slipping him some ham (I repeat, floozy). #Grandmachronicles

Sunday, January 11, 2015 at 12:10pm
I got hacked again. So, ignore the email, please, if you received one.

Sunday, January 11, 2015 at 12:52am
There has been a parallel narrative to the Grandma tales, the parable of sorts, of the call rising out of the dark hollow in the woods. Sometimes the call gets answered and it gets weird. I once spent a night in a tie-dye teepee keeping a man safe. He had no clue where he was, but he wanted spaghetti, thought my breasts were radio knobs and wanted to turn up the volume VERY LOUD. The thing is, I was there with him. The only other option (and consensus in the camp) was to duct tape him to a tree so he'd be unable to stumble through campfires. I'd give up a thousand nights to keep someone lost and alone from being tied to a tree. I'd turn the volume up and find the spaghetti. And in the morning if he walked away, I'd say again and again, "Love you. Welcome home."

Saturday, January 10, 2015 at 4:45pm
In the midst of chaos. Wait for it...pop goes the #Grandmachronicles

Friday, January 9, 2015 at 11:52pm
Conversation with My Grandmother:
>Grandma: JAN-MARIE, DID YOU EVER SEE ANYTHING LIKE THIS BEFORE? (Grandma holds out a napkin filled with something she is amazed by She opens it.)
>Me: Sure, why?
>Grandma: IT SMELLS SO PRETTY! SMELLY WOOD! (She stuffs the napkin in my nose)
>Me: It's potpourri, Grandma. Where'd you get that?

Grandma: I STOLE IT FROM THE BATHROOM AT THE
SALVATION ARMY.
THIS is why I drank many bloody Mary's this afternoon.
#Grandmachronicles

Friday, January 9, 2015 at 6:24pm
Grandma likes to talk--even in the loo when no one else is around. I
found her talking to Naked Allen Ginsberg earlier today, " Buddy, you'd
feel better if you'd put on some pants. It's damned cold," she said. (It's a
poster in my office). #Grandmachronicles

Friday, January 9, 2015 at 9:00am
Grandma's all tuckered out. Not sure why. I'm the one having to take
muscle relaxers for the spasms. She fell out right after announcing that
she wants to go to the beach today. #Grandmachronicles

Friday, January 9, 2015 at 12:55am
Not a Grandma Chronicle, but a parable of sorts. I remember the first
time I fell asleep at a Rainbow Gathering in a tent by myself. It was an
inky black night, and I might have been scared, but I knew if it got too
freaky, I could call out "Shanti Sena" and someone would come running
to help. It didn't get scary that night, I fell asleep to all these voices in the
woods shouting out "welcome home" and "love you." Woke up the next
morning and found I'd pitched my tent next to the shitters. So, I was
sleeping right next to some scary shit all night and didn't know it til
someone squatted behind the tent and hollered out that I might like flies
a little too much for my own good.... This all only makes sense if you
look at the metaphor Also, this post might have something to do with
being blessed by first, back spasms, followed by muscle relaxers and
exhaustion. This is all compounded by how distance tends to multiply
volume when it is broadcast from a hollow in the woods. Grandma will
be up at seven for coffee. I'm going to sleep now. LOVE YOU.
WELCOME HOME. #nofliesonus

Thursday, January 8, 2015 at 4:53pm
Jan Becker added 2 new photos.
Selfies and giggles at IHOP. #Grandmachronicles

Thursday, January 8, 2015 at 4:04pm
Destination, let alone destiny is uncertain when venturing out with
Grandma. Our trip to the pier became a trip to Festival Flea Market.
Grandma fancies the wigs. Fun fun. #Grandmachronicles

Thursday, January 8, 2015 at 2:18pm
That was 45 minutes of bliss. Off to Pompano Pier (I need coffee).
#Grandmachronicles

Thursday, January 8, 2015 at 1:07pm
Spring syllabus is written. Grandma and Mom are off on another
adventure, this time to Dollar Tree. Grandma has discerning taste. Last
night at Publix, she insisted on buying white bread for sandwiches. I'm
not cutting the crusts off for her. Since they are out, and my syllabus is
done. I am going to take a power nap and dream of dense hearty loaves.
I'll need my energy for when they return. #Grandmachronicles

Wednesday, January 7, 2015 at 5:27pm
Only with my Grandma could a trip to the Salvation Army turn into a
live sex show. We ran into a locked-together pair of puppies in
housewares. Oy vey. #Grandmachronicles

Wednesday, January 7, 2015 at 1:07pm
My upstairs neighbor also has a visitor. She has been on the balcony on
her phone for close to an hour discussing conspiracy theories related to
the Patriot Act. According to this woman the government has installed
devices on our household appliances to spy on us. This is true, because
Jesse Ventura said so. Grandma would like her. #Grandmachronicles

Wednesday, January 7, 2015 at 10:51am
This status update was written in the john, where everything is so quiet, I'd like to stay forever. Grandma had plans to sleep all day. But then I uttered the magic words, "Salvation Army, Whacky Wednesday," and she's rallied. God help me. #Grandmachronicles

Wednesday, January 7, 2015 at 8:53am
Grandma was up at 7 AM playing LOUD reggae music. At least it was Toots. #Grandmachronicles

Tuesday, January 6, 2015 at 9:44pm
Grandma and Mom are all tucked in for the night. They had a long, rough day that started at 3:30 AM, of disgruntled wheelchair pushers, shady car rental agencies, and I-95 between Fort Lauderdale and Pompano Beach during rush hour on the Epiphany. The Feline is happy to see his Great Grandma. She slipped him some chicken at dinner, on a napkin. #Grandmachronicles

Tuesday, January 6, 2015 at 5:16pm
I got a call from my mother that they've arrived in South Florida. She and Grandma are lost somewhere in Wilton Manors. My mother sounds like she could use a shot of something. I will too. #Grandmachronicles

Tuesday, January 6, 2015 at 1:32pm
Grandma's flight was delayed. This is good. I'm beginning to realize it's probably smart to clean the apartment more than just when they come to visit. #igotthefunk #Grandmachronicles

Tuesday, January 6, 2015 at 10:16am
Grandma and Mom land in three hours. I need coffee like six hours ago. #Grandmachronicles

Monday, January 5, 2015 at 4:10pm
Best part of my day: Seeing status updates from friends, who were
formerly disenfranchised by the draconian same-sex marriage ban in
Florida, FINALLY having unions recognized by the state. LOVE WINS!

Sunday, January 4, 2015 at 6:25pm
All I wanna do is make hats.

Saturday, January 3, 2015 at 9:25am
Not sure which of these is the most unfortunate part of my morning: 1. I
was attacked by noseeums overnight, so woke to welts everywhere. 2.
Tipped the fan over, knocked the fan blade loose, and when I tested it to
see if it was working, the fan blade shot across the room of its own
volition. 3. The Feline snagged a nipple with his claw while begging for
treats (Yes, I just said nipple. I'm not ashamed. We all have them.).

Friday, January 2, 2015 at 7:19pm
It just occurred to me that Grandma is landing the same day that Florida
starts issuing marriage licenses for same sex couples. THIS could be an
epic first night for her vacation if I plan the dinner venue wisely.

Friday, January 2, 2015 at 11:26am
The Chef's first business day of the New Year has been filled with phone
calls to the Postmaster General. I had no idea they had a general in
charge of the postal service; nor did I know that one could initiate an
investigation into where our mail has been going when it doesn't come
to our mailbox. Now I can't get the image of the little general from the
car insurance commercials out of my head. Also, The Chef is the only
person I know who files a complaint when the bills don't arrive.

Thursday, January 1, 2015 at 8:07pm
Found this at Publix, from Port au Prince. It's in the curry pot...gone.

Thursday, January 1, 2015 at 12:49pm
The Chef's car has been out of commission, so we've been sharing my old
Toyota. Our routine has been that he comes in from work, and I head to
Dania Beach to catsit. The past two or three trips, I've been confused,
because by the time I reach Fort Lauderdale, my eyes have started
swelling, and my skin feels tingly and pin-pricked. Last night, when he
got home from his shift, The Chef asked if I'd noticed anything funny
about my steering wheel. I confirmed that indeed, it has felt like I'm
allergic to something in the car. He explained he's been working with
Scotch bonnets (The Chef considers food his colleague. Sometimes he'll
come home and say he worked with salmon.) and didn't wash up after
chopping them up (He typically feeds between 500 and 1000 people
during the holidays). I asked him why he wouldn't wash up afterwards.
"I kinda like that feeling," he answered. Sabotage, I say. Sabotage.

Wednesday, December 31, 2014 at 10:33pm
I need to get to Kentucky.

Tuesday, December 30, 2014 at 6:06pm
Another tough lesson from today: When putting extremely hot peppers
in baby food jars to store in the cupboard, it is wise to wear ventilation
gear. #whollyhotstuff

Tuesday, December 30, 2014 at 3:08pm
Happy New Year.

Tuesday, December 30, 2014 at 3:00pm
Lesson I have learned after being attacked by mosquitoes and then
compared to a turkey by The Chef: I was not aware I possessed this
much dark meat.

Monday, December 29, 2014 at 8:17pm
I showed The Chef a mosquito bite in a particularly delicate area. His
reaction was to comment that if I were a turkey, the mosquitoes had
selected the choicest, tenderest portion for their feast. #notaturkey

Monday, December 29, 2014 at 10:15am
Jan Becker likes Medicinal Mushrooms.

Sunday, December 28, 2014 at 5:56pm
The Feline is terrified by the Disney channel. I made the mistake of stopping as I was browsing channels, and he fled the room, cowered under the bed and whimpered. Weirdo.

Saturday, December 27, 2014 at 9:10am
Every car rental place in South Florida is sold out for the weekend. This means The Chef will be using my car to commute to work today. He doesn't appear to have a good record with vehicles this week. Please pray for my Toyota.

Friday, December 26, 2014 at 9:59pm
And then The Chef calls because the loaner has broken down. Montgomery Clift will have to wait. Sigh.

Friday, December 26, 2014 at 9:22pm
I can't believe I went almost 45 years without seeing From Here to Eternity. This is one of those shameful status updates I post from time to time where I confess one of my darkest sins. Quite possibly, not seeing this film is among my most egregious offenses, and I'm just at the 10 minute mark and already know this. Thank you, John Dufresne, for teaching me about the 10-minute mark.

Thursday, December 25, 2014 at 7:52pm
Conversation with a pair of blokes at Walgreens (because of course we ran out of toilet paper on Christmas):
> Me: Excuse me, could I reach past you? I just need to grab some T.P.
> Bloke #1: Yeah, sure...Wait a minute, $4.49 for a 4-pack of toilet paper? Is that right?
> Me: It's Scott Tissue.

Bloke #1: Yeah, but it's $4.49. Look, you can get this one for $1.99 for four.
Me: Yes, I know, but it's not Scott Tissue. I only buy Scott.
Bloke #1 looks down, shakes his head...
Bloke #2: Man, that's some serious shit.

Thursday, December 25, 2014 at 4:03am
Wait...Storing poop in one's pants is an option?

Wednesday, December 24, 2014 at 4:10pm
Poor Chef came home early, all flustered. The transmission died on his Honda. Lucky for him, his loaner (from a friend) is a Corvette. AND we're having curry for dinner (like there was another option).

Tuesday, December 23, 2014 at 11:32pm
Live in Florida? Please take a look at the Floridians' Clean Water Act.

Tuesday, December 23, 2014 at 8:46pm
Becker's Festivus looking towards 2015 moment of disillusion with our collective future, and all the predictions from my childhood: Where the hell is the transporter technology?

Tuesday, December 23, 2014 at 2:34pm
I love The Chef, and I love when he has a day off (like yesterday) and cooks me dinner. However, the next time I find he's been grinding peppercorns, coriander, fennel, and fenugreek in the coffee grinder (and then not wiping it out), I'm going to replace his single malt scotch with maple syrup. #passiveagressivecoffeesnot

Sunday, December 21, 2014 at 8:47pm
I spent the solstice in the Everglades with Love the Everglades Movement (which you should check out if you've not done so yet). Other than "Thank You," I'm not sure what to say--except that in the scope of things, I am small, and the planet (even just the spot the Everglades occupies) is big and diverse, and in need of some <3 & attention.

Sunday, December 21, 2014 at 8:40pm
Jan Becker shared Love the Everglades Movement's photo.

Sunday, December 21, 2014 at 9:16am
Happy Winter Solstice!

Saturday, December 20, 2014 at 12:33pm
My agenda today involves things which delight The Feline, like the vacuum cleaner, moving the furniture around, and most especially, cleaning solvents. He is scowling on the balcony right now, guarding his cat grass like a dragon in a treasure cave. If he doesn't cheer up soon, I may wash him as well.

Friday, December 19, 2014 at 7:38pm
Message on answering machine from The Chef's friend, who is sending us hot peppers. Confused the hell out of me first time I listened to it: Hey Chef. Hey Jan. It's Bud. Keep an eye out for package from Postal service. Finally got this year's crop dried. Heard you were running low. Sending you purple dragon, purple thai and I threw a little purple cayenne in there. Until he got to the purple cayenne, I was completely lost.

Friday, December 19, 2014 at 7:11pm
Jan Becker shared Equality Florida's photo.
I have mixed feelings about this decision. While I'm happy the Supreme Court is refusing to delay the marriages, I'm worried that the 11th circuit court could potentially strip people of their marriages once they've gotten married. Still, I'm holding out hope that the 11th circuit court rules on the side of justice and equality when they make their decision...and if you need an officiant, I'm ordained.

Friday, December 19, 2014 at 4:03pm
I survived the DMV. That is all.

Friday, December 19, 2014 at 1:25pm
There are 85,003 people on line at the DMV. Approximately, 93% of them are obnoxious. The other 7% seem medicated. We're all standing behind a stanchion. Feels like a cattle drive at the slaughterhouse.

Friday, December 19, 2014 at 10:46am
Other than the first bout of contact (initial license, driver's exams, first vehicle registration), is anyone thrilled about going to the DMV? Also, why does my vehicle title hide when I need it to go there? It's sort of like when I try to take The Feline to the vet and he hides under the bed.

Thursday, December 18, 2014 at 6:17pm
According to Officer Favitta of the Broward Sheriff's Office, there is a slight chance I may get pulled over tomorrow on my way to the DMV to get a new registration. Since my plate is now in the system as stolen, he tells me it would be a felony stop, involving drawn weapons and a frisk/search (and he gave me instructions on how best to respond in that event). Apparently, I am becoming a randy old woman, because my inner voice, on hearing this said very loudly in the cavern of my brain, "That frisk might not be so bad, Jan Becker."

Thursday, December 18, 2014 at 5:19pm
Spending my evening with the Broward Sheriff Department. Fun Fun. (License plate has gone missing).

Thursday, December 18, 2014 at 10:45am
The Chef brought me my first dreidel last night. Where was this wonder of fun all my life?

Tuesday, December 16, 2014 at 11:07pm
Message From Bullhorn Backyard by Lake Just Now: "ALL DETAINEES, PLEASE RETURN TO YOUR ASSIGNED HOUSING UNITS." Suddenly, the management style in my building makes much more sense.

Tuesday, December 16, 2014 at 10:18am
Happy Chanukah!

Monday, December 15, 2014 at 6:36pm
Yeah, so I just decided to make a menorah while I'm at it.

Monday, December 15, 2014 at 1:23pm
It's been at least 20 years since I've had a Tannenbaum in my home. I'm
not an adherent of one particular religion. However, I like that most of
the holidays that are celebrated in December are hopeful and focus on
the return of light to a dark time, so I made this little tree (it's crocheted)
as a reminder that the dark days will pass. I'll light candles starting
tomorrow too. Though I don't own a menorah.

Monday, December 15, 2014 at 9:06am
Conversation from this Morning's Convention of Maintenance Men
Outside My Bathroom Window as I Was Drying Off From My Shower:
> NOT Creepy Maintenance Man: "Blah, blah, blah, weekend,
> weather, cold snap, Christmas, parking situation...Trash Guy is
> here! Did they finally get that turkey out of the trash chute?
> Should we go down and see if he needs any help?"
> Creepy Maintenance Man: "You go ahead. I want to stand right
> here for a few minutes."
Happy Monday.

Monday, December 15, 2014 at 2:56am
The guest bed arrived this week (not the bed of nails I'd been threatening
for The Winemaker). It's a futon mattress. It takes about a week to
decompress from the vacuum pack they shipped it in. Mom and
Grandma are coming in the New Year and I'll be sleeping on it while
they are here. The thing is too big to store anywhere in the apartment,
except on top of my mattress, so my bed is now twelve feet tall (honest).
The Feline is enjoying the view of his domain from the superior height.
When I finally get in there, it will be like The Princess and the Pea (sans
legume). I'm still too intimidated by the potential level of comfort to try

just yet. I may never climb back out...Unless...I could build a slide for it...or a firefighter's pole!

Sunday, December 14, 2014 at 12:56pm
I should have thought of all the screaming children who live here before I took the third shot of corn liquor. Ouch.

Saturday, December 13, 2014 at 10:39pm
Jan Becker feeling the holiday spirit.
And then I got into the corn liquor...

Saturday, December 13, 2014 at 1:55pm
Yes, I am making another pot of curry. Don't judge.

Friday, December 12, 2014 at 11:48pm
I finally gave in and got the new monitor. And a keyboard. I feel like I'm in a fun house. Or a puzzle house. It all feels too big and ergonomic.

Thursday, December 11, 2014 at 1:52pm
Some sad facts: 1. An infant grows too quickly. 2. No matter how short my time away from home, if I step out the front door, The Feline will give me hell when I return.

Thursday, December 11, 2014 at 3:03am
Of course this was in Florida, and of course her name was Creamer. The holidays are when families come together, after all.

Wednesday, December 10, 2014 at 3:39pm
Why would they bother trying to track down taggers during Art Basel when all the walls are being painted anyway?

Wednesday, December 10, 2014 at 12:29pm
Fourth graders are cool. They see eyes "green like the Incredible Hulk."

Wednesday, December 10, 2014 at 5:20am
GAH! I am facing a day filled with 140+ fourth graders on about 45 minutes sleep. THIS will be interesting.

Tuesday, December 9, 2014 at 6:14pm
Spent the day dodging opera in the living room and wrestling with my manuscript. The Chef had another day off, but things are about to get intense in the writing room. He is going out. I am putting on the writing uniform. Cat in the Hat t-shirt and fuzzy Cookie Monster pajama pants. And as soon as that front door closes, I'm all about the business.

Monday, December 8, 2014 at 12:48pm
Thoughts on finishing the book for a Fall graduation after hearing back from my thesis director: I think I can. I think I can...

Sunday, December 7, 2014 at 9:41pm
Thoughts on finishing the book in time for a Spring graduation: I think I can. I think I can. I think I can...

Sunday, December 7, 2014 at 8:15pm
If you are free tomorrow afternoon, I highly recommend this talk with Joshua Safran. He's written one of the best memoirs I've read--ever. Josh is one of my favorite people on the planet too. Mega mensch.

Sunday, December 7, 2014 at 10:32am
Some wonderful things: 1. The Chef is working a double shift, so plenty of quiet for gardening and other misadventures (i.e., write like a motherfucker). 2. The Feline is fiercely guarding his catnip plant, which I intend to replant today (there will be blood). 3. There are children screaming by the lake, which might annoy me sometimes, but today, they seem to be necessary disruptions to the quiet of Sunday morning.

Saturday, December 6, 2014 at 11:23am
This Might Be the Fever Talking: This bug I have, whatever it is, is trying
to lodge in my chest. I hate not being able to breathe freely. Especially
this week. It's like every time I try to take a breath, I'm thinking of Eric
Garner-- and this hurts much more than bronchitis is supposed to. I've
been quiet about the recent legal decisions, not because I don't care, but
because I'm so sad, it doesn't seem like anything I can say would make
much of a difference. And I've been busy listening to the rhetoric that the
folks in Ferguson are thugs, that the police are hell-bent on genocide.
Here's the thing. I live my life by the ideal that everyone on the planet is
connected to me. Eric Garner, Trayvon Martin, and Michael Brown were
my brothers. And they're dead. And they were killed by my other
brothers--and I am sad for them as well. It seems like no one is using the
word "We" (as in The People) anymore in the rhetoric surrounding these
deaths. We've all lost someone here. We're all diminished. It's not an "us"
and "them" issue. The divided house We are trying to defend is
crumbling around us while We point fingers at one another and waste
time being distracted by a fallacy that there is not enough on our little
blue marble to sustain us all. I have to believe there is bounty enough if
We get our shit together and start treating one another as if every person
is a beloved family member. I'm still working on that last part...

Friday, December 5, 2014 at 10:01pm
While doing some research on the Chapman family (mother's side) I
found a family motto: "Crescit sub pondere virtus." It's Latin for "Virtue
thrives under opression." Might be time for a tattoo.

Thursday, December 4, 2014 at 7:30pm
I just want to put very hot things on my face today.

Wednesday, December 3, 2014 at 11:02pm
Aside from everything that went into my pot for the curry (turmeric,
ginger, garlic, cinnamon, garam masala, tomatoes, coriander, cayenne,
ghost bite peppers, red bell peppers, onions, every other assorted hot
pepper I could find in my pantry, curry powders from Durban and

Madras, coconut milk and cumin), the most wonderful thing in the world is this box of Puffs Plus with Vicks.

Wednesday, December 3, 2014 at 4:20pm
Weird thing: I live in South Florida, where there are large populations of people who eat very hot peppers regularly. I went to three different grocery stores and none of them carry dried chile peppers. That's whack.

Wednesday, December 3, 2014 at 4:11pm
Unless it gets held up on appeal, love and freedom and equality win out--it's about effing time.

Wednesday, December 3, 2014 at 3:46pm
Jan Becker likes Jai-Alai Books.

Wednesday, December 3, 2014 at 11:26am
I am going to cook up the fiercest pot of curry I can muster today in an effort to kill off the slithy toves that are breeding in my sinuses.

Wednesday, December 3, 2014 at 9:29am
How many sneezes does it take to get to the end of this rhinovirus? The world will never know. (I'm an English major, can't count that high)

Tuesday, December 2, 2014 at 2:18pm
Two Confessions for today: 1. When stuck in traffic on I 95 because of an armed carjacking, my primary concern was whether I'd make my appointment, not that I might get shot. 2. From Thanksgiving. I put the turkey in the oven, fell asleep and woke up 6 hours later to a burnt bird. I threw the bird down the garbage slot where it became wedged between the 2nd and 3rd floors, and stayed there, stinking over the entire holiday weekend. So, I ate tofu for Thanksgiving, and collard greens. This might drive me to vegetarianism, I feel so guilty.

Monday, December 1, 2014 at 5:30pm
The Chef is doing something in the kitchen. I'm not sure what--but it's amazing, whatever it is. I can taste it three rooms away.

Monday, December 1, 2014 at 12:48pm
I <3 Missouri Review. I had to withdraw a submission from them and they took the time to write and thank me for allowing them to read it, and also asked me to send in more work. This never happens to me. I almost never need to withdraw, and when I do, I never get a note like that. Whatever bug I have is rebounding today, but that cheered me up.

Sunday, November 30, 2014 at 2:19pm
The Feline is all tuckered out from nursing me through this illness--it's tough looking cute and being available for cuddles 24/7. I'm starting to finally come around. I even unpacked my suitcases from the Book Fair and cooked breakfast for The Chef, whose boss gave him the next couple of days off to make sure he is fully recovered. I'll remember to kick him in the shins the next time I see him.

Saturday, November 29, 2014 at 5:37pm
I'm finally feeling well enough to try to drink a protein shake. It tastes nasty, possibly the worst thing I've ever consumed. Might take me a few hours to get through it, but I'm determined. YUCK.

Saturday, November 29, 2014 at 10:26am
I woke up thinking I had to be behind a registration desk right now somewhere in Miami. I'm still not convinced I don't need to be there. The Chef is feeling better as I get progressively worse. I'm a much better nursemaid than he is. As soon as I gather the energy, I'm firing him. He's playing loud klezmer music in the living room. I have nothing against klezmer, but it's far too intense for my pounding head right now, and is making me weepy.

Friday, November 28, 2014 at 7:36pm
Jan Becker feeling sick.

The Chef is very generous with everything including his virus. I am guessing this strain is not one the vaccine covers. Yuck.

Friday, November 28, 2014 at 12:29pm
My strategy for dealing with the Chef's illness is to keep him as full of Nyquil as is safe. I just checked on him, and the covers were soaked through. I changed those for him and got him hooked up with some thick wool Pendleton blankets. Soup is on the stove bubbling away. And I've got the reserve bottle of PA corn liquor at the ready should he show the slightest sign of waking. That will knock not only him out, but this terrible flu. Glad I got my shot early this year. This bug looks nasty.

Friday, November 28, 2014 at 9:20am
Shopping for carrots and celery for soup stock for a very sick Chef doesn't count as contributing to capitalism on Black Friday, does it?

Thursday, November 27, 2014 at 10:36pm
It appears that our beloved Chef has the flu. He came home early from work. He NEVER comes home early from work--nor takes a sick day. I'm praying for a speedy recovery for him, because I am the world's worst nursemaid, and he, the world's most cantankerous sick-boy.

Thursday, November 27, 2014 at 8:16pm
My computer monitor is about to die. I'm not shopping for a new one tomorrow, or on Cyber Saturday. I'm all about the bah humbug this year.

Thursday, November 27, 2014 at 4:47pm
Oh, yes, I did just sleep until 4:30 in the afternoon. I'd still be napping if the neighbors didn't speak to one another in screams.

Wednesday, November 26, 2014 at 11:04pm
About the male creatures I cohabit this apartment with: The Feline is like a mean drunk when he's been in the catnip. The Chef is covered with burns, though he considers them routine. He's feeding 1,000 tomorrow. I feel bad for all those turkeys. One of the things I love most about him is

that he works so hard. And despite how hard he works, The Chef still compliments my collards.

Wednesday, November 26, 2014 at 5:30pm
Finally made it home. Be careful! I picked up some thread for a project and got a live catnip plant for The Feline. The Chef is working a double shift tomorrow. The cat and I plan to sit home and get stoned (on catnip) and hook. I'm thankful I don't have to see anyone tomorrow. Sheesh.

Tuesday, November 25, 2014 at 10:24am
I've been out of the classroom as an instructor since May, and most of the time, I've been so busy I didn't notice enough to miss it, but I'm subbing today for a friend, and so excited to be back, even for one day that I'm having a hard time containing myself. Those poor students! I hope they can handle Jan Becker's exuberance.

Monday, November 24, 2014 at 8:43pm
Jan Becker likes Stonewall National Museum - Wilton Manors Gallery.

Monday, November 24, 2014 at 11:15am
George Clinton just hugged me good-bye!!!

Monday, November 24, 2014 at 6:12am
I'm going to miss all these writers, sure, but it was especially difficult to say good-bye to the woman who's been making me cappuccino in the lobby each morning.

Sunday, November 23, 2014 at 3:36pm
OH MY GOD! GEORGE CLINTON JUST KISSED ME!

Saturday, November 22, 2014 at 6:30am
The voice on my morning wake up call sounded just like Rosie Perez. This is a very effective voice.

Friday, November 21, 2014 at 8:24am
Subtle racism/classism/any-isms should not occur anytime, but at 7am, I cannot be expected to hold a civil tongue in my head. And no, I won't explain. I'm not awake enough yet to wrap my head around that mess.

Wednesday, November 19, 2014 at 10:05am
I'm Miami-bound in a few hours on a secret mission that will span several days. Too much to do in the meantime. Will be back Monday, maybe...I might just become Secret Agent Jan.

Tuesday, November 18, 2014 at 2:07pm
Here is how you know I love someone/something. I will wear Spanx for you. #MBFI31

Tuesday, November 18, 2014 at 2:40am
Yes, I am up at quarter to 3 reading articles on trauma and genetic predisposition to PTSD. Fascinating.

Monday, November 17, 2014 at 12:11pm
In other news, snowbirds have infected The Chef with their filthy rhinovirii. This, just in time for Miami Book Fair. I am making him sleep on the porch til this passes. #nobugsallowedbookfairweek

Monday, November 17, 2014 at 9:07am
I wonder if by "progressive" bifocals they mean that I progressively move from double vision to normal as soon as I get some coffee in me, because two months in, I still see double before I get my joe.

Sunday, November 16, 2014 at 7:13pm
I still have not found those Spanx. I plan to walk around the next week chanting "SPANX SPANX SPANX SPANX SPANX SPANX SPANX SPANX " like the Monty Python "SPAM" skit. If you see me, just ignore me. This too shall pass.

Sunday, November 16, 2014 at 6:50am
An exciting twist on my new habit of getting up to go to the bathroom
and waking up hours later still seated on the toilet: Getting up to go to
the bathroom and falling asleep there for hours and then falling into the
bathtub, thereby wrenching my back and other sordid bits. Sigh.

Saturday, November 15, 2014 at 1:26pm
I just love the headlines for any story about Uranus.

Friday, November 14, 2014 at 6:28pm
Today was an awful exercise in waiting. The mail carrier never came, the
phone didn't ring, and on and on. Problem is I never know when to stop
waiting and get back to business. I feel like I'm trapped in a Beckett play.

Wednesday, November 12, 2014 at 1:37pm
The Feline usually leaves my yarn alone. Unless he's stoned on catnip.
Then, it's the most wonderful pile of wool in the world, and he, the
world's most efficient felter.

Monday, November 10, 2014 at 9:03am
I find it disconcerting that I make one offhand comment about Spanx,
and all of a sudden I get ads with offers for $25 dollars in "Booty Bucks."

Sunday, November 9, 2014 at 6:41am
Jan Becker likes The Crochet Lounge.

Sunday, November 9, 2014 at 12:51am
Anybody else think it's weird that this popped up right as the snowbirds
arrived? I know a guy from Binghamton named Willie the Worm (true
story). He used to come down for the winter. Had a rough time in
Vietnam, and couldn't get used to being confined to a house after he
came "home." Funny how when it's a soldier off at war, the notion of
"home" is the entire country. WELCOME HOME: "... And here again,
Fort Lauderdale leads by example. Complementing the anti-feeding law

are $25,000 earmarked to buy one-way bus tickets for homeless people to, well, anywhere. The honest message: Get out of town or starve."

Saturday, November 8, 2014 at 11:03pm
Unnecessary Censorship moment of the evening: Channel 10 News bleeped out the first half of cockroach. Sigh. Really?

Saturday, November 8, 2014 at 10:49am
Sometime ago there was a child in my building who screamed every day, all the time. She moved out. I needn't have missed her (I probably haven't). There are many children here now that have replaced her, and they all seem to scream every day, all the time.

Friday, November 7, 2014 at 8:48pm
Management is trying to interfere with The Winemaker's Annual Migration, and have imposed a 24-hour limit on guest parking, along with restrictions on the vehicles that belong to the people who live here. An example: I can't park in the lot if I have a FOR SALE sign on the car. I think they also may plan to assign parking spots. Next will be the retinal scan, a DNA sample from The Feline, and fingernail clippings. Weird. Feels like I'm living in an Aldous Huxley novel.

Friday, November 7, 2014 at 10:04am
I know this is a little behind the times, but I watched Frozen, and have been thinking. I don't understand why Elsa is getting all the Halloween costumes and product marketing. Sure, she was cryokinetic, but Anna did all the work to save that kingdom. I think it might have something to do with blonde hair. Trust me, being a blonde is way overrated.

Thursday, November 6, 2014 at 1:25pm
Because the fire alarm testing is not loud enough, a murder of crows has landed in the live oak outside my office and is screaming, "Nevermore!" at The Feline (he is intimidated).
BONUS: Creepy Maintenance Man Encounter Knock Knock (knock, knock)

Me: Who's there?
CMM: I'm here to inspect you. Me: Sigh...

Thursday, November 6, 2014 at 9:05am
Management is running its annual smoke alarm test for the building.
This means there will be a Creepy Maintenance Man encounter at some
point, as they must enter the apartment. Fire Alarm tests before 9AM:
There ought to be a law against that.

Wednesday, November 5, 2014 at 9:20am
The Chef's birthday, and he's having it rough this morning, because we
both feel like we drank too much and woke up to find Rick Scott hogging
the bedcovers, and Pam Bondi doing foul things in our lavatory.

Wednesday, November 5, 2014 at 1:49am
Is it just me, or is this the kind of law they set up for non-humans. For
example, feeding alligators will get you arrested...Somehow, I don't
think this is supposed to apply to people.

Wednesday, November 5, 2014 at 12:01am
I endorse the proposal bandied about South Florida Counties to secede
from North Florida and form a separate state. Can we do this? Please?

Tuesday, November 4, 2014 at 11:23am
Today's voting "high" light: obviously stoned man saunters into the
polling place and hollers out, "THIS IS WHERE I VOTE FOR LEGAL
WEED, RIGHT?!?" Sigh. America.

Tuesday, November 4, 2014 at 9:32am
Here in Florida, I've noticed that I feel more pressured to do this "early
voting" thing than I have ever felt anywhere else I've lived. I understand
the impulse to urge people to go vote early, especially with the creeps we
have in office--and important ballot initiatives that need to be decided
each election cycle. I don't do the early voting thing though, because it
means I would miss my favorite part of the process--walking into our

local ballot place hand-in-hand with The Chef (it's okay, you can groan, I know it's schmaltzy), and having my ID checked by the volunteer I call the colonel (I don't know his name, he just looks like a colonel), who recognizes me on sight now. I like being with neighbors, even if many of them are voting the opposite of how I want the election to go. I can't get that by driving to a courthouse in Ft. Lauderdale and waiting in a long line. Besides, I'm in Florida. I don't have a lot of faith that my vote would count if I stepped out of my yearly routine. I've never missed an election; it's way too important to skip. Besides that, as a military brat, I grew up with an intimate understanding of how much protection of freedom to vote costs. So, I'll be there today. I've been waiting a whole year for this.

Monday, November 3, 2014 at 7:07pm
Holy cow. I think I need to figure out a way to get some condoms around my inbox. I'm experiencing a sudden proliferation of emails. It's like a rabbit farm in there.

Saturday, November 1, 2014 at 6:31pm
Jan Becker with Omar Figueras and Hector D. Junior.
Ay! Que guapos! Lucky gal with these two dates.

Friday, October 31, 2014 at 8:51pm
I am growing fond of the Brazilian church lady, who, tonight did not suggest I might be an unemployed, drunk prostitute, but still stopped by with comics about Christ--and Skittles (I swear. SKITTLES).

Friday, October 31, 2014 at 8:20pm
I am placing myself in voluntary quarantine tonight due to the cruciferous vegetables. Trust me, it's better this way. Also, Dear Master Class with Richard Blanco I'll be attending tomorrow. I offer my apologies in advance.

Friday, October 31, 2014 at 10:02am
This probably has a lot to do with why I keep running into that demon spawn Jeb Bush here...

Wednesday, October 29, 2014 at 11:18pm
Conversation with The Feline:

> Me: Happy Day of the Cat, Romeo.
> Feline (penetrating gaze)...
> Me: You know, some folks would be happy to have a whole day dedicated to celebrating their existence.
> Feline: (yawn)...
> Me: I guess you think every day is Day of the Cat, huh? Feline: (Penetrating gaze...licks his balls.)
> Me: Sigh.

Sunday, October 26, 2014 at 7:02pm
The glory of FINALLY being able to open the windows when weather breaks here in South Florida is cruelly tempered by the mass hatch of noseeums, who are particularly attracted to the taste of my blood.

Sunday, October 26, 2014 at 4:23pm
It took me all day to figure out what was missing from my Sunday. No knocks on the door from the lady from the Brazilian church with prayers for my soul or that I'll give up the drunkenness and prostitution that I may have fallen into. I feel a little lost.

Saturday, October 25, 2014 at 2:58pm
Only 18 more minutes of this mercury retrograde crap!

Saturday, October 25, 2014 at 1:33pm
I had the pants on, for about 30 seconds. I'm just not ready to commit to a full day of pantaloons.

Saturday, October 25, 2014 at 12:16am
I may finally put on a pair of pants this week. It's been since April...I might not, but I'm entertaining the idea.

Wednesday, October 22, 2014 at 5:16pm
The Infant's Canine has declared all-out war on the squirrel population of South Florida.

Wednesday, October 22, 2014 at 10:46am
I am working on creating a Rube Goldberg device that will deliver French press coffee to me in the morning on a timed schedule.

Tuesday, October 21, 2014 at 10:23am
I woke up with a craving for authentic, homemade egg foo yung. Instead, for breakfast, I opened a big can of chaos.

Monday, October 20, 2014 at 11:59pm
I think this is relevant in light of FIU's acquisition of 60 (yes, 60) assault rifles, a bomb sniffing dig and an armored anti-assault vehicle.

Monday, October 20, 2014 at 12:51pm
I'm conducting experiments to determine the content of yarn marked "UNKNOWN FIBER." Bleach does some pretty freaky things to wool.

Monday, October 20, 2014 at 10:34am
You know how sometimes you have a problem, and you think you're the only one in the world with that problem, and the problem might be shameful so you walk around thinking no one else could possibly have that problem, but it makes you feel a little lousy about yourself? I have one of those problems. I suspect I'm not the only one who gets up in the middle of the night, falls back to sleep on the toilet, and wakes up hours later with a sore back. Am I the only one who ever does this? It's not making for a very pleasant day after.

Sunday, October 19, 2014 at 6:45pm
The Feline is in heaven. He's high on catnip and I'm organizing yarn stash.

Sunday, October 19, 2014 at 1:32pm
The woman from the Brazilian church, who came a few weeks ago and was worried about my job, came back. Apparently, she thinks I have more serious issues than not having a real job. Why can't I just get visits from the Mormons and Jehovah Witnesses like most folks?

Sunday, October 19, 2014 at 8:51am
Someone told me we "fall back" this weekend. That was a big fat lie. And worse, I have a feeling the people I spread this vicious rumor to are, like me, walking around completely befuddled at how unfair it is to be stuck in the hour between Fall and Winter. (First weekend of November).

Saturday, October 18, 2014 at 2:10pm
Since the invention of the early afternoon nap, there have only been five naps that were rated the most restorative, the most necessary, the most pure. This one left them all behind.

Friday, October 17, 2014 at 7:38pm
Weird day. The landfill sent me paperwork for a settlement because they make the air smell like poop. They also promised to try harder not to make the air smell like poop. Hmm. I think it's worth a lot more than $500.00 not to have to smell poop in the air.

Thursday, October 16, 2014 at 5:56pm
Best location in Miami for a yarn bomb? Freedom Tower?

Thursday, October 16, 2014 at 7:46am
Along with progressive politics, here in South Florida, our city councils are consistent with their pragmatic solutions for dealing with the homeless population. (please note the sarcasm there). Along with paying millions to relocate a homeless shelter to a barren edge of Broward, Fort Lauderdale deals with street folks by destroying their self-built shelters (cardboard dwellings) and personal belongings (shopping carts filled with personal things), because they are not aesthetically pleasing. Seems to me intolerance isn't very pretty either.

Thursday, October 16, 2014 at 1:41am
Something I think I'll be processing in my dreams tonight: William S. Burroughs was once a copywriter.

Wednesday, October 15, 2014 at 2:47pm
Something that made me giggle with delight today: Creepy Maintenance Man recently bought a very manly, Ford F-350, with an extended cab, and manly-man hubcaps, and, hell, the whole truck just screams "overcompensation." Here's the part that make me giggle: The solar shades he uses to keep the cab cool are decorated with pastel butterflies and flowers. (I like a man who likes butterflies and flowers, might have to rethink my relationship with CMM).

Tuesday, October 14, 2014 at 9:51pm
Today felt like I lived in six different genres. You know what I mean?

Tuesday, October 14, 2014 at 11:55am
This is one of those days when I have to hide the fact that I have no clean laundry by overdressing for the occasion. Funny how that works.

Monday, October 13, 2014 at 11:24pm
The Feline watched Life of Pi tonight. He thinks Richard Parker's a prick.

Monday, October 13, 2014 at 9:17am
I woke up this morning with an urge to reverse engineer something (anything/nothing particular). There are a few conundrums here: 1. I have zero propensity for the logic and/or mechanics of this endeavor. 2. I don't have a project suitable to disassemble. 3. If I entertain this sudden urge, I may find myself venturing into all sorts of random, impulsive projects that bear no practical purpose in my day-to-day life. For example, I might walk into the kitchen one morning and decide spontaneously that I need to take apart the disposer or discover how freon is stored in the refrigerator, and I do not have time to investigate the mechanics of kitchenry. I guess the lesson here is that I need to tamp

down my more deviant urges. (This is what happens when I answer Facebook status prompts honestly. I understand it makes no sense...so little does, less than halfway into my first cup of coffee.)

Sunday, October 12, 2014 at 10:41am
I have awakened on a morning of accurate onomatopoeia: The birds are really chirping; every car alarm just activated with a resounding beep (simultaneously in response to the dumpster trucks roar); and The Feline—he did really just barf in the hall.

Saturday, October 11, 2014 at 9:13am
Hooey, the Miracle Wonder Chair is going to have to step up if I'm going to get through this weekend. The negative ion generating, magical jade pendants in its heating pad are throwing off less "waterfall energy" than Max promised when I bought the chair. It feels more like a Judas' Cradle than an ergonomic wonder device.

Thursday, October 9, 2014 at 10:15am
Just as my game returned, building management saw fit to bring in a portable crane to rip out the ceiling to the building with saws and other very loud power tools, just outside my window on the floor above me. I believe my next essays will be informed by construction worker butt, which is similar to plumber butt, but perched high above the ground, and a little more tanned than the average plumber.

Thursday, October 9, 2014 at 7:09am
I'd forgotten what a good eight-hour night of sleep felt like (because of insomnia, not stress--OK, maybe a little stress). Watch out world! Becker's got her game back.

Wednesday, October 8, 2014 at 3:28pm
Methinks that infants and crotchety old men have much in common.

Wednesday, October 8, 2014 at 8:33am
Is it just me? Or is it kinda creepy when someone views your Linked In profile, and they don't tell you who it was? I get a little creeped out.

Sunday, October 5, 2014 at 5:08pm
Conversation with the woman who just came to the door:
> Me (In my sock monkey pajamas): Hello
> Lady: I have an especial invitation to you from our church. Do you speak English or Portuguese?
> Me: English. Lady (hands over a flyer): We having a special blessing next Sunday with our Bishop from Brasilia. He's flying in to bless your water. It will make a lotta good changes for your life. You look like you need a job. This blessing might help you find a job.
> Me: Actually, I'm working right now, from home. I was working when you knocked.
> Lady (surveys my sock monkey pjs, looks me up and down): Ahh, Sure, well you come, maybe he can help you find a real job. Sigh.

Friday, October 3, 2014 at 2:23pm
The woman who cleans the hallways here has a rough job. She works outside in rotten heat all summer, and has to put up with the messes people here leave behind (Like the elevator urinator). She's elderly too, so I imagine it's even harder on her body than it would be for a young person. Every time I see her, she wants to chat. I was fond of her up til today, when she stopped me in the hallway, pointed to my Green Eggs and Ham shirt and told me she had no respect for Dr. Seuss, and that Dick and Jane was a superior children's series. (Effing critics, man).

Friday, October 3, 2014 at 12:43pm
Only in Jan Becker's world does it take three hours to get ready to go to the store for Half & Half.

Thursday, October 2, 2014 at 12:24pm
The Feline loves his phallic shaped toys.

Thursday, October 2, 2014 at 10:36am
Facebook is finally allowing me to like things. This makes me happy.

Thursday, October 2, 2014 at 10:36am
Jan Becker likes Beating Windward Press.

Wednesday, October 1, 2014 at 6:59pm
The Feline tears up his catnip filled chili pepper stuffy birthday boy gift.

Tuesday, September 30, 2014 at 9:47am
Yes, I know I've been hacked. Sorry. You don't need hair extensions (though if you did want them, I'm sure they'd look wonderful). I'm not really held in a prison in Djibouti, and don't need bail money--at least this week. (Mercury goes into retrograde Oct. 4th).

Saturday, September 27, 2014 at 11:55am
When I came home from babysitting, The Chef was clutching a half-full carafe of coffee and had an already filled mug. I asked if I could pour a cup. "No," he answered," I need it all." I think we may have just hit the first rough patch in our domestic partnership.

Friday, September 26, 2014 at 5:30pm
I may be covered in blisters, but I'm totally rocking these new bifocals!

Friday, September 26, 2014 at 9:04am
I had some highly inappropriate dreams last night. Jimmy Fallon was involved (I don't even watch Fallon).

Thursday, September 25, 2014 at 9:47pm
Random copy-editing hiccup: Why do we use "ones" to indicate many things? For example: He made many mistakes in his life--many serious

ones. Isn't "one" singular by definition? I may have to go off on a crusade against the use of "ones."

Wednesday, September 24, 2014 at 8:02pm
I find it fitting that Facebook has chosen to block me from liking anything during Banned Books Week. I was blocked for liking an independent publisher and fiber artists.

Wednesday, September 24, 2014 at 7:13pm
Facebook wants to know what's on my mind. I've been blocked from "liking" any pages for thirty days, AND they've removed every page I've liked for the last thirty days. Facebook, if I told you honestly what was on my mind, I'd get blocked from doing much more than liking pages. So, I'll just say Happy New Year, and leave it at that.

Tuesday, September 23, 2014 at 10:10am
I had a dream a long time ago in which a badger whispered a secret in my ear. I've wondered, why a badger? Why would it come to me in a dream? Why whisper its secret? Last night, I watched the honey badger episode on PBS' Nature, and I decided if some random animal shows up in my dreams and whispers in my ear, I'm glad it is an animal who is intelligent, can take on a lion, nurtures kids way past what is normal for any other weasel, sends off a powerful stench from its anal pouch when intimidated, and can castrate a charging water buffalo with its claws.

Monday, September 22, 2014 at 12:33pm
Things I am pondering this afternoon: 1. "Poet laureates" or "poets laureate"? 2. Can I catch an incurable disease if I eat the two-year-old protein bar I found at the bottom of my backpack? 3. What if it's just a curable disease? Should I risk it then?

Sunday, September 21, 2014 at 5:18pm
My allergies have been acting up, so The Chef suggested I try saw palmetto. It's amazing! Not only are my sinuses all cleared out--my prostate also feels wonderful!

Saturday, September 20, 2014 at 6:22pm
Facebook is asking what's on my mind. I'm thinking of my second toe on my right foot and feeling a little sad for it today. It always stayed home.

Friday, September 19, 2014 at 5:56pm
I was feeling down about all the rain here lately, but then I turned on the Weather Channel, which for some reason was running a segment about Binghamton. They said you poor Binghamtonians were waking up to 36° weather this morning. Cheered me right up.

Friday, September 19, 2014 at 3:38pm
New glasses. Please ignore the zit on my forehead and the hair. I'd just gotten trapped in a thunderstorm.

Friday, September 19, 2014 at 12:41pm
I hate picking out new glasses. It's like selecting a new face.

Friday, September 19, 2014 at 11:52am
Jan Becker played ORCS for 23 in Words With Friends.

Friday, September 19, 2014 at 1:33am
In the continuing theme of the day, when I got home, Crystal Lake Drive and Military Trail were both roadblocked and there's a helicopter overhead with a searchlight flying low over the apartment building. Reminded me of CW McCall. "The smokies were thick as bugs on a bumper. They even had a bear in the air." I'm going to sleep. At least I didn't run into any tanks.

Thursday, September 18, 2014 at 9:20am
Jan Becker played SALE for 20 in Words With Friends.

Wednesday, September 17, 2014 at 7:57pm
I'm home, and it's quiet. The Chef is back to work. The Feline is out on
the balcony chasing geckos. I'm taking the night off, watching bad TV
and putting my feet up.

Wednesday, September 17, 2014 at 11:09am
Jan Becker played HUNT for 24 in Words With Friends.

Wednesday, September 17, 2014 at 10:13am
Jan Becker feeling blessed.
Again, I woke this morning all tied up in my sheets. No hairbrushes in
my belly though, and no trips to member states of the Axis of Evil in my
dreams last night. The Chef's two-week vacation is over!

Tuesday, September 16, 2014 at 12:30pm
Jan Becker played JEST for 39 in Words With Friends.

Tuesday, September 16, 2014 at 7:41am
I dreamt last night that I traveled to North Korea and wore high heels.
When I woke this morning, my back was out, I was tied up in my
bedsheets and had a hairbrush's bristles embedded in my belly. I have
no clue how the hairbrush got into the bed, but The Feline is looking
vengeful this morning.

Monday, September 15, 2014 at 1:22pm
Hazel the cat drank my coffee...Happy Monday.

Monday, September 15, 2014 at 9:50am
Jan Becker played ZA for 22 in Words With Friends.

Monday, September 15, 2014 at 7:02am
There is more morning than my cup of coffee can conquer.

Sunday, September 14, 2014 at 8:08am EDT
Jan Becker played VOID for 21 in Words With Friends

Friday, September 12, 2014 at 8:59am
The Chef and I planned to go to Key West this weekend. We've been saying we'll go there for fifteen years now. However, after looking over the weather report for the weekend, we're putting it off again. I could be bummed out, but after some thought, I've reached the conclusion that spending most of the weekend home in my sock monkey pajamas is probably even more wonderful than a weekend in the keys.

Friday, September 12, 2014 at 8:21am
Jan Becker played SAFE for 21 in Words With Friends.

Wednesday, September 10, 2014 at 11:55am
Building management sent me an email that they are painting our walkways and no one can walk in or out of the apartments til 4. I'm dilated. Need to take a shower before Chef and I formalize our domestic partnership AT FOUR PM! BAD timing! I may be covered in paint.

Wednesday, September 10, 2014 at 9:40am
Not sure why I feel this way, but getting an eye exam feels more invasive to me than a visit to the gynecologist.

Wednesday, September 10, 2014 at 9:27am
Jan Becker played GAZE for 25 in Words With Friends.

Tuesday, September 9, 2014 at 1:10pm
There is a man outside my apartment pressure-washing the building. I'm tempted to open my windows and save myself some time cleaning.

Tuesday, September 9, 2014 at 10:29am
Jan Becker played HO for 22 in Words With Friends.

Monday, September 8, 2014 at 11:58pm
Pinterest does not know me at all. They sent me an email with boards for preppers and planners, with DIY nuclear and apocalypse preparedness

kits. I'm not prepared for the next five minutes. If a nuclear catastrophe comes, I'm planning to wing it. It's worked for me so far.

Monday, September 8, 2014 at 9:51am
Jan Becker played JAM for 29 in Words With Friends.

Sunday, September 7, 2014 at 5:14pm
Meanwhile, on Crystal Lake Drive: Sometimes I'm the one who gets to experience the schadenfreude instead of providing it. The Chef is having Sunday laundry room adventures, complete with people removing his clothing. Also, the mariachis have vacated the building. If I'd known they were moving, I'd have sung "Vaya Con Dios" as they pulled away.

Sunday, September 7, 2014 at 3:22pm
Something I wish I had known in my previous life: Copy editing for long stretches can trigger vivid hallucinations.

Sunday, September 7, 2014 at 8:34am
Jan Becker played OM for 29 in Words With Friends.

Sunday, September 7, 2014 at 8:11am
I need to lay off the Brussels sprouts. Sheesh.

Saturday, September 6, 2014 at 10:09am
Jan Becker played AXED for 33 in Words With Friends.

Friday, September 5, 2014 at 9:21pm
Is there a critter in South Florida similar to Punxsutawney Phill (I mean in its predicting ability, not necessarily a rodent) that gives some sort of sign of when the humidity is going to break?

Friday, September 5, 2014 at 8:02am
Jan Becker played BURNT for 20 in Words With Friends.

Thursday, September 4, 2014 at 8:14pm
Blank page 0 - Jan Becker 1. Essay submitted. Now I shower and sniff rum. (No drinks. I'm still recovering from the coconut mojito incident)

Thursday, September 4, 2014 at 4:31pm
I am not required to be thankful, but today, I find myself grateful for Jamaican friends who travel home and bring me back bottles of rum.

Thursday, September 4, 2014 at 11:24am
CVS has me in an isolation booth. It looks similar to the blank page.

Thursday, September 4, 2014 at 7:50am
The blank page is taunting me.

Thursday, September 4, 2014 at 7:31am
Jan Becker played DUNE for 27 in Words With Friends.

Wednesday, September 3, 2014 at 9:46am
Good news is car is not majorly messed up. Bad news is they are making me reschedule another appointment for the air conditioning. Ugh.

Tuesday, September 2, 2014 at 9:03am
The Chef and The Feline are negotiating a peace accord. We have company coming. To The Chef, this means The Feline's bed gets thrown into a pile on top of his catnip toys in a corner where he can't access them. The Feline is taking this as a personal affront and has taken to raising his hackles and hissing whenever The Chef enters the room. It occurs to me that The Chef does not speak feline. I finally got through to The Chef. "He will pee on your laundry pile if you toss his bed in the corner," I explained. Funny how fast the bed came back out of the catnip toy pile. (Of course, he would not pee on his laundry, but sometimes peace requires bold lies).

Monday, September 1, 2014 at 1:46pm
The Florida sun is god's way of messing with a hungover head. Too bright!. Too loud this sun!

Monday, September 1, 2014 at 5:07am
Oh. holy hell hangover, mojitos.

Sunday, August 31, 2014 at 6:58pm
Whoo! Coconut mojitos with The Chef. Holy alcohol.

Friday, August 29, 2014 at 8:11pm
Now is not the time for the "check engine light" to rear its ugly head. Let's hope it's just that I forgot to tighten the gas cap.

Wednesday, August 27, 2014 at 5:23pm
I guess it'd be smart to check on a number before texting a friend about going to an art installation on public sex in Hialeah. WOOPS. SORRY GRANDMA.

Wednesday, August 27, 2014 at 2:54pm
Another reason babies should rule the world: Sometimes it is wise to just meditate on the intricacies of one's receiving blanket. So simple, yet so complex, the weave that warms.

Tuesday, August 26, 2014 at 10:35am
Kindest words The Chef has ever said to me: "Coffee's Ready, Honey."

Monday, August 25, 2014 at 10:54pm
They're going to drop love bombs!

Monday, August 25, 2014 at 9:17am
Jan Becker played GONER for 24 in Words With Friends.

Monday, August 25, 2014 at 7:51am
Random morning moment of joy: Popping last dose of steroids out of the blister pack. Been fun, but Jan Becker on steroids is too much. NO MAS!

Sunday, August 24, 2014 at 11:03pm
Part of my response to the former student (a high school senior): "Keep in mind, Grasshopper, you are trapped within the common core right now. They show you the rules. I'll teach you how to break them. You still need to know those rules, and master the 'boring ass stuff'. A warrior is mightiest when skilled in a variety of creative and rhetorical weapons."

Sunday, August 24, 2014 at 1:30pm
Jan Becker played GIST for 27 in Words With Friends.

Sunday, August 24, 2014 at 1:30am
Jan Becker feeling vindicated.
Today's random moment of joy: Opening email from a former student, who told me in her last emails that she'd need therapy to recover from my creative writing class last fall (favorite student email ever). This one started, "I didn't do any of the things you suggested I do with my writing and regret it, and now I'm not writing, can you help me out?" Hehehe....

Saturday, August 23, 2014 at 1:58pm
So, I didn't sleep all the way through to Sunday as I'd planned, but I made it more than halfway through Saturday. Boy, did I need that.

Saturday, August 23, 2014 at 1:15am
I had so much fun tonight at the Reading Queer Inaugural Reading. But, I'm exhausted. I am going to sleep til Sunday. (And of course, this minute is when The Feline decides he would like to play fetch with me).

Friday, August 22, 2014 at 1:54pm
Squawling baby. Tried teether, no go. Diaper? Dry. Wanna be held? Na ah. ANDREW MCCARTHY MOVIE? INSTANT BLISS. Kid's got taste.

Friday, August 22, 2014 at 11:05am
My plan to introduce The Infant to Mel Brooks is taking an unexpected turn. She's goose-stepping in her froggy chair to The Producers and plotting her own Broadway debut.

Thursday, August 21, 2014 at 10:12am
Jan Becker played HIVES for 20 in Words With Friends.

Thursday, August 21, 2014 at 9:56am
This morning was phone calls to the landfill following my enlightening conversation with poison control last night. Poison control had a surprising amount of information on landfill gases ("Oh, hydrogen sulfide? That could kill you!"). I found out this morning that there is no monitor on my side of the mountain to detect dangerous gases, even though this is the way the wind blows during storms. That's changing today. They're putting one in right next to the building. I also tried to convince the landfill manager they should open the vents when they burn DEA seizures, but he thought I was kidding...

Thursday, August 21, 2014 at 8:54am
Jan Becker played DELVE for 60 in Words With Friends.

Thursday, August 21, 2014 at 1:24am EDT
The folks at the poison control hotline are very friendly to talk to if you ever accidentally overdose on an inhaled steroid. I've been assured I won't die from this either. Though I can expect some lovely tremors. #helluvaweekhere

Wednesday, August 20, 2014 at 6:49pm
Jan Becker feeling pumped.
Went to the doctor today for lingering breathing issues related to the landfill fart (hydrogen sulfide is made of people). She gave me steroids. Hehehe, I have a new appreciation for the Incredible Hulk...

Wednesday, August 20, 2014 at 12:33am
Sometimes Google is a curse. For example, tonight I learned Mt. Trashmore's farts are made of hydrogen sulfide, which may have been responsible for a mass extinction during the Triassic era. I don't need to know this. Not when I am heading to bed anyway.

Tuesday, August 19, 2014 at 10:01am
Observations on sitting with an infant: 1. Tummy time sucks. 2. Teething is a bitch. 3. Figuring out how to sleep can be a puzzling task. 4. Protest for a 4-month-old involves spitting up formula. 5. Half-digested formula smells worse than a landfill in Florida in August. #tiajuanablues

Monday, August 18, 2014 at 5:47pm
Jan Becker played PUTZ for 34 in Words With Friends.

Monday, August 18, 2014 at 5:46pm
Jan Becker played ZIT for 24 in Words With Friends.

Sunday, August 17, 2014 at 11:12pm
I am happy to report that the only substantial deviance from the norm I've noticed since the landfill farted is that I glow in the dark. But that's just a general abnormality, unrelated to the landfill.

Sunday, August 17, 2014 at 12:09pm
Something's up with mountain today (I live downwind from a landfill). The Chef seems fine, but The Feline and I are wheezy and red-eyed. It smells better (they bring out giant trucks that spray disinfectants to mask the odor--really, that sounds crazy, but it's true). I hear I am not being exposed to anything radioactive, but don't be shocked if I've sprouted gills and perform telekinetic parlor tricks the next time you see me.

Sunday, August 17, 2014 at 10:09am
If you haven't yet checked out Reading Queer, you should...

Sunday, August 17, 2014 at 7:54am
Jan Becker played RIPE for 23 in Words With Friends.

Saturday, August 16, 2014 at 11:04am
I want to replace the sign that management erected out back--the one
which reads, "NO BOATING NO SWIMMING NO FISHING." The
replacement would read: "NO GURU NO METHOD NO TEACHER."

Friday, August 15, 2014 at 11:24pm
The Chef is concerned rutabagas do not fulfill their maximum potential
via conventional preparation. I think of rutabagas quite often myself .

Thursday, August 14, 2014 at 3:07pm
The Feline would like me to find a solution to the violence of
thunderstorms. Poor kitty. Power's out too. Poor Jan.

Thursday, August 14, 2014 at 1:32pm
Silence is dangerous. I was built for cacophany.

Thursday, August 14, 2014 at 10:19am
Jan Becker played ABORT for 24 in Words With Friends.

Thursday, August 14, 2014 at 2:45am
What the heck is going on with Ferguson? They're arresting reporters?
The police are driving around in tactical armored gear? Jesus. Basta.

Wednesday, August 13, 2014 at 9:26pm
In other news, The Feline has a sudden fascination with Hooey the
Miracle Wonder Chair's power cord. The only cord in the place he thinks
is appetizing. I think it might have something to do with negative ions.

Wednesday, August 13, 2014 at 4:10pm
Jan Becker played DAB for 24 in Words With Friends.

Wednesday, August 13, 2014 at 2:17pm
I'm hesitant to post this for many reasons. It's a difficult article to read. It takes a compassionate view on treating pedophilia, and the anger that crops up around this issue is understandably justified, but often also prevents a compassionate reaction. However, I don't believe in treating pedophiles as monsters, for many reasons, but especially, because I think it gives them more power than they are entitled to, and robs the victim in a way. I don't see people as evil, but as very sick (in the pathological sense of the word). I've decided to go ahead (obviously) and post this, and here's why: If the man who sexually abused me had been able to get help, if he had not spent much of his life with a terrible secret--I might not have spent years working through the issues I was left with after surviving the abuse (still working), and for that reason, because it's a taboo that needs to be broken, I'm going to go ahead and post.

Tuesday, August 12, 2014 at 8:55pm
It is good sometimes to step away from everything and grab The Feline, and look at the great big moon winking back down at me (and then maybe whistle--you know how to whistle, don't you?).

Tuesday, August 12, 2014 at 12:30pm
Jan Becker played PIES for 21 in Words With Friends.

Monday, August 11, 2014 at 5:10pm
Jan Becker feeling loved.
The Chef is taking this menopause thing rather seriously. It's his day off and he's cooking--edamame. Because, "We really need to get some estrogen into you--RIGHT NOW!"

Monday, August 11, 2014 at 2:59pm
People in my building take the laundry room way too seriously.

Monday, August 11, 2014 at 11:24am
Jan Becker played SAVED for 29 in Words With Friends.

Monday, August 11, 2014 at 1:23am
Tonight my muse is whispering the most wonderful words in my ears:
"Go to sleep. You've had enough for today, Becker." And as usual, she's
correct. Zzzzz

Monday, August 11, 2014 at 12:13am
Jan Becker played ZEST for 24 in Words With Friends.

Saturday, August 9, 2014 at 8:17pm
Someone's teething. #HOLYMOTHEROFPISSEDOFFKID!

Saturday, August 9, 2014 at 10:58am EDT
Last night at 2AM my muse said, "You need to research the history of the
peninsula in Hawai'i you lived on when you were a kid." And like a fool,
I listened. I discovered some things. 1. The peninsula I lived on,
"Mokapu" (also the name of my school). means, "What lies here is sacred,
keep out." 2. It was the site of what would be the equivalent to the
Garden of Eden in the Judaic creation myth. The site where the god Kane
breathed life into the Hawai'ian first man. 3. I remembered seeing signs
when I was a kid that some of the places I played were sacred burial
grounds, and I was always very respectful of those places (and drawn to
them, yeah, they were quiet and good, contemplative places). But what I
didn't realize was that the military had set up a sand mining operation
on the base, and when they stored the sand in dunes for later use, they
weren't so careful about scattering the bones of the ancestors all over the
base, or re-burying them under tarmac for landing strips when they
brought in their backhoes and front loaders. All this makes me very sad.

Friday, August 8, 2014 at 8:52pm
I have a feeling I was on this guy's delivery route. He had letters with my
zip code on them. Even now, I have trouble getting my mail. Our carrier
will just not show up at all for days at a time--or show up, stop at the
office and skip past the bank of mailboxes downstairs.

Friday, August 8, 2014 at 12:40am
Dear Muse, Thank you for showing up at close to one in the morning, when I'm about to go to sleep. I'm planning to listen as you whisper in my ears, and I'll do the transcription you're demanding, but it would be nice if you didn't traipse in just as I'm about to go to bed in the future....

Thursday, August 7, 2014 at 8:23pm
Jan Becker played MUSE for 63 in Words With Friends.

Wednesday, August 6, 2014 at 9:44pm
Found out Grandma's menopause lasted ten years. I'm pulling out the vise grips and tackling the plumbing in an attempt to cope with this.

Tuesday, August 5, 2014 at 1:15pm
So, I went to the shrink this morning, the same doctor who told me Jesus cured his asthma on the radio and has conspiracy theories about Jeb Bush and Osama bin Laden. Today he was talking to me about menopause and Adam and Eve, and somehow the conversation shifted to the role of Muslim women in marriages. And there I was with this doctor, who should not be as ignorant as this doctor was, and I found myself saying, " That's a very narrow view of Islam you've got going there, Doc." And he was like, "No it's true. They stone their women. ALL THOSE WOMEN ARE OPPRESSED" So then, I found myself saying, "I was married to a Muslim man, and he never treated me poorly." I'd be pissed if I wasn't worried about other impressionable college students this doctor treats. He should know better. #iwasoneofTHOSEwomen

Tuesday, August 5, 2014 at 8:32am
Jan Becker played SHAMES for 22 in Words With Friends.

Monday, August 4, 2014 at 1:12pm
Jan Becker played DRIFTED for 24 in Words With Friends.

Monday, August 4, 2014 at 1:01pm
I know why Santa Claus lives at the North Pole. Mrs. Claus +
menopause.

Sunday, August 3, 2014 at 6:55pm
I may be moving into the beer cooler at Wegman's for the next five years.

Sunday, August 3, 2014 at 10:50am
Jan Becker played ZA for 45 in Words With Friends.

Sunday, August 3, 2014 at 10:44am
File this under "indelicate status updates/TMI": Apparently I have
reached THAT age--the "perimenopausal" age. And while I am not quite
ready for a croning ceremony just yet, I would totally dry hump an
iceberg for relief from a hot flash.

Sunday, August 3, 2014 at 10:35am
Jan Becker played OFFED for 28 in Words With Friends.

Sunday, August 3, 2014 at 10:27am
Jan Becker played ABIDE for 53 in Words With Friends.

Saturday, August 2, 2014 at 12:52am
I just realized it's August. NO PANTS TIL SEPTEMBER! (Subject to
renewal at end of term of agreement).

Friday, August 1, 2014 at 10:30am
This is a good (?) sign that today will be über-productive: Party boat is
out on the lake (has been for the past two hours), dragging water skiers
around. They're playing a marvelous soundtrack though--and loud
enough that all my "lady lumps" are reverberating....

Thursday, July 31, 2014 at 7:04am
Jan Becker played PUTTED for 20 in Words With Friends.

Tuesday, July 29, 2014 at 6:57pm
Above his love for canned food, catnip, being petted and phallic-shaped objects, The Feline appreciates being brushed. This too comes with its hazards. After an hour-long brushing session, I have learned The Feline has a tendency to shart on me. I think it's his way of telling me he loves me. I can think of preferable ways of conveying appreciation...

Tuesday, July 29, 2014 at 1:56pm
Jan Becker likes Gilligan's Island.

Tuesday, July 29, 2014 at 11:21am
Jan Becker played LIQUOR for 41 in Words With Friends.

Monday, July 28, 2014 at 5:16pm
I'm impressed. The mailman managed to cram Norman Mailer into my mailbox. All 1057 pages of him.

Sunday, July 27, 2014 at 2:10pm
Somehow, I managed to sleep until after 1PM. The Chef woke me up as he was leaving for work (I may have been sleep Facebooking earlier). Still no morning coffee in me. This is an ugly situation--or rather, now, I am an ugly situation.

Saturday, July 26, 2014 at 11:44am
The Feline is terrified of The Chef's big feet (size 13). Sometimes we catch him sitting in a corner, staring with great terror at The Chef's ankles. This morning, while giving The Feline his fish (which Romeo loves more than anything, even prodigious piles of catnip snipped fresh from the pots outside), The Chef decided to tap-dance in the kitchen (he's no Gregory Hines). This was two hours ago. The Feline has been MIA since.

Saturday, July 26, 2014 at 11:26am
Jan Becker played JETTY for 32 in Words With Friends.

Thursday, July 24, 2014 at 4:21pm
I'm disturbed at a trend I'm seeing among some good friends who equate support for the Palestinians with anti-Semitism. Palestinians are as Semitic as anyone living in area--and this is not just a Jewish vs. Muslim fight. Both countries have citizens of different faiths living within their borders. I'm praying for peace, not for Palestine, but for the whole world. What's good for Palestine is good for Israel also. That's how compassion works. Conversely, murdering another kills a part of the murderer.

Thursday, July 24, 2014 at 11:02am
This is a morning for getting funked up.

Wednesday, July 23, 2014 at 8:00pm
There is a disabled gecko in the bathroom. I suspect The Feline. It's missing two legs and a tail.

Wednesday, July 23, 2014 at 1:32pm
I am beginning to believe Max was being truthful when he said Hooey, My Miracle Wonder Chair would alter my body's chemistry. I've been a little light-headed all morning and breaking into sweats. It could be the onset of menopause, or I drank a gigantic cup of coffee in one gulp when I woke up, but if I can lay the blame on this chair, I'll stick with it. He said this thing throws off the same kind of energy one finds at waterfalls and the beach. I'm not feeling THAT quite yet, but I'll give it some time.

Tuesday, July 22, 2014 at 3:59pm
Jan Becker played SLAM for 24 in Words With Friends.

Tuesday, July 22, 2014 at 2:04pm
Finally, I am in my new desk chair! It came with an infrared heating thing that utilizes jade as the heat conductor. The guy who sold it claims I don't need to have heat on for the jade to fill me with negative ions and unicorn dust, and to counter EMFs in my toxic environment. He says I will need to drink water as I detox with the aid of the miraculous properties of new chair, which will heal all that ails me. Since the chair is

miraculous, it needs a name. I am dubbing it Hooey. Hooey, My Miracle Wonder Chair. I need another degree just to figure out how to adjust it.

Tuesday, July 22, 2014 at 9:27am
About The Feline: Despite his propensity to eat poems and crochet patterns, he does this thing that completely disarms me--The Feline greeting common to most cats where they rub their nose on your hand. No matter how bad he's been, when he does that, I have to forgive him, because it makes me feel like a princess who's getting a hand-kiss from Prince Charming. (Also, his name is Romeo, so it works).

Tuesday, July 22, 2014 at 8:27am
Jan Becker played BOGIE for 30 in Words With Friends.

Monday, July 21, 2014 at 11:25pm
Sometimes even The Chef gets surprised. Tonight, he was introduced to the roasted Brussels sprout. I thought everyone knew about those.

Monday, July 21, 2014 at 9:46pm
Jan Becker likes Broward College.

Monday, July 21, 2014 at 9:45pm
Jan Becker likes Seminole Hard Rock Hotel & Casino - Hollywood, FL.

Monday, July 21, 2014 at 12:13pm
It should not be this difficult to pick up an office chair. Tomorrow now. Sigh. #ican'tgetno

Monday, July 21, 2014 at 7:06am
Jan Becker played FUZED for 38 in Words With Friends.

Monday, July 21, 2014 at 6:59am
Only 3 1/2 hours til I pick up the new chair. I haven't been able to sleep all night. It's sort of like waiting for Christmas morning.

Sunday, July 20, 2014 at 6:26pm
After the hairball incident, The Feline ate my crochet patterns.

Sunday, July 20, 2014 at 1:30pm
Jan Becker played PLAQUES for 55 in Words With Friends.

Sunday, July 20, 2014 at 12:49pm
There are so many books to read and so little time. If I survive Moby
Dick, I plan to tackle at least one Mailer, but have no idea where to start.
Also, Capote. Tackling dead white men seems to be my latest diversion.

Saturday, July 19, 2014 at 5:35pm
Jan Becker likes Game of Thrones.

Saturday, July 19, 2014 at 12:21pm
Jan Becker played PIETY for 20 in Words With Friends.

Saturday, July 19, 2014 at 9:02am
SUCCESS! I have made an incident-free morning cup of java, from Java,
and am drinking it while checking emails. Life is good. Whatever
celestial boondoggle was plaguing me yesterday is lifted! And finally a
decent song trapped in my head!

Friday, July 18, 2014 at 7:35pm
Tonight's amazing kitchen disaster involved an exploding pie plate.
Thankfully, the apple, cherry, rhubarb pie had been removed and the
plate washed before I put it on the stovetop to dry while I heated water
for the coffee I so desperately need. I should have probably looked to see
which burner I turned on. Sigh.

Friday, July 18, 2014 at 3:25pm
Jan Becker played SEEDS for 23 in Words With Friends.

Friday, July 18, 2014 at 1:48pm
I believe The Feline is trying to tell me Timmy is trapped in the well again. He keeps finding me, where ever I go--last incident was in the lavatory, where I was trying to squeeze in a chapter of Moby Dick (on a side note, Pequod and Queequeg are the best words were ever written) -- and he bashes his head against my calf and mewls loudly, and then leads me to nowhere. It's all very confounding. I still haven't gotten a full cup o' joe in me. This morning it was cotton yarn from Turkey waiting to be signed at the door (how does yarn arrive from Turkey one day after the order goes in? Black Magic), The Chef asking for eggs for breakfast (he's a chef--this is very strange of him to request), then vitamins from USPS that needed a signature (bonus--the vitamin company sent an "OBESITY DAY" reusable shopping tote—let's say classy and fashionable?). I hate this morning, now almost 2PM. I'm hitting the reset button, right after I rescue Timmy. This is all to say, if I owe you email, please be patient....

Friday, July 18, 2014 at 12:29pm
I have issues with communicating prior to caffeine, please bear with me as I reach my optimum awake level.

Wednesday, July 16, 2014 at 10:37pm
Jan Becker played DEEJAY for 36 in Words With Friends.

Wednesday, July 16, 2014 at 7:50pm
As punishment for stealing my pens and tearing the liner off the box spring, The Feline is lounging in his handmade Italian wool cat bed after feasting on snow crab.

Wednesday, July 16, 2014 at 6:11pm
Jan Becker played ACID for 42 in Words With Friends.

Wednesday, July 16, 2014 at 9:39am
I'm a bit hung over from writing. Bear with me as I sort out my brains.

Wednesday, July 16, 2014 at 9:01am
Jan Becker played PAID for 61 in Words With Friends.

Tuesday, July 15, 2014 at 11:02pm
Jan Becker feeling crazy.
I managed to meet the deadline. As is oft the case, I'm now completely wired on the writing, higher than the moon on endorphins, and will annoy both The Chef and The Feline until dawn.

Tuesday, July 15, 2014 at 5:00pm
After consulting with my muse (this involves a half hour session of pressing my hand on his tummy while he purrs hard enough to make the room rumble), I've taken my shot of liquid iron <hiccup>, am brewing the Burundi Kirimiro microlot (I keep it in reserve for desperate situations), and opening the damn Word document.

Tuesday, July 15, 2014 at 12:40pm
Does this happen to anyone else? I have an 11:59 PM deadline for something I'm writing (it's self-imposed), and all I want to do is pull out my toenails. Or maybe give The Feline a bath (he has not had a full bath in at least 6 years), or, I could clean the grout in the bathroom with a toothbrush. Or, clean out the storage unit (which I've not been in in at least 2 years). Or, I could finally get started on reading Moby Dick. Or anything, except write this thing I'm working on....

Monday, July 14, 2014 at 7:37pm
Jan Becker played BLOC for 33 in Words With Friends.

Monday, July 14, 2014 at 5:01pm
Another reason working as a copywriter makes me happy: It's 5pm and I'm still in my sock monkey pajamas.

Monday, July 14, 2014 at 9:34am
Jan Becker played WHIFF for 36 in Words With Friends.

Monday, July 14, 2014 at 1:31am
Jan Becker likes The Working Poet Radio Show.

Sunday, July 13, 2014 at 9:40pm
This is the part of writing nonfiction that gives me the biggest issue. I
wish I could just tell the story and not reflect on it.

Sunday, July 13, 2014 at 9:25pm
The Feline believes I am equipped with a button, and if he bumps it with
his nose enough times, a treat will come out of me.

Sunday, July 13, 2014 at 2:00pm
Because we don't have nearly enough Walmarts and condos in Florida.

Friday, July 11, 2014 at 5:24pm
Jan Becker played JIVERS for 39 in Words With Friends.

Friday, July 11, 2014 at 4:48pm
Dear Wholly Unmerciful Hell that is South Florida on a sunny summer
day with no AC in the car, thank you for the ecstatic visions you
provided me during my bout of hallucinatory heat stroke. I can now
cross sweat lodge, vision-quest, and peyote ritual off my list of things to
do before I die. Seems I covered (or approximated) all three today.

Friday, July 11, 2014 at 12:32pm
The Chef is weeping in the living room. Lebron James has broken his
heart. Sigh.

Friday, July 11, 2014 at 10:01am
If not for the patience requirement, I'd likely be a virtuous woman...No...
I wouldn't be virtuous then either.

Friday, July 11, 2014 at 2:42am
The Feline just filched a honey/peanut and Greek Yogurt South Beach
Diet protein bar. Weird.

Thursday, July 10, 2014 at 5:03pm
Jan Becker played KEG for 35 in Words With Friends.

Thursday, July 10, 2014 at 3:57pm
Thank you, Universal Material Continuum for delivering! I'll be picking up, but that's fine with me. Here's the chair I went with.

Thursday, July 10, 2014 at 10:23am
I have a tentative response from the universe regarding an office chair. Will know more in a couple of days.

Wednesday, July 9, 2014 at 7:25pm
Dear Universal Material Continuum, New chair or not, I shall still write like a motherfucker. Just easier if I wasn't seated on the Iron Throne.

Wednesday, July 9, 2014 at 2:10pm
Consider this status update a call to the universal material continuum: Jan Becker needs a good sturdy desk chair with decent support for very little money. I know I find excuses not to write all the time. If you hook me up, Universe, I will write like a motherfucker.

Monday, July 7, 2014 at 10:57pm
The Chef is disgusted by my selection of horseradish hummus, but satisfied with the Ethiopian shade grown organic coffee. I read the ingredient list for this "speculoos cookie butter" stuff I've heard so much about. Here's my take: It's probably not a good idea to eat anything that sounds like it's involved in pelvic exams or PAP smears.

Monday, July 7, 2014 at 10:31am
It should be illegal to be as excited about going to Trader Joe's as The Chef is now. After the coffee, I'm all for exuberance, but not just yet.

Sunday, July 6, 2014 at 6:00pm
I have discovered the joy of shooting pits with the cherry pitter. My life
will never be the same.

Sunday, July 6, 2014 at 4:19pm
Jan Becker shared Dalai Lama's photo.

Sunday, July 6, 2014 at 3:18pm
Jan Becker played URBAN for 20 in Words With Friends.

Sunday, July 6, 2014 at 3:03pm
Jan Becker feeling like Rodney Dangerfield.
I like owning a very old car (2000 Toyota), because I don't have to worry
about a high insurance bill or that every little dent and ding is going to
devalue it. However, after discovering the rather large scrape on my rear
bumper just now, I'm finding myself quite irked that no one left a note.
I'd have just told the other car owner to forget about it, but I'd at least
like the courtesy. This irkedness (is that even a word?) is similar to the
time I parked next to a truck and left plenty of room, and the driver
REPEATEDLY flung her door open wide and dented my passenger side,
then walked off without even acknowledging it. My car may be an old
clunker, but dammit, it's my old clunker. I'd hope for a little respect.

Sunday, July 6, 2014 at 10:37am
Good Morning, Mother Nature! There's an impressive storm outside.
The Feline is hiding somewhere. I am reminded of how my Mom used to
wake me for school. That was a bit like a large thunderclap too.

Saturday, July 5, 2014 at 8:46pm
Jan Becker played BLIP for 48 in Words With Friends.

Friday, July 4, 2014 at 5:18pm
I hope they canonized the person who discovered epsom salts.

Friday, July 4, 2014 at 2:50am
The crochet related injury is rather severe; I'm going to sleep for a coupla days. Ouch.

Thursday, July 3, 2014 at 12:34pm
Two things: 1. The Feline does not approve of laundry day (neither do I). 2. Creepy Maintenance Man has the rare ability to speak loudly without ever opening his yap. An example: I ran into him in the hall just a few minutes ago. I was carrying a basket filled with four loads of laundry. (Today he is wearing a reggae colored doo rag.) He didn't say a word. Not even his usual grunt of hello. He just looked at me. But the look he gave me said, "You dirty, dirty girl." #Creepy.

Thursday, July 3, 2014 at 11:16am
Jan Becker played VIEWER for 25 in Words With Friends.

Wednesday, July 2, 2014 at 6:53pm
Jan Becker played LOONS for 37 in Words With Friends.

Wednesday, July 2, 2014 at 12:59pm
Yesterday, The Chef and I went out for dinner in Fort Lauderdale, and I haven't been able to stop thinking about the "WE BUY GOLD" sign holder since. This was no ordinary sign holder. He was wearing a gold lamé belly shirt, and black satin hot pants, and he didn't stand there holding his WE BUY GOLD sign. He PRANCED. He sashayed and twerked. He dropped it like it was hot (And lord, was it hot!). He clenched a bouquet of gold silk roses between his teeth, and astonished me with unfettered exuberance. I have no gold to sell him, but that sign holder on the Corner of Oakland Park Blvd made my whole evening.

Monday, June 30, 2014 at 5:47pm
I misplaced my blog! Also, I broke the alphabet, and discovered there is such a thing as fermented cod liver oil. Today is weird.

Monday, June 30, 2014 at 7:07am
I woke from an intense nightmare, went through my coffee routine, sat down at the computer, and wanted to price kimchi crocks. I typed "fermentation c..." and "fermented cod liver oil" popped up. Suddenly, that nightmare I had has lost all its power.

Sunday, June 29, 2014 at 2:14pm
The neighbor with the conspiracy theories is packing up to move. In other news, I am wondering how dangerous it is to ferment cabbage in my kitchen (kimchi).

Sunday, June 29, 2014 at 7:13am
Jan Becker played HUMID for 24 in Words With Friends..

Saturday, June 28, 2014 at 9:20am
Jan Becker played POO for 21 in Words With Friends.

Friday, June 27, 2014 at 1:38pm
Just when I thought it was safe to go outside...I haven't seen Creepy Maintenance Man in a couple of months. He caught me today in the elevator. He was wearing a black dew rag with electric blue skulls on it. "Hey," I said, "I haven't seen you in a long time." "I've seen a lot of you," he answered. #Creepy.

Friday, June 27, 2014 at 5:37am
Jan Becker played JESTER for 28 in Words With Friends.

Tuesday, June 24, 2014 at 5:03pm
In honor of St. Jean-Baptiste Day, I feel like I should be wearing a hair shirt, eating grasshoppers and dunking folks in the lake out back.

Tuesday, June 24, 2014 at 4:37pm
Jan Becker played KIND for 30 in Words With Friends.

Tuesday, June 24, 2014 at 12:19pm
Jan Becker likes Peter Dinklage.

Monday, June 23, 2014 at 11:22pm
I learned tonight that it is also possible to do an inordinate amount of damage to oneself with a crochet hook.

Monday, June 23, 2014 at 1:58am
Conversation with The Chef:

> Chef: Have you ever eaten pickled pigs feet?
> Me (look down, flick a dustball off my leg) Why? Have you?
> Chef: Eww. No, I tried once when I was eleven, it was too disgusting. Tell me though, have you?
> Me: Why, yes, when I was young I did.
> Chef (look of absolute horror on his face): Why?
> Me: Because I grew up with Marines.
> Chef (horror still on his face, coupled now with confusion): Why would Marines eat pickled pigs feet?
> Me: Duh. Because pigs feet are disgusting.

Sunday, June 22, 2014 at 2:55pm
Suicidal jet skier redux out on the lake today. Yesterday, we got nailed with a gigantic cluster eff of a storm that flooded out my road, and tore up a bunch of the trees. Leaves everywhere. The jet skis continued through the lightning and thunder. Today so far, no storms, but clouds are building. Funny how every fall, I begin to forget how violent the weather down here can become, but then summer hits with thunder like bomb blasts. I just wish these people wouldn't drag their kids around on rubber tubes through the storms.

Sunday, June 22, 2014 at 1:25pm
Jan Becker played TOXIC for 30 in Words With Friends.

Saturday, June 21, 2014 at 9:59am
Jan Becker played PIXIES for 27 in Words With Friends.

Saturday, June 21, 2014 at 8:28am
Happy Solstice!

Wednesday, June 18, 2014 at 10:55am
I guess there's more than one way to skin a football team.

Tuesday, June 17, 2014 at 11:51pm
Today seems to be a day of twos. Two more things before midnight: 1. It is possible to do an inordinate amount of damage with a pair of tweezers and four broken watches. 2. Baby kale and escarole with black-eyed peas make me forget why I thought I needed a watch to begin with.

Tuesday, June 17, 2014 at 4:50pm
This might explain why I feel such a strong sense of kinship to manatees.

Tuesday, June 17, 2014 at 1:18pm
Jan Becker played BOVINE for 52 in Words With Friends.

Tuesday, June 17, 2014 at 1:04pm
Two things I learned this morning: 1. It is possible to do an inordinate amount of damage with a pumice stone. 2. If I ask very nicely, occasionally The Chef will agree to cook me dinner. This sort of makes #1 much less painful.

Monday, June 16, 2014 at 3:24pm
Jan Becker played PRIED for 26 in Words With Friends.

Monday, June 16, 2014 at 3:01pm
The Chef is not entirely convinced that I can find a practical use for the bastard sword I told him I would like to purchase.

Sunday, June 15, 2014 at 2:48pm
It is World Cup time. The Brazilian market up the street is completely sold out of beer, and the port selection is looking mighty meager.

Sunday, June 15, 2014 at 10:30am
Jan Becker played DEUCE for 20 in Words With Friends.

Saturday, June 14, 2014 at 2:14pm
So far today, I've consumed about a gallon of coffee, 3000% the daily recommended allowance of B vitamins, iron, drank a big nasty protein shake, and all I want to do is climb back in bed and go to sleep.

Friday, June 13, 2014 at 6:16pm
Bad Idea = Jan Becker + 1 leaky faucet + 1 roll of plumber's tape + 1 pair of vise grips - any plumberly knowledge.

Friday, June 13, 2014 at 11:57am
Jan Becker played SEXY for 26 in Words With Friends.

Friday, June 13, 2014 at 11:14am
Phone's out. Internet's spotty. Happy solar-flares-during-a-supermoon-mercury-retrograde-Friday-the-13th! Also, can someone explain why there's a guy out on Crystal Lake rowing around in a hockey mask???

Thursday, June 12, 2014 at 11:29pm
Jan Becker shared Orion Magazine's photo.
I have a feeling that between the giant full moon, solar flares and Friday the 13th, things are going to get a little freaky here on Crystal Lake.

Thursday, June 12, 2014 at 6:14pm
Guess who has jury duty on Monday.

Wednesday, June 11, 2014 at 9:13am
Jan Becker played VAIN for 28 in Words With Friends.

Tuesday, June 10, 2014 at 2:03pm
The Feline and I are in the midst of an estrangement. This happens every time I shower. He crawls under the bed and refuses to come back out for hours. It's a little lonely without him. Thankfully, I don't shower often enough for it to put a serious strain on our relationship.

Monday, June 9, 2014 at 11:23pm
So, I was randomly browsing a FAQ on US copyright laws and came upon this page. Everything's going well, the questions and answers are all informative/helpful and I run into Question#10: HOW DO I PROTECT MY SIGHTING OF ELVIS? Our government gave an answer!

Monday, June 9, 2014 at 7:54pm
Seems like the whole day I couldn't tell whether the sky was black with clouds or swampfire.

Monday, June 9, 2014 at 11:21am
The stars are testing me with odd confluence of NBA finals and World Cup. On one side, there is The Chef, rabid in his admiration for The Miami Heat-- on the other, the entire neighborhood of Brazilians I live in. I think I'll be listening to a lot of Gloria Gaynor the next few weeks.

Monday, June 9, 2014 at 4:02am
Jan Becker played ZITI for 46 in Words With Friends.

Monday, June 9, 2014 at 3:29am
Jan Becker played SATIRE for 31 in Words With Friends.

Sunday, June 8, 2014 at 8:45pm
In a previous life, I crocheted hemp bikinis and sold them at harvest festivals and Woodstock reunions and such.

Sunday, June 8, 2014 at 3:14am
I should not Google things in my neighborhood that pique my curiosity at 3am if I want to get any sleep at all. The search results too often lean toward the disturbing. #norestforthewicked

Friday, June 6, 2014 at 10:19pm
I made a pot of beans today bigger than the average 4-year old. It's part of my writing ritual, and I'm about to go deep into revisions. I asked The Chef to taste it, and he asked for a full-sized portion. That was a good sign, but then he complimented my mirepoix. He said I executed excellent knife work. Booyah! Incidentally, along with being a handy expression of joy, 'booyah' is a Midwestern-American/Belgian stew.

Friday, June 6, 2014 at 5:31pm
I feel for The Feline. It's afternoon. The sun is out. The air conditioner has him fooled into thinking it's a lovely spring day. He just wants to bask in a sunbeam on the balcony. He can see butterflies and whatnot through the glass. I'd let him out, but he'd melt.

Thursday, June 5, 2014 at 6:30pm
I've begun to receive robo-calls from a voice asking me to hold the line so an operator can speak to me about my troubling menopausal symptoms. I prefer this to the voice who asks me to hold for the operator who wishes to discuss my prostate issues.

Thursday, June 5, 2014 at 10:25am
Jan Becker played BONG for 20 in Words With Friends.

Wednesday, June 4, 2014 at 6:51am
I was held in contempt in all my dreams last night. Off to court.

Tuesday, June 3, 2014 at 8:23pm
Two things: 1. I am now insisting that The Chef call me "Madam Forewoman." 2. We were stopped in the hallway by a neighbor who has

a conspiracy theory related to the number of moving vans on the premises this past weekend (there were 7 outgoing).

Tuesday, June 3, 2014 at 1:23pm
The Chef claims I will be a lousy juror. He says anyone who says they "joyfully anticipate fulfilling their civic duty" has something seriously wrong with them (18 hours til I report! I remain joyful).

Monday, June 2, 2014 at 8:47pm
Jan Becker played DUCATS for 48 in Words With Friends.

Monday, June 2, 2014 at 8:39pm
I'd like to thank my genius blunt-smoking neighbors for contact high I got from riding elevator, but it occurs to me there are kids in the building and so, alas, it's probably not wise for them to hot-box the elevator.

Sunday, June 1, 2014 at 1:24pm
Jan Becker played GOTHIC for 26 in Words With Friends.

Thursday, May 29, 2014 at 9:51pm
Scripps spelling bee is more entertaining than the NBA division finals.

Thursday, May 29, 2014 at 3:13pm
Jan Becker played HUNG for 38 in Words With Friends.

Thursday, May 29, 2014 at 10:03am
Ugh, pollen counts.

Thursday, May 29, 2014 at 1:11am
Jan Becker played DUSTED for 47 in Words With Friends.

Wednesday, May 28, 2014 at 6:46pm
Fabienne Sylvia Merritt, is a super-brain. About two summers ago, I waged an all-out war with ghost ants, who were swarming The Feline's dinner dishes. She suggested I put his food dishes in bowls filled with

water, because ants can't swim, and would drown trying to get to his food. That worked for two years, but I'm sad to report, the ants have learned how to swim, and it looks like I'll be going back to war. #FelineChronicles

Wednesday, May 28, 2014 at 1:48pm
Jan Becker played HEX for 24 in Words With Friends.

Wednesday, May 28, 2014 at 11:25am
I feel like I've lost another mother. Thank you, Maya. You helped a whole flock of birds find the way out of our cages. <3

Wednesday, May 28, 2014 at 12:20am
Conversation with The Chef:
> Chef: What were you doing up at 3am?
> Me: I was looking at blueprints of the Starship Enterprise.
> Chef: Which one?
> Me: All of them, and Klingon Bird of Prey
> Chef: Klingon Battle Cruiser too? Any others?
> Me: The Millenium Falcon
> Chef: (throws head back) Oh! Hahaha! The Millenium Falcon? HAHAHA! That's not real!

Tuesday, May 27, 2014 at 12:15pm
I rarely ever sleep a full eight hours. I did last night, woke up around quarter to noon. Here's what I don't get: Why is it that on those rare occasions that the Sandman blesses me, do I wake up feeling like a giant chew toy that just spent 8 hours in the mouth of a teething leviathan?

Monday, May 26, 2014 at 4:25pm
Jan Becker played SEXIST for 22 in Words With Friends.

Sunday, May 25, 2014 at 3:09pm
I give up. In addition to the mockingbirds, I've been trying to work over the din of motorboats towing terrified and shrieking children, reggae-

samba competing with bad country music (as opposed to good country music), barking dogs (NO DOGS ALLOWED), and a crowd of very loud picnickers. Even the iguanas are out there sounding barbaric yawps. I'm going to go mop the damn floor.

Saturday, May 24, 2014 at 9:18pm
So, the internet is back. In other news, one of the reasons the manager of the building gave for keeping the windows closed is that we'd avoid bugs if we were all sealed up tight. Now that we've battened our windows, an army of ants is colonizing the kitchen. Sigh.

Saturday, May 24, 2014 at 9:45am
(After Yeats, but before coffee) An aged Jan is but a paltry thing, a tattered coat upon a stick...

Friday, May 23, 2014 at 4:25pm
Observations on running errands in a hot car in South Florida: 1. I am much tougher than I thought. 2. The most magnificent being in all of Creation is the giant live oak in the Publix parking lot. 3. On the highway in a traffic jam, an 18-wheeler throws a lot of shade. Use it. 4. There is a special place in hell for anyone who leaves their pet in a car here. 5. Maybe it's time to get that estimate I've been avoiding.

Friday, May 23, 2014 at 1:28pm
In preparation for the errands I need to run today (in the car with no AC), I stepped outside to see how hot it is. Yikes!

Thursday, May 22, 2014 at 8:35pm
They're blocking Mos Def from entering the US? What the hell?

Thursday, May 22, 2014 at 4:35pm
Ok, a move may be in order. I just received an email with a lease addendum that says we must keep the windows closed "at all times." I don't think I can live in a closed-up box all year-round. Summer maybe, but all year? Sheesh.

Thursday, May 22, 2014 at 8:34am
Right now, The Feline is being mocked by the bird. I'm halfway into my first cup of coffee, and just remembered that last night, as I was getting ready for sleep, above the mockingbird, I heard the oompah, the guitar, and the accordion. Seems the mariachis ARE still around, though I'm not sure why they choose to practice at 1am.

Wednesday, May 21, 2014 at 8:11pm
I should have stayed in pajamas all day. (Why can't we live in our pjs?)

Wednesday, May 21, 2014 at 5:27pm
Why is it that now that I've sworn off pants til August, I find myself changing my outfit four times a day? #nopantstilaugust

Wednesday, May 21, 2014 at 10:25am
Off to Miami. Let's hope I don't roast somewhere along the way. #hellisnoacinSoFL

Wednesday, May 21, 2014 at 2:55am
I miss mushroom hunting.

Tuesday, May 20, 2014 at 9:01pm
All it really takes to make my day turn wonderful is a pair of new pajamas--even if they don't have sock monkeys all over them.

Monday, May 19, 2014 at 9:50am
Conversation with The Chef on the balcony last night: (clear night, light breeze, a large object flies over the lake)
> Chef: Look! It's the Starship Enterprise!
> Me: Mmm-hmm (no moon yet, low light pollution, we see a shooting star)
> Chef: Oh no! They're firing on them.
(He also sees the Enterprise when he looks at Marlins stadium. Anything big and shiny = The Starship Enterprise)

Sunday, May 18, 2014 at 4:25pm
Gorillaz on the hifi. Toasting nuts in the oven. Chutney on the cooktop.

Saturday, May 17, 2014 at 6:11pm
My moment of Schadenfreude for the day: Finding a copy error in a New York Times Book Review.

Saturday, May 17, 2014 at 2:32pm
From an email the building manager sent me regarding new parking regulations and copies of documents she requested I send her: "We are doing this tedious requirement to detect secret unauthorized residents and stop residents to turning our lot in a car dealership." (I'm not making fun of her English; there are other things more worthwhile to mock here). What this means: 1. We are no longer allowed to have guests who stay for five weeks at the crunch time of spring semester (plus!) 2. We are no longer allowed to have a 'for sale' sign on our cars (okay, free speech guarantees don't apply here. We're already not allowed to hold conversations by the mailbox--seriously). 3. 'Secret unauthorized residents,' I'm intrigued. 4. You may be able to get a deal on a used car in my parking lot if you act quickly. I am guessing there will be a going out of business sale.

Saturday, May 17, 2014 at 1:32pm
Jan Becker played FLUID for 33 in Words With Friends.

Friday, May 16, 2014 at 7:52pm
I will never wholly miss The Winemaker. There's no need. He migrated North the beginning of March, and today, in the middle of May, the vacuum is still picking up sand in the rug. Or perhaps, it's Winemaker Pixie Dust. #winemakerchronicles

Thursday, May 15, 2014 at 10:09am
Again, in answer to the Facebook prompt, "what's on your mind? I love my cat. That's all I've got this morning. I adore him. He's a good boy. He never gives me much grief (even when he eats my poems--he's right, that poem was too abstract, and the other? It was gushing with sentimentality). He sits in his own chair next to me as I type. When he thinks I've been at it too long, he'll reach out his little paw, and tap me on the shoulder. He's got a catnip problem, but he's not driving, and he doesn't have to go to work, so I don't think the addiction is an issue. So, Facebook, that's what's on my mind. I love The Feline. I wish you'd ask different questions.

Thursday, May 15, 2014 at 10:01am
Jan Becker played ZEN for 23 in Words With Friends.

Wednesday, May 14, 2014 at 3:05pm
Ok, now mail woman is just rude. She stopped by, picked up mail from the office, and then left without delivering anything to anyone. Sigh.

Wednesday, May 14, 2014 at 8:05am
Answers to the Facebook prompt, "What's on your mind?" 1. Geckos should know better than to enter the home of 'The Mighty Hunter' (The Feline) as it will not be a pleasant experience for them--or me. 2. What book should I take in for jury selection? Soul on Ice? Steal This Book? Papillon? American Psycho? (It's only three weeks away; decisions must be made) 3. When Ann Coulter, Rush Limbaugh and Pat Robinson look in the mirror, is the image greeting them as grotesque as what I see when I look at them? Also, were they breast fed by succubi? 4. What do those Nigerian schoolgirls dream about, if they get any sleep at all?

Tuesday, May 13, 2014 at 4:09pm
Other things that arrived in the mail while I'm waiting for something important: 1.A fundraising packet for Marco Rubio (BWA-HA-HAHAHA! As if I'd ever...how the hell did I get on that mailing list?) 2. A sales flyer for the local Brazilian meat market (Picanha is on sale) 3. A

summons for jury duty (I'm actually excited about this. I've been waiting years to fulfill my civic duty.)

Tuesday, May 13, 2014 at 12:58pm
Jan Becker played QUOTAS for 34 in Words With Friends.

Tuesday, May 13, 2014 at 9:41am
My Grandma Becker used to say I was clumsy as a cow with four left feet. It sounds mean, but she was right. Somehow, I twisted my ankle in my sleep. That's pretty clumsy.

Monday, May 12, 2014 at 3:27pm
It seems that whenever I'm waiting for something important to come in the mail, all I get are offers for funeral home services and coupons for Depends bed and chair pads. But hey, $2 off!

Monday, May 12, 2014 at 12:39pm
Jan Becker played ANUS for 25 in Words With Friends.

Sunday, May 11, 2014 at 8:13am
My thoughts on reading this: 1. Whoa. One can get high on embalming fluid? Gross/ cool/ creepy 2. How did this happen outside of Florida?

Sunday, May 11, 2014 at 7:42am
Happy Mother's Day! I decided when I was very young that I would never be a mother. The job's too tough, and I'm way too self-centered. Yes, the job is tough, and the pay is literally crap sometimes, but it's important, so thank you.

Saturday, May 10, 2014 at 3:37pm
I think I-95 S had a record-breaking day in cars totaled, also, 441 N, I-95 S. Everywhere, accidents. The good news is that because I spent so much time in traffic with my arm hanging out the window, I can no longer tell

where the bug bites end and my sunburn begins. (that's a blister on my blister, I am NOT happy to see you)

Saturday, May 10, 2014 at 7:07am
What no one has said ever: You look mighty fine in ointment. #biteme

Saturday, May 10, 2014 at 5:57am
I'm blaming this noseeum thing on The Feline, who has developed the skill to open the door to the balcony, which I found wide open this morning when I got up to make coffee. I am considering putting him in a straitjacket before bed each night to see just how talented my little Houdini-like escape artist is. #IloveyouSnugglebearsosorryImalignedyou

Friday, May 9, 2014 at 7:31pm
Note to Self: While investigating the cause of your itch, do not under any circumstances do a Google image search for noseeum bites.

Friday, May 9, 2014 at 4:31pm
Jan Becker feeling itchy.
Ok, so scapegoating the Snuggle Bear was a bit premature. I'm just allergic to everything.

Thursday, May 8, 2014 at 6:09am
First thought on waking this morning (second time waking this morning): Freelance has lance at its root, like the long pole weapon, a spear for a mounted warrior + free. So, to be a freelancer is sort of like being a sword for hire. Only, the pen is so much mightier.

Thursday, May 8, 2014 at 2:28am
So much better after a few Zzzzs. But now it's 2:30AM and I'm wide awake. It's just nice to not be so itchy.

Wednesday, May 7, 2014 at 5:15am
I don't think it's the world to which I'm allergic after all, but the Snuggle fabric softener. Eventually, this will make me happy. Right now, I just

wish I'd figured that out before I did all the laundry and missed a whole night's sleep scratching myself up. #damnyouSnugglebeardamnyou

Tuesday, May 6, 2014 at 2:02pm
It occurred to me today on my way to Miami in a car with no air conditioning, that it may never be necessary to wear pants again--at least if I'm in South Florida. #nopantstilAugust

Monday, May 5, 2014 at 1:18pm
Jan Becker feeling itchy.
I am allergic to the world.

Sunday, May 4, 2014 at 10:37pm
Two thoughts: 1. If there is poi for me anywhere in South Florida it will be here. 2. I checked out the lineup and "Special guests King Kukulele and Marina the Fire Eating Mermaid will also perform." Holy mother of god, I think I must go.

Sunday, May 4, 2014 at 3:30pm
Off on a hippie hike. Just to the Brazilian market, but there are some interesting developments in the jungle I mean to investigate by hoof.

Saturday, May 3, 2014 at 7:31pm
It occurred to me, while I was walking to the trash chute in my sock monkey nightgown and housecoat, that this hiatus I am taking from pants is also a prime opportunity to seriously rock the Mrs. Roper look. #nopantstilAugust

Saturday, May 3, 2014 at 12:00pm
Despite his foibles, I am consistent in my adoration of The Feline, even if he eats my poems and leaves mutilated gecko corpses on the balcony.

Friday, May 2, 2014 at 11:06pm
The brood of iguana appears to have vacated my sinuses. The Chef came home to a cold bottle of Rogue's Special Creamery 8th Anniversary Ale. He was expecting grapefruit juice.

Friday, May 2, 2014 at 11:31am
It feels like a brood of iguanas is squatting in my sinuses.

Friday, May 2, 2014 at 12:18am
Yay! More rejections!

Thursday, May 1, 2014 at 1:07am
Oh, no. I've made it to THAT wedding episode in Game of Thrones everyone was freaking out about last year. Good god, that's a bit bloody, isn't it?

Wednesday, April 30, 2014 at 4:07am
I think I just woke up the whole building with my whoop of delight! Grades are finally in! WHOOP! NO PANTS TIL AUGUST!

Tuesday, April 29, 2014 at 12:11pm
The Chef's drama with the Hialeah heist continues, and I have a migraine and grading to finish today. It is not easy under these conditions. When The Chef becomes agitated he turns into a combination of Tony Bourdain and Gordon Ramsay at their most vituperative. I hope they fix this soon at the bank. I much prefer his normal state, which is pleasant, like living with Two Fat Ladies.

Monday, April 28, 2014 at 8:01pm
Gah. I have reached my limit of grading for the day. OR, I have suffered long enough today wondering what is about to happen in the land of 7 kingdoms.

Monday, April 28, 2014 at 4:41pm
I just got "dorm" as a verb. Students who dorm...Another thing I am taking personally, but should not.

Monday, April 28, 2014 at 2:45pm
GASP! I will not take it personally that my student chose to use Comic Sans on a targeted resume. (Ok, so that was a lie. I am taking this very personally!)

Sunday, April 27, 2014 at 11:48pm
Binge-watching Game of Thrones will not make me a better person.

Sunday, April 27, 2014 at 12:06pm
The Chef breaks laptops often.

Saturday, April 26, 2014 at 12:46pm
In South Florida, there is a low threshold for what a thief deems worthy of stealing. I went downstairs just now and my car was broken into sometime last night. A cursory glance shows they grabbed my GPS. BUT JEEBUS I DON'T EVEN HAVE AIR CONDITIONING IN MY CAR! Aren't there Rolls Royces around that would look a little more tempting? #jackasscarcrooks

Saturday, April 26, 2014 at 8:56am
Jan Becker played TREASON for 44 in Words With Friends.

Saturday, April 26, 2014 at 8:53am
Jan Becker played YUCK for 60 in Words With Friends.

Friday, April 25, 2014 at 11:04pm
Jan Becker feeling sick.
The Chef asked me to do his laundry today (he is very good about doing his own). I noticed there was a towel that smelled about as foul coming out of the dryer as it did going into the wash. I mentioned this to The

Chef tonight when he squealed with delight that I'd folded his clothes (he is not so good at folding). Here's the weird part (there is always a weird part with me), the wretched towel whose stench cannot be removed is the one The Winemaker used. It's been nearly a month since he left us. It's been washed four times, and still, The Winemaker lingers. #winemakerchronicles

Friday, April 25, 2014 at 2:18am
Oh, good gravy, Along with my recent discovery of Pinterest, the universe has directed me to three-plus seasons of Game of Thrones that are demanding I watch them. I'm sensing an impending quagmire of distraction. #damnthedevilboxes

Tuesday, April 22, 2014 at 11:04am
Happy Mother (Earth) Day!

Monday, April 21, 2014 at 10:28pm
This may be inappropriate to admit, but I kind of enjoy the delirium of a spiking fever.

Monday, April 21, 2014 at 1:44pm
Ugh. It's not even flu season. Avoid Jan Becker if at all possible. She is virulent.

Saturday, April 19, 2014 at 6:49pm
I was not supposed to barbecue myself (I'm okay).

Friday, April 18, 2014 at 4:03pm
One of the pitfalls of being a copyeditor: Random telephone consultations from friends newly off their "Lenten Wagon" seeking advice on drunken correspondence. My advice: Save a draft. Look at it in the morning.

Thursday, April 17, 2014 at 11:15am
Creepy Maintenance Man and Creepy Exterminator Guy have left. They were joined by the building manager who has ordered us to close all our windows and turn on the air conditioner. I don't think her order is enforceable, nor do I believe her when she says it is the solution to insects in South Florida. Besides, I like a breeze, even a swamp breeze.

Thursday, April 17, 2014 at 10:15am
Jan Becker played SHEETS for 49 in Words With Friends.

Thursday, April 17, 2014 at 7:49am
What I am looking forward to today: A visit from Creepy Maintenance Man and Creepy Exterminator Guy. If I've never mentioned Creepy Exterminator Guy, it's because we only see him once a year during the "Annual Pest Control Visit." An Annual visit for bugs in South Florida is one of the funniest things I've ever heard, as it is pathetically inadequate. And Creepy Exterminator Guy is always in and out very quickly, but I don't like the look he gives The Feline. It's sort of the same look The Feline gives to rodents.

Tuesday, April 15, 2014 at 10:57pm
Jan Becker likes Cabin Porn.

Tuesday, April 15, 2014 at 9:07pm
Undergraduate logic is sometimes puzzling. I thought the lesson on logical fallacies would help, but with (some) undergrads, everything is a non-sequitur.

Monday, April 14, 2014 at 2:39pm
Jan Becker likes Florida International University.

Monday, April 14, 2014 at 1:57pm
GAH! I can't adequately express how momentous it feels to sign and deliver my first professional copywriting contract! I'm about to explode

from happiness! (You have been warned. It may be wise to keep some distance from me, lest I blow up and spew joy all over you!)

Sunday, April 13, 2014 at 2:36pm
Jan Becker feeling queasy.
In other news, I had a good time at the Lip Service: True Stories Out Loud show in Fort Lauderdale last night. However, Jack Daniels and I have had a serious falling out.

Sunday, April 13, 2014 at 10:54am
The Chef got hijacked by some credit card fraudsters in Hialeah. Ay dios mio.

Sunday, April 13, 2014 at 12:22am
Here, on Crystal Lake, there are rules regarding conversation 'on' the hallways.

Saturday, April 12, 2014 at 6:50pm
Random narcissistic habit I've opted to adopt: Any song with the word "man" in its title, I'm changing to "Jan." For example, "I am a Jan of Constant Sorrow" or "Rocket Jan." This is what occupies my cerebral space.

Friday, April 11, 2014 at 12:59pm
Jan Becker played RISKY for 22 in Words With Friends.

Friday, April 11, 2014 at 10:06am
There should be a rule about Creepy Maintenance Man arriving before the coffee is brewed.

Thursday, April 10, 2014 at 10:27am
The poor Feline is besieged by the battle cries of scrub jays every time he tries to nap on the balcony. There is no peace on the lake this morning. Even the ospreys are on patrol.

Wednesday, April 9, 2014 at 8:42am
I had absolutely no desire to fish, swim or boat on the lake until that
damn sign went up. Now, all I want to do is jump in the lake with a
fishing pole and push a boat around while doing the backstroke. Sigh.

Tuesday, April 8, 2014 at 11:46pm
There's a new development out on the lake. Someone has posted a sign
that says, "No Fishing. No Boating. No Swimming." So far, it does not
appear that anyone has read the sign; it's still as full of boats and
swimmers and anglers as ever. Signs, signs, everywhere signs.

Tuesday, April 8, 2014 at 12:45pm
In my opinion, the word "ogle" is utilized far too infrequently.

Monday, April 7, 2014 at 11:57pm
Jan Becker played QUEER for 26 in Words With Friends.

Monday, April 7, 2014 at 10:00pm
Jeeze, I've believed in fairies for years.

Monday, April 7, 2014 at 8:51pm
While we are on the subject of parties, I came home from work, to find
"The Island Man" here. The Island Man is a very loud friend of The
Chef's. We seldom see him (there is probably a reason for this...) I called
to The Feline earlier to let him outside, "Romeo, Romeo..." and The
Island Man stretched out his arms to embrace me, puckered his lips,
blew me a kiss and hollered out, "I'm right here, Baby!"
#Islandmanchronicles

Monday, April 7, 2014 at 12:31pm
The mercury is at 84° right now, with 63% humidity and a heat index of
88°. By the time I leave for work this afternoon, I expect the heat index to
be about 94°. With no air conditioning in my car, I think I can safely
predict the heat index inside will rise to somewhere around 112°. This
may result in delirium, heat stroke, and ecstatic visions. While I am not

diametrically opposed to ecstatic visions, I prefer not to hallucinate while teaching, or whilst traveling to work. Therefore, I shall sacrifice any possibility of maintaining a professional demeanor and let my hair blow in the wind. And should some curious student ask, "Jan, why are creatures from the Everglades residing in your hair?" I shall answer, "because they heard there was a party going on."

Sunday, April 6, 2014 at 8:29pm
Sherman Alexie must be doing it right.

Sunday, April 6, 2014 at 5:30pm
Just when we all thought it was over...The post-Winemaker refrigerator cleaning has commenced. We are preparing the culture dishes for testing. #Winemakerchronicles

Sunday, April 6, 2014 at 12:29pm
I've been wracking my brains trying to find an effective way to teach proofreading/copy-editing to my students. Then this morning, I received an email from Mr. Henry Salami, a solicitor from Nigeria who has a very large inheritance to send me. I realized Mr. Salami could use some help with his persuasive memo.

Saturday, April 5, 2014 at 11:41am
Ladies' Night was great (it always is). But family in PA, please allow me to explain. Ladies' Night means it's likely I won't get to sleep til 5am when you are waking up. I love you too, but this doesn't mean I am capable of speech prior to noon. I do appreciate that you didn't call at 7AM, I'll concede that much.

Friday, April 4, 2014 at 9:29am
I'm stocking up on the Honey Maid.

Thursday, April 3, 2014 at 4:07pm
I have a confession. I have developed a very complicated relationship with Lyndon Baines Johnson.

Thursday, April 3, 2014 at 1:42pm
Things like oil changes and recharging cell phone plans should be much easier than this.

Tuesday, April 1, 2014 at 1:51am
I just ate a Meyer lemon that was so sweet, I had to go back and eat another--like I'd eat an orange! You Northerners are missing out. I'd say come visit, but I think the past month has shown I am not a good hostess.

Monday, March 31, 2014 at 11:30am
If you see a CDC truck parked in front of my building, they are investigating a new strain of influenza called 'The Winemaker Flu'. I am hoping they will place me in quarantine. #Winemakerchronicles

Sunday, March 30, 2014 at 9:53pm
The Winemaker left us with the flu. The Chef is all holed up in bed. I pumped him full of Nyquil and Vitamin C. I am burning things.

Sunday, March 30, 2014 at 4:53pm
I had barely finished my last chronicle, when The Winemaker knocked on my office door and announced he was leaving. Poof! just like that, he has left to Binghamton for another year. This is unusual behavior, but The Feline is happy to stretch and access the outdoors unhindered once more. I am not sure what I think. Godspeed, Winemaker, I suppose I'll just admire your ability to write a surprise ending to this year's visit. #Winemakerchronicles

Sunday, March 30, 2014 at 3:56pm
I am still suffering the after-effects of my evening in the bathtub with Mr. Bates. My head is a screaming me-me. The Winemaker is back from his last trip to the beach (this year). I'm going to suggest he pack up the sand he just dragged in and take it home with him when he leaves tomorrow. It would be impossible for us to forget he's been here. All the living room

furniture is covered with a fine layer of Winemaker sweat, suntan lotion, and Eucerin skin cream. It will take at least a year to scrub that off. #Winemakerchronicles

Sunday, March 30, 2014 at 6:58am
It doesn't happen often, but I sleepwalk occasionally. I just woke up in my bathtub, from a dream about Mr. Bates (Downton Abbey). Ouch, stiff back. I should have poured some epsom salts and hot water first.

Saturday, March 29, 2014 at 6:12pm
Jan Becker played HINTED for 20 in Words With Friends.

Saturday, March 29, 2014 at 4:38pm
The Winemaker leaves Monday. He's packing his bags right now. Glory glory hallelujah! #Winemakerchronicles

Friday, March 28, 2014 at 3:36pm
I have made an executive decision regarding The Winemaker's next annual visit. If he plans to return for a month next year, I am going to fly my grandmother in, and have her stay here too, for the full month, in the living room, with The Winemaker. I think that will at least make things a little more entertaining. Noah spent 40 days and 40 nights in the rain; Jesus spent 40 days in the desert. I am on day 31 of my own trial of spirit. So far, no angelic beings, or olive branches have shown up to give me any hope. The thought of Grandma here for the whole month of March next year, that makes me smile. #Winemakerchronicles

Friday, March 28, 2014 at 12:59am
Somehow, The Winemaker misjudged my capacity for taking directives, and ordered me to drop my crochet hook and watch The Great Gatsby (I am capable of multi-tasking through a movie) ... I think that might have been Daisy's downfall. She listened when someone gave the order to drop her hook. Jan Becker does not take orders. I did not drive my crochet hook deep into The Winemaker's gullet when confronted with

his imperative, but I did not put the crochet hook down either, and made it halfway through a curtain tonight. #Winemakerchronicles

Thursday, March 27, 2014 at 8:56am
I woke this morning with a mystery rash on my forearm that is crawling rapidly towards my shoulder. It looks like poison ivy, though I've not been exposed to any recently. Somehow, I am certain the houseguest is involved. #Winemakerchronicles

Wednesday, March 26, 2014 at 10:50pm
I'm not sure what is happening in the livingroom. Basketball is involved, and that's never a good sign, not when The Winemaker is calling the game louder than the announcers, louder perhaps than power drills (and still, this pounding head). I'm going to sleep. Coffee at 4am ;)
#Winemakerchronicles

Wednesday, March 26, 2014 at 2:11pm
Funny how there are never power drills until my head starts pounding.

Tuesday, March 25, 2014 at 9:24pm
There have been some interesting developments in diplomatic relations between The Feline and The Winemaker. When I returned from a day of cupcakes and gluten-free lavender sorghum birthday cakes, I found The Feline had been locked in my office. This seemed to suit him just fine. (I'm planning to brew coffee at 5am...) #Winemakerchronicles

Tuesday, March 25, 2014 at 10:20am
Good Morning, Facebook. Thank you all for all the happy birthday wishes. I'm trying to keep up with them all. I do this every year, and usually miss saying thank you to someone. So, thank you. Here, there is a surly Winemaker in my living room, a happy cat chasing geckos on the balcony, and fun ahead. I'm teaching a creative writing class for a friend today. That makes me happy :D

Monday, March 24, 2014 at 1:29pm
Compound words are the bane of my existence.

Monday, March 24, 2014 at 1:09am
It was all going splendidly until someone pulled out the scissors and started trimming my hair. #Winemakerchronicles

Sunday, March 23, 2014 at 8:58pm
The Winemaker found it necessary to phone me today to remind me he is out of the house. He may not be in the apartment, but somehow, he is still all around me. #Winemakerchronicles

Saturday, March 22, 2014 at 9:18pm
Conversation with the Winemaker:
> Me: Winemaker, could you do something about all the sand you bring in every day?
> Winemaker: What do you mean, JB?
> Me: Well, our rug is black, and sand is not. Your brother just vacuumed. (I point to the dunes on the living room rug.)
> Winemaker: It's all part of the equation, Becker.

And this, my dear friends, is why I am not a mathematician. #Winemakerchronicles

Friday, March 21, 2014 at 4:17pm
The Winemaker is watching golf. I am doing laundry, which means I am also watching golf while I fold. I do not understand The Winemaker, nor do I understand golf. I do understand the importance of laundry, especially since I just washed The Winemaker's towel. I am happy to report that I have not yet died. #Winemakerchronicles

Thursday, March 20, 2014 at 7:55pm
Conversation with The Winemaker, in which he attempts to assert an existential crisis onto my weekend:
> WM: What's your fallback position, JB?
> Me: What do you mean?

WM: I mean, this writing thing--that's not a real job. What are you going to do for work?

Me: Write...I'm a writer. Writers write, right?

#Winemakerchronicles

Wednesday, March 19, 2014 at 8:16pm

I would like a bigger F-bomb to drop on today.

Tuesday, March 18, 2014 at 10:13pm

I told The Chef that I heard about this wonderful thing called "the four-night rule" for guests. He didn't believe it was true. We can still dream, can't we? #Winemakerchronicles

Tuesday, March 18, 2014 at 6:33pm

The people outside are throwing each other in the lake, whining about how cold it is. It's 80° outside. Hehehe, they never stood under a Pennsylvania mountain waterfall in April. That's cold.

Monday, March 17, 2014 at 7:56pm

I needn't have worried. There are 150 screaming children in the building.

Monday, March 17, 2014 at 1:02pm

Jan Becker played BRATTY for 21 in Words With Friends.

Monday, March 17, 2014 at 11:03am

The Winemaker just revolutionized the art of vacuuming. I wish I could explain this further (there is so much I wish I could explain regarding our annual visitor). #Winemakerchronicles

Sunday, March 16, 2014 at 12:26am

Of course, the wannabe in a reality show singing competition mother and her screaming child are moving out. Of course they are. And of course, they have to slam the door every time they take something to the truck. Of course, they do. Am I happy about this? OF COURSE I AM!

Saturday, March 15, 2014 at 1:25pm
Conversation with The Winemaker: (I was looking for quiet; he was disturbing me)

> Me: I think you fail to understand how difficult it can be to teach and write.
> WM: Try working a job where you put your life on the line every day.
> Me: You mean like when I release grades to the students?
> #Winemakerchronicles

Friday, March 14, 2014 at 8:45pm
Isn't the purpose of literature to trigger something?

Friday, March 14, 2014 at 7:53pm
The trouble with being a writer is all the existential crises.

Wednesday, March 12, 2014 at 10:16am
I love watching weird old PSAs

Wednesday, March 12, 2014 at 8:57am
The Feline and I have a morning routine we've been following for years. We wake up, I start the water for coffee and give him fish. He eats his fish, and by the time the water is boiling, he wants to go out. If there is any change to this routine, The Feline becomes aggrieved. He begins to pace. He meows, at first quietly, then with increasing intensity and persistence. The Winemaker's boudoir is in the living room, right near the door to the balcony. The Feline does not understand etiquette. His vocabulary consists of only four words: Fish, OUT, Bad, and Good boy. And so this morning, when I grabbed the yowling Feline, inches from The Winemaker's bed, where the volume and pitch of his cries to be released from an interior lacking in geckos and songbirds had reached the level one might expect in a performance of La Traviata, I picked him up, and whispered, "good boy." #Winemakerchronicles

Tuesday, March 11, 2014 at 11:53pm
Jan Becker likes Kevin Smith.

Tuesday, March 11, 2014 at 8:46am
The Feline is on the balcony, which means every songbird on the lake is
protesting. Meanwhile, The Winemaker has not yet fully emerged from
his slumber. The protests are growing louder outside. You can see where
this is going, right? #Winemakerchronicles

Monday, March 10, 2014 at 7:38pm
Now is also when we begin to reflect on what we have lost and what we
have found during the Winemaker's stay. What we have lost: The small
saucepan. What we have found: Peanut M&M candies between the sofa
cushions. #Winemakerchronicles

Monday, March 10, 2014 at 12:07pm
Every year during The Winemaker's annual trip, about this time, we find
ourselves asking the same questions we ask every year: Shall we survive
this visit? How shall we survive it? And most importantly, do we have
enough toilet paper to muddle through this? #Winemakerchronicles

Monday, March 10, 2014 at 12:03pm
Jan Becker played MULCH for 21 in Words With Friends.

Saturday, March 8, 2014 at 3:10pm
Question from a student in my class: Are you qualified to teach
Technical Writing for Computer Majors? Answer: I used to play
Dungeons & Dragons. I think you'll be okay with me.

Friday, March 7, 2014 at 8:32pm
I'm having issues with the insects again. First, I was once more stalked
by a bee. I ran screaming like a little kid into the bathroom this time, so
no stings. But my face is COVERED with bug bites. I'm like one giant
welt. Methinks these are no ordinary insect bites. These are swamp grade
stings, super-villain bug bites.

Friday, March 7, 2014 at 11:04am
So much depends upon the right ice cube tray filled with tap water beside the veggie burgers. #Winemakerchronicles

Friday, March 7, 2014 at 4:03am
Costs of racism on the US economy? Almost $2 trillion. Per year.

Friday, March 7, 2014 at 3:39am
3am, I find myself doing the "walk of shame" thing (at least it felt like it) into my own apartment. #Winemakerchronicles

Thursday, March 6, 2014 at 7:50am
Morning: Trash trucks, slamming doors, trash trucks, not one, not two, but three screaming children, trash trucks, scrub jays in the live oaks squawking, school bus, some guy who finds it necessary to beep his horn repeatedly to signal he's come for a pickup, another car's alarm, police siren, helicopter--all that, and all The Winemaker hears is me, in the kitchen, boiling water for coffee (BOILING WATER?!?) "Becker can't you keep it down?" he asks. Poor guy can't sleep. I haven't the heart to tell him I slipped a pea under his mattress. #Winemakerchronicles

Wednesday, March 5, 2014 at 10:20am
I sometimes forget that The Winemaker and The Feline are natural enemies. Last night, The Feline wanted to go out on the balcony for late night gecko hunting (He rarely catches one). The Winemaker was trying to sleep on his air mattress on the living room floor, and normally I would make Romeo wait. However, it had been a long day for him inside, and I tried to slip him past The Winemaker to let him out. The Winemaker was roused by The Feline's plaintive cries, sat straight up in bed, and declared, "It was all very civil until just now!" (Uh-oh). I can report that The Feline survived the event, but alas, no late-night geckos. In other news, a "Christ-centered Church" was handing out free bottles of water at the corner of 151st St and Biscayne Blvd yesterday. I wonder if that means it was holy water? #WinemakerChronicles

Monday, March 3, 2014 at 8:53pm
So, the last thing mercury did before it went direct was set a gremlin loose on my air conditioning in the car. This coincides with getting a surprise call to go in and teach a course in South Miami. This is good, because I've missed teaching so much, I've been randomly bursting into tears since the semester started. My route runs parallel to the Eastern edge of the Everglades, which means I must drive about an hour with the windows open on the edge of a giant swamp. An open window seems to act like a vacuum to every critter in the swamp. By the time I get to campus, not only is my hair all frizzed out and messy (think Dee Schneider), it's likely got a few castaways in it. I will say this. I stood in front of a class tonight for the first time in months, and then I picked up a dry erase marker and wrote on the board. And up there with my hair all crazy (and maybe crawling a little), I got my superpowers back.

Monday, March 3, 2014 at 12:40pm
Random crochet trivia in honor of National Crochet Month: During the potato famine, Irish women saved families from starvation by picking up their hooks and making Irish lace to adorn the necks of wealthy Americans and Europeans. I like a craft that can save the skin of a nation.

Monday, March 3, 2014 at 9:33am
Jan Becker played FONTS for 20 in Words With Friends.

Sunday, March 2, 2014 at 10:30am
The Winemaker has had his Sunday morning repast, cold pizza and Stephen A. Smith, and has left for his morning jaunt. In other news, most of my friends are prepping for a long flight back from Seattle. Godspeed, friends. I'm glad you've all had adventures. When you've recovered from your AWP hangovers, I'll be waiting to be regaled by your tales.

Friday, February 28, 2014 at 10:54pm
An unexpected bonus observation in The Winemaker's absence: I heard his soft-sided Igloo cooler making noise on top of the fridge earlier. What

does The Winemaker have on his iPod? Green Day "Awesome as F**k" <---His asterisks, not mine. #Winemakerchronicles

Friday, February 28, 2014 at 7:15pm
The Winemaker asked me for a band-aid this evening. "It's hard work walking on the ocean." He tells me. "The ocean?" I asked, "you walk on water?" The Winemaker has a full dance card tonight. I think there's a lounge singer involved. #Winemakerchronicles

Thursday, February 27, 2014 at 8:08pm
I never need to go to the beach when The Winemaker visits. He brings the beach home with him. Ahh! The sand between my toes! #Winemakerchronicles

Wednesday, February 26, 2014 at 11:36am
The Winemaker and The Chef were out at a show last night (Darkstar Orchestra). I woke this morning to feta cheese on the kitchen floor. Sometimes it is best not to investigate. Sometimes it is best to just remove the feta cheese from the floor and wait for the coffee to brew.

Tuesday, February 25, 2014 at 8:31pm
I saw The Winemaker briefly on my way out the door today. He was upset that I was missing a hubcap on my tire. I am rarely concerned about hubcaps. My car is 13 years old, but I guess being a Buick owner, our Winemaker has standards.

Tuesday, February 25, 2014 at 12:39pm
Funny, The Winemaker's pending arrival makes me want to grab a megaphone and announce: Let the games begin! (21 minutes til landing).

Tuesday, February 25, 2014 at 8:02am
Jan Becker played HONED for 30 in Words With Friends.

Monday, February 24, 2014 at 6:36pm
I was a military brat. I went to 9 different schools during my time in compulsory education (and I probably had it easy). But if you couple this information with the 28% increase in domestic violence that occurred in military homes between 2008-2011, the evidence seems to suggest there is a whole demographic of our society we need to love if they are to be productive in their adult age. (We should probably nurture all children, but brats seem particularly vulnerable).

Monday, February 24, 2014 at 3:53pm
Just finished up another two-hour service visit with Comcast. Third time my cables have been rewired in 6 months. Each time they come, they drill new holes through the wall. I think this is just fine. We can use the extra ventilation. And a bonus! I've gotten to know the cable guy so well, he's like a part of the family.

Monday, February 24, 2014 at 10:50am
The Winemaker arrives tomorrow. It seems like just yesterday we were seeing him off.

Saturday, February 22, 2014 at 5:59pm
Jan Becker played EVILS for 28 in Words With Friends.

Saturday, February 22, 2014 at 5:52pm
Jan Becker played PITCHY for 40 in Words With Friends.

Saturday, February 22, 2014 at 5:45pm
Jan Becker played MURDER for 21 in Words With Friends.

Friday, February 21, 2014 at 10:58pm
My upstairs neighbor waited until now to turn on the power saw.
#creepynightsoncrystallake

Wednesday, February 19, 2014 at 9:50pm
If you're in Seattle for the AWP conference, stop by our booth at the Book Fair (location C9). Joe Clifford, will be signing copies of his books with Melanie Neale McLendon, Friday from noon - 1pm. In the meantime, you can read this interview, in which I grilled Clifford about his sleep habits, his remarkable publishing streak, and the mysteries of the Florida International University roof top.

Wednesday, February 19, 2014 at 4:42pm
Universe is back to normal. The Chef informed me The Winemaker's migratory urge struck early this year. He'll be arriving the 25th, which coincides with the last day of the current retrograde. We are considering a correlative study of Punxatawney varmint shadow castings on Candlemas and variations in Winemaker road trip embarkment dates.

Wednesday, February 19, 2014 at 1:33pm
I was going to make a Pussy Riot pun, but I'll pass.

Tuesday, February 18, 2014 at 8:54am
Jan Becker likes Space.

Tuesday, February 18, 2014 at 8:48am
I am not sure what the universe is up to. Mercury is in retrograde, but suddenly, things are working more in line with how they should. I'm just going to keep my mouth shut about mercury and go about my business. Oh, and thank you, Universe. Jan Becker is grateful, if shocked.

Monday, February 17, 2014 at 3:52pm
Jan Becker played NIX for 38 in Words With Friends.

Monday, February 17, 2014 at 3:04pm
I'm considering going outside to educate the young men fishing on the dock about two things: 1. It is probably not a good idea to fish in a lake less than 1/2 mile from a giant landfill. 2. One probably will not catch any fish if one spends one's entire time screaming one's fool head off.

Monday, February 17, 2014 at 2:18pm
Jan Becker played ZANY for 48 in Words With Friends.

Friday, February 14, 2014 at 11:35pm
Every so often, The Chef surprises me. He came home tonight and asked
if I knew the poem about the cinnamon peeler. Here it is. I love how
poetry shakes out from unexpected places. I knew he was okay when he
asked if I was "contemplating jazz" over in the corner. I asked him what
made him ask me that, and he said, "Oh, well, I figured, since you're an
'angel headed hipster'." A man who doesn't mind Naked Allen Ginsberg
hanging above the bed, who surprises me with Michael Ondaatje, and
thinks Moms Mabely is hotter than Beyonce is fine with me.

Thursday, February 13, 2014 at 9:54am
Ahh, that Chef of mine! He put two new front tires on my car...<3

Monday, February 10, 2014 at 10:39pm
I think I hit a pothole tonight that was a porthole to another dimension.
It was that big. It ate my tire...and the rim...and my hubcap...and possibly
something integral to the front end, like an axle, or something like that....

Monday, February 10, 2014 at 3:24pm
Signs Mercury may be in retrograde (and an unexpected blessing from
the universe): 1. Trip to the post office to drop off pre-paid packages took
one hour, because the guy in front of me was sending international faxes
and the fax was broken. 2. Trip to the pharmacy to pick up prescriptions
I called in three days ago took one hour because the computers were
down. 3. Came home, took the elevator, and found myself standing in
front of eviction notices taped to the front door. <---- This is the
unexpected blessing part. I'd gotten off on the wrong floor. The notices
were not for me, but for the family, directly below me. AKA- The Child-
Who-Screams-All-Day-Everyday and her mother--the one who sings "I
Will Always Love You" in a mangled key. Normally, I would not be

happy for someone else's misfortune, but I will not deny my Schadenfreude, not this one time.

Sunday, February 9, 2014 at 5:46pm
Jan Becker played OGRE for 24 in Words With Friends.

Sunday, February 9, 2014 at 11:58am
I finally got around to purchasing The Chef's 2014 calendar. I got him Classic Star Trek. The calendar boy for February is George Takei, naked to the waist gripping a rapier in full attack mode. The caption reads 'Naked Time'. Neither The Chef nor I can stop staring... #februaryyou'reourlittlevalentine.

Saturday, February 8, 2014 at 10:42pm
Jan Becker shared James Baldwin's photo.

Wednesday, February 5, 2014 at 4:57pm
Jan Becker played EDITOR for 31 in Words With Friends.

Saturday, February 1, 2014 at 9:45pm
Epsom salt and ammonia pastes, oatmeal poultice, Baking soda poultices, mashed banana poultice, onion poultice, ginger/garlic poultice, ice, wet heat, and Appalachian Heal-All salve with chickweed, nettle, chamomile, calendula, lemon balm, plantain leaves, lavender flower, honey and beeswax. Honey and beeswax from the creature who killed himself in me, and mashed bananas, which contain a substance called isopentyl acetate, the same chemical a bee releases when it stings. It signals the other bees to attack, and I smeared it on my kneecap.

Saturday, February 1, 2014 at 4:34pm
Jan Becker likes Bryan Cranston.

Saturday, February 1, 2014 at 4:34pm
Jan Becker likes Fyodor Dostoevsky.

Saturday, February 1, 2014 at 3:34pm
Jan Becker played HUG for 22 in Words With Friends.

Saturday, February 1, 2014 at 3:02pm
While searching for home remedies for bee stings. I found this. I may try it, if only to grow mushrooms on my knee: Cow manure!

Friday, January 31, 2014 at 8:27am
Happy Year of the Horse. I'm a little worried. I have a history with horses involving getting thrown and having my delicate bits squashed by them. I celebrated the new year by being stung by a bee. I'm sort of allergic to bees. Not the can't breathe, my tongue is swollen kind of allergic, but I swell up miserably and often ooze when stung. Anyhow, here is what a good friend does when a bee crawls up your pant leg in January (in the middle of a downpour) and stings you on the knee and you find yourself screaming that your pants need to get off RIGHT NOW. A friend doesn't run in the other direction, she helps you out of your pants, gets the activated charcoal paste and feeds you Benadryl, then hooks you up with a bed, so you can sleep the Benadryl off. Thanks Corey and Kacee. Let's hope that was just the leftover bad energy from the year of the snake. Venus is direct. It has to get better (at least for a week, until mercury goes retrograde).

Thursday, January 30, 2014 at 6:52am
Lest you think it is ever all quiet and peace in my neck of Pompano, The Winemaker has made contact. He will be arriving in roughly 32 days. The childproofing has begun....

Tuesday, January 28, 2014 at 8:50am
Here at Casa Del Crystal Lake, the mockingbirds whistle bars of "Cielito Lindo" in the morning (Viva Los Mariachis de Mi Tierra!).

Monday, January 27, 2014 at 9:28pm
I should probably be nicer to Creepy Maintenance Man. For example, considering that he will be back tomorrow to grout the tile in my very

tiny bathroom, the ghost pepper chili I had for dinner was a less than compassionate decision.

Monday, January 27, 2014 at 1:02pm
Creepy Maintenance Man is here for the repair work. He's a close talker. #Creepy

Saturday, January 25, 2014 at 3:48pm
Jan Becker played CURE for 30 in Words With Friends.

Friday, January 24, 2014 at 1:30pm
Creepy Maintenance man is here servicing our AC unit. I asked him, "Are you going to need to go through the whole apartment?" His response: "I have to service the AC. Then I'm going to go through everything and check out your plumbing." #Creepy

Wednesday, January 22, 2014 at 2:10pm
It occurs to me that tax preparation and creative writing are not entirely dissimilar.

Monday, January 20, 2014 at 4:30pm
Jan Becker played PENILE for 45 in Words With Friends.

Sunday, January 19, 2014 at 1:27pm
I woke this morning with a strange hankering for some poi. It's been more than thirty years since I've even seen a bowl of poi. I'd appreciate it if someone in South Florida would serve poi on their menu. I'd like a choice too, between two finger and three finger poi.

Saturday, January 18, 2014 at 9:34pm
Darkstar says the upcoming mercury retrograde is going to feel like a magic mushroom trip. This also will require some reflection...

Saturday, January 18, 2014 at 8:19pm
I touched a Gucci leather bag for the first time in my life today. This is going to require some reflection...

Saturday, January 18, 2014 at 8:18am
Mom and Grandma are flying back to PA today (they've been at my uncle's the past two weeks). Godspeed! Hope to see you again soon. <3

Saturday, January 18, 2014 at 7:53am
Jan Becker played FLAKY for 57 in Words With Friends.

Friday, January 17, 2014 at 1:12pm
I woke up this morning to 40° weather...and mosquito bites all over my belly. WTF?

Thursday, January 16, 2014 at 8:15pm
Jan Becker went to Virginia Key GrassRoots Festival of Music, Art & Dance, February 20-23!

Wednesday, January 15, 2014 at 8:58pm
Sometimes, I just want to head over to the American Legion, and hang out with a bunch of cranky old men, sip a bourbon and listen to stories.

Monday, January 13, 2014 at 9:38am
I'm trying hard not to be a jerk, honest.

Sunday, January 12, 2014 at 10:23am
Jan Becker likes Joan Didion.

Sunday, January 12, 2014 at 12:28am
There is a lack of subway in South Florida. Damn.

Saturday, January 11, 2014 at 2:07pm
Jan Becker played FREAK for 65 in Words With Friends.

Friday, January 10, 2014 at 3:19pm
I had a DNA profile done more than a year ago, and when it was done, I looked at the results, which were surprising, started studying Scandinavian culture, and accepted that my ethnicity was vastly different than what I was told growing up. The lab has sent me new results, and I have to figure it out all over again, because it's all changed. Thank you, Ancestry DNA. I needed another identity crisis. I think this time, rather than immerse myself in cultural studies, I'll just call myself a mutt and focus on being human.

Friday, January 10, 2014 at 1:58am
Amiri Baraka has long been one of my favorite poets; I read my first Baraka poem when I was 9 years old. I loved this man. I loved how pissed off he was--how pissed off he made me sometimes; I loved how he loved America. Love sometimes speaks indignation, but it's history, man. Thank you, Amiri Baraka for leaving behind your words.

Tuesday, January 7, 2014 at 9:39am
Oh, good. It's finally cold enough to wear this big-ass coat from that thrift shop down the road.

Saturday, January 4, 2014 at 9:17am
Grandma wanted two things out of this trip. 1. Spaghetti and meatballs from The Chef (who is doing doubles this weekend, and won't be able to help us out there). 2. A trip to the thrift store. I introduced her Macklemore and Ryan this morning. Quinn and I are calling her O.G. from here on out; she's got the moves for it.

Friday, January 3, 2014 at 11:57pm
Grandma talks all the time, even in her sleep. Earlier, I heard her murmuring," Too skinny...Jan's gotten too damn skinny." Silly Grandma, it took me too long to figure this out, but I'm just right.

Friday, January 3, 2014 at 7:34am
LOVE is a leaky air mattress. #SunshineChronicles

ACKNOWLEDGEMENTS

Seven and a half years ago, when I moved to South Florida to pursue a graduate degree at Florida International University, I had no way of knowing what a wonderful, strange place I was moving to. Nor did I know that I'd find in South Florida the community of book-loving freaks I'd sought my entire life. Thank you for making me feel welcomed & at home at last. I would like to thank my 717 Facebook friends, who've tolerated my status updates these last nine years, & have consistently encouraged me to continue being weird. Thank you also to the cast of characters who inherit & work in my apartment building & give me plenty to ponder, & thank you, Winemaker, Grandma, & Mom, for your long, sometimes awful annual visits. Lynne Schneider, Josh Keiter, & Carolyn Fargnoli, someday there will be CAKE again together. Laura McDermott Matheric & Walter Matheric, thank you for procreating, & birthing The Infant, who became The Toddler, & is rapidly becoming a Big Girl, then the second Infant who will also one day be a Big Girl. It has been a joy & an honor to serve as their Tia Juana. Hopefully their therapy bills won't bankrupt you. Thank you to the faculty in FIU's MFA program: Les Standiford, John Dufresne, Campbell McGrath, Deborah Dean, Denise Duhamel, & especially, thank you to Lynne Barrett, & Julie Marie Wade who both told me to do something with my weird Facebook posts. Terese Campbell, thank you for also telling me to do something with these weird daily dispatches, but even more, for random hugs on days when I needed them most. Thank you, Barbara Swan, for shipping me off to Los Angeles, & for love. Betty Jo Buro, Juleen D. Collins, & Gabriel Suarez, thank you for being my buddies, reminding me sometimes to "settle down" & insisting that quitting is never an option. Kacee Belcher, thank you for adventures & for always being there in a moonshine emergency. Thank you to all my classmates in the MFA program, who are too many in number to name individually, but whose names are written somewhere more sacred than on the page. Corey

Ginsberg, Fabienne Josaphat, Karen Kravit, Melanie Mochran, Ruth Ann Ward, Louis K. Lowy, Kathy Curtin, Marina del Pruna, Nick Garnett, Esther Kenniff, & MJ Fievre, Marci Calabretta- Cancio-Bello, Mary Slebodnik, Leenie Moore, Betty Jo Buro, and Barbara Swan, thank you for out of school workshopping, writerly conversations, & most of all your encouragement, & keen insight. Thank you, Jon Buckley & Callie Brunelli for opening your home to me & giving me peace & coffee & memories, I love you more than I can say. Kevin Baker, thank you for signing on as my agent. Thank you, Girls' Club, of Fort Lauderdale, for your support during my writer's residence. A HUGE note of gratitude to Neil De La Flor, JV Portela & Reading Queer for bringing such joy into my life—I've been so blessed already, becoming a fairy godmother in the Miami queer community has meant more to me than I can express. Thank you, Godfather of Miami Literature, & Venerable Pope of the written word, Mitchell Kaplan, for fostering & nurturing such a wonderful community of writers, & especially for proving that successful business & community are not mutually exclusive. Thank you, Lissette Mendez, for many things, for hiring me for my first job as a writer, for being the absolute best boss a woman could wish for, but also thank you for being a great friend, & for telling me there was more in my Facebook posts than I saw at first. Nick Garnett, thank you for being my partner in writerly crimes, & letting me rant, & thank you & Denise Schiavoni for your help when it was most needed. Thank you, Luis Berros, for lending your beautiful Coppertone Girl for the cover art, and Marlene Lopez, for your brilliant cover design. Thank you, Matt (The Chef) for helping me create a safe, nurturing environment in which to live, for never doubting my crazy goals, & for never balking or complaining when I write about you. & most especially, thank you to my editor on this project, J.J. Colagrande & Jitney Books. I knew seven years ago when I read the name "Thelonious Horowitz" in your first novel *Headz* that you had to be a mad genius—you have proven yourself abundantly freaky. Thank you for loving my words into book form. Tu eres mi hermano, siempre. Te amo.

BIO

Jan Becker is from a small coal mining town in Pennsylvania. She didn't stay there very long. She grew up in a Marine Corps family, on military bases all over the United States, and wandered the US for many years before settling in South Florida. She is currently an MFA candidate at Florida International University, and has taught courses there in composition, technical writing, creative writing and poetry. She is also on the regular faculty at Reading Queer Academy, where she teaches a Boot Camp for Queer Writers and serves as a mentor. Her work has appeared in *Jai-Alai* Magazine, *Colorado Review, Emerge, Brevity Poetry Review, Sliver of Stone,* and the *Florida Book Review.* She is the 2015-2016 Writer in Residence at the Girls' Club Collection in Fort Lauderdale, and winner of the 2015 AWP Intro Journals Award in Nonfiction.

76380442R10183

Made in the USA
Columbia, SC
05 September 2017